PRACTICING LEADERSHIP

Principles and Applications

THIRD EDITION

ARTHUR SHRIBERG
Xavier University

DAVID L. SHRIBERG
Miami University (Ohio)

RICHA KUMARI
Shriberg & Associates

John Wiley & Sons, Inc.

Associate Publisher   Judith Joseph
Senior Acquisitions Editor   Jayme Heffler
Senior Editorial Assistant   Ame Esterline
Marketing Manager   Heather King
Production Manager   Pam Kennedy
Production Editors   Kelly Tavares, Sarah Wolfman–Robichaud
Managing Editor   Kevin Dodds
Illustration Editor   Benjamin Reece
Cover Designer   Jennifer Wasson
Cover Photo Credits   boardroom: © Royalty-Free/Corbis; international flags: Photolink/Getty
Images; scales: © Royalty-Free/Corbis; pyramid and sphinx: © Thinkstock/Getty Images; Mount
Rushmore: Brand X Pictures/Getty Images; wind turbines: Getty Images; royal guard: Royalty-
Free/Corbis; Parthenon: Adam Crow/Getty Images.

This book was set in New Caledonia by Leyh Publishing Services, and printed and bound by
Courier–Westford The cover was printed by Phoenix Color.

This book is printed on acid-free paper. ∞

To order books or for customer service call 1-800-CALL-WILEY (225-5945).

ISBN   0-471-65662-3

Printed in the United States of America

10   9   8   7   6   5   4   3

ABOUT THE AUTHORS

Arthur Shriberg is the Downing Professor of Management at Xavier University and a well-known leadership and management consultant. He has degrees from Columbia University (Ed.D.), Boston University (M.A.), Xavier University (MBA), and the Wharton School at the University of Pennsylvania (B.A.). He has served as vice president and/or dean at four universities. He has assisted more than fifty companies with various organizational challenges.

David L. Shriberg received his B.S. from Cornell University, and his M.S. and Ph.D. from Northeastern University. He is a currently an assistant professor of school psychology at Miami University (Ohio), and a well-known writer and consultant.

Richa Kumari is a consultant and trainer and has received an MBA from Xavier University. She also has degrees from Delhi University, India (B.S.) and Institute of Management Development and Research, India (MBA).

Ryan Allio is a graduate of the University of Akron, Ohio, with a BA in Psychology focusing on leadership. He is currently pursuing a master's degree at Xavier University.

E. Paul Colella received his bachelor's, master's, and doctorate degrees from Fordham University. He is a Professor of Philosophy at Xavier University and an accomplished musician.

Stephen R. Covey is the founder and chairman of the Covey Leadership Center. His book, *The 7 Habits of Highly Successful People,* has sold more than 2 million copies.

Tonya Huggins is Director of Diversity at the Health Alliance of Greater Cincinnati and has extensive experience dealing with cultural and diversity issues. She received her Master's degree from Northwestern University.

Timothy Kloppenborg received his bachelor's, master's, and doctorate degrees from the University of Cincinnati. He is professor of management at Xavier University and a consultant in project management, quality and teaming. He is the lead author of *Project Leadership* (Management Concepts, 2003).

James M. Kouzes and **Barry Z. Posner** are the authors of the critically acclaimed *Credibility* and many other well-known management and leadership books.

Stephen Mullin is a retired officer in the U.S. Marines. He is currently senior portfolio manager at U.S. Bank.

John E. Pepper served as chairman of the board, president, and CEO of Procter & Gamble. He has chaired numerous international, federal, and community boards.

Judy L. Rogers is a well-known educator and director of graduate services in Student Personnel Administration at Miami University (Ohio).

Amy Burke Shriberg, a professional writer, has a B.A. from the University of Illinois, an M.A. from Georgetown University, and a Ph.D. in political science from Brandeis University. She is currently a researcher and writer for the Kettinger Foundation.

Michael Shriberg received his B.S. degree at Cornell University and his Ph.D. at University of Michigan. He has written extensively in the fields of sustainability and environmental management. Michael is currently the coordinator of the Great Lakes program for the Public Interest Research Group.

Linda Treviño is a well-known authority on ethical management issues. She is a professor of organizational behavior and chair of the department of management and organization at Penn State University and holds a Ph.D. in management from Texas A&M University.

ACKNOWLEDGMENTS

The initial text and the second edition have been a collaborative effort including a great many dedicated people. David L. Shriberg, my son and co-author, was the primary writer of several chapters and profiles, and he helped coordinate all aspects of the project. He wrote most of the *Leadership Moments, Create Your Own Theory,* and *Questions for Discussion and Review.* We have added the multi-talented Richa Kumari as a co-author for this edition. She wrote the chapter on teaming and leadership. She also wrote several profiles and took primary responsibility for updating the Instructor's Manual and coordinating Web support. I wrote the new opening chapter, rewrote two other chapters, and edited the entire publication. Special thanks to Carol Lloyd and Mary Lynn Williamson who made significant contributions to the first and second editions of the book.

Judy Rogers, Linda Treviño, Tonya Huggins, Michael Shriberg, Amy Burke Shriberg, Paul Colella, Steve Ruedisili, Megan Clough, Steve Mullin, and Gordon Barnhardt all wrote initial drafts that were used as the basis of chapters in this or previous editions, while Tim Kloppenborg helped write parts of chapters in this edition. We are particularly grateful to Lou Kruger, Professor at Northeastern University, John E. Pepper, former Chairman of the Board of Procter & Gamble, and well-known leadership authors James Kouzes, Barry Posner, and Stephen Covey for their original contributions to this text. We thank Ann Harbison, Steve Reudisili, and Meagan L. Clough whose contributions to the second edition were used by Tonya Huggins in her new chapter, "Leadership in a Multicultural and Global Society."

Researchers involved include Katia Zhestkova, Eddie Bitzer, Nikkil Kockhar, David Keszei, Ryan Allio, Laura Schwarber, Mrinalini Kamaraju, Libby Nash, and Joyce Cerejo. Assistance was also given by Marjorie Shriberg, Rebecca Shriberg, Steven Shriberg, Emma Shriberg, Ena Vazquez-Nuttall, Mauricio Munoz, and many of my students who wrote reviews of the first and second editions. Valuable typing assistance was given by Shirlee James and Donna Waymire.

We also appreciate the work of the staff at Wiley, including Pam Kennedy, Judith Joseph, Jayme Heffler, Ame Esterline, Heather King, Kelly Tavares, and Sarah Wolfman–Robichaud.

—*Art Shriberg*

TABLE OF CONTENTS

INTRODUCTION

It seems that everyone is always talking, writing, theorizing about—and searching for—leadership. We have only to look at the abundance of literature, popular videos, and seminars to see how captivated we are by the notion of leadership. Leadership development is now considered an increasingly important part of a college education, as evidenced by the burgeoning number of graduate and undergraduate leadership courses and the new centers and schools for leadership established at numerous universities.

Actually, however, our fascination with leadership is nothing new. Long before the psychologists and management scientists of the twentieth century worked at defining and measuring leadership, Plato, Machiavelli (see Chapter 7 for more detail on Pre-Industrial influences on leadership), and Shakespeare offered images of leadership cast in the context of their times. And yet there is still no common agreement on what leadership means. James McGregor Burns (1979) captured the elusiveness of the concept when he noted that "Leadership is one of the most observed and least understood phenomena on earth."

Whatever it is, we need it, desperately. We yearn for great leaders who can foresee what we must know and do to negotiate the constant change and ambiguity facing us in this increasingly dangerous world. We also bemoan the absence of great leaders who can give us rock-solid answers.

Because it is generally agreed that leadership is vital for our survival as a society, we should need to prepare people to be leaders. It is in this context—the call for leaders and leadership—that we set about writing this book.

✦ WHY THIS BOOK?

Why add to the already towering pile of books on the subject? We offer a fusion of several different ways to examine leadership in an unconventional leadership text. Although we include most of the traditional perspectives, we put these leadership theories and approaches in a more comprehensive context and help the reader not only to understand their source but also to see how they can be and are applied.

Not simply a collection of theories, this book considers the approach and theory to practicing or "doing" leadership. While skills are important, this book does not take a skills-only approach. Don't look to this text as *The Five-Minute Leader*. Although we certainly incorporate suggestions and ideas that our readers can readily use for practicing leadership, we have **not** written a how-to book.

Finally, this book is not about finding the ideal model. We haven't found the perfect leader we can all simply study and emulate. We don't think there is such a person. However, we have included profiles or snapshots of people practicing leadership in a variety of settings and cultural contexts. In each case, the profiles illustrate points addressed in the chapter.

✦ OUR METHODS FOR FRAMING LEADERSHIP

Although the lives and decisions of the people profiled teach a powerful lesson, our goal is not for our readers to become the next Nelson Mandela or Miep Gies. Nor do we expect our readers to adopt the personal leadership styles of the authors of this text. Rather, our approach to leadership mirrors our belief about learning: Just as we see no universally accepted theory of leadership, just as the information age has cast doubt on the image of leader as omnipotent hero, we do not pretend to have all the answers about leadership. Students of leadership are experts in their own right. Readers bring with them unique backgrounds, experiences, and perceptions that are important to the discussion of leadership. We see learning about leadership as melding the ideas and experiences of our readers with our ideas as authors of this text, as well as with the ideas of the scholars whose works we present. In this way, learning becomes a relational activity, a dialogue. We seek to engage readers in examining the material, their own perspectives, and those of current leaders to make sense of this phenomenon called leadership.

We have included several pedagogical features in the text that underscore our belief that knowledge is socially constructed. We use a puzzle as a metaphor for how we have come to understand leadership over the centuries. We will give you frequent reminders of where you are on solving the puzzle, where common roadblocks can be found, and much commentary about the challenges you face. Be prepared for challenges in the task.

Some other guidelines for the task:

- We have attempted to integrate the implications of ethics, diversity, and internationalism throughout the text and we have created two new chapters entitled "Ethical Leadership" and "Practicing Leadership in a Global and Multicultural Society."

- We don't hesitate to pose questions—questions without one clear answer. We want to engage you in the process.

- And speaking of process, the way in which we developed this text illustrates the notion of practicing leadership. The authors are a mix of managers, administrators, and professors from several disciplines and practitioners in a variety of settings.

- At the start of each chapter, we use *Leadership Moments* to demonstrate how individuals face leadership challenges every day.

- The text does not necessarily have to be read sequentially. Different instructors may want to highlight different aspects, depending on the backgrounds of students and their own teaching strengths.

- You will learn about current leaders—including some who are well known and some who are not—and we will describe their contributions to leadership. Their leadership profiles are intended to bring to life how one's closely held assumptions about leadership directly shape the behavior of leaders.

- A *Create Your Own Theory* section will prompt readers to personalize the main message of the chapter and either use or discard it in their own emerging theory. *Leadership Skills* boxes highlight skills and principles illustrated in the chapter. We complete each chapter with a Summary, Key Terms, questions for discussion and review, and links to self-assessment tools that can be found on the Internet and/or a closing exercise.

- Finally, in the closing chapters, we encourage readers to develop their own comprehensive, integrated theory about leadership, as well as their action plans for practicing leadership. Leaders and collaborators in the twenty-first century must be able to reflect on what they believe and why, make sense of situations from multiple perspectives, and form sound conclusions about what actions to take based on those interpretations.

- We give the instructor added cases, tools, references and activities, as well as Teaching Notes and multiple-choice and essay test questions in our *Instructors Guide* and on our Web site.

A central point of this book is that while each of the disciplines we discuss has made a contribution to our understanding of the concept of leadership, none can stand alone as the defining set of assumptions. By viewing leadership through multiple lenses, we come closer to understanding it and become more skilled in practicing it in different contexts.

This point can be illustrated by the Indian tale of the six blind men and the elephant. The first man felt the elephant's trunk and announced that the animal was a snake. The second, feeling a leg, said it was a tree. Grabbing a tusk, the third asserted the animal was a spear; a fourth patted the elephant's side and claimed it was a wall. Holding onto the tail, the fifth man said it was much more like a rope, while the sixth, having seized the elephant's ear, pronounced it closer to a fan.

Although each man's perspective held some truth, we can see that none on its own captured the reality of the elephant. Only by combining these views do we begin to understand this phenomenon called elephant.

The metaphor suggests that each person, depending on his or her position in relation to the "elephant," can contribute some important information to the task of describing an elephant; however, each can only "see" the animal from a narrow vantage point. Each has only a partial perception. These restricted views would lead each person to reach very different conclusions about the nature of an elephant and its possible use in their lives.

Thomas Kuhn (1970) describes the utility of paradigms in much the same way. We use paradigms as tools to make sense of nature, as a means to create knowledge. "To be accepted as a paradigm, a theory must seem better than its competitors [at describing reality], but it need not, and in fact never does explain all of the facts with which it is confronted" (Kuhn, 1970, pp. 17–18).

A paradigm that is widely accepted becomes a foundation for research and practice; consequently, it shapes what we see and also what we study and how we study it.

An example is Louis Pasteur's introduction of the rabies vaccine. The vaccine represented a paradigm shift in medicine. Prior to that time, blood-letting was the favored approach to cleanse the body of its evil invaders. Pasteur's discovery completely reversed this set of assumptions by showing the value of actually introducing a virus into the body to spur the development of immunities.

Yet, as Kuhn tells us, no paradigm can explain all the facts that confront it. We see certain things about the world because of this new perspective, but are unable to perceive others. In this way, competing paradigms coexist and some eventually fade away. Newer ones come onto the scene and more fully describe the reality of the moment.

In the same way, the stories about leadership in this text should be viewed with the understanding that there are no universal truths about leadership. Our purpose in offering multiple stories of leadership for critique and evaluation is to help you become your own leadership theorist. It is vital that you retain the images of leadership that hold the most power for you, for these images shape your behavior and eventually become part of how you practice leadership. The way you practice leadership is a direct result of how you imagine it.

✦ OUR ASSUMPTIONS

We are convinced that we must begin thinking about leadership in new ways in the twenty-first century. The old prescriptions are not as useful as they used to be. Our approach is built on ten basic premises:

1. *Where we are in our understanding of leadership is a function of where we have been.* We must learn from our past attempts to understand leadership. Most texts trace leadership back to only the middle of the twentieth century, but this one returns to Plato and considers the evolution of leadership. Looking at historical approaches to leadership allows us to examine their hold on our perceptions, weigh their merits, and if necessary, demystify them so we can advance our thinking about what leadership is and is not.

2. *There is no one formula for leadership.* This is so even though many bestsellers such as *The Leadership Challenge* by Kouzes and Posner and *The 7 Habits of Highly Successful People* by Covey, among a plethora of others, suggest techniques that are helpful. Practicing leadership involves a multidimensional integration of theory, process, and practice. What is effective in one situation may not be useful in another. Leadership comes in many shapes and forms.

3. *Leadership is not differentiated by setting.* Currently, most leadership texts are written primarily for a specific market such as education, management, the military, and nursing. We assert that *practicing leadership* applies in all settings, so this multidisciplinary text speaks to the concept rather than to a particular setting. We draw from many disciplines in both our theoretical discussions and our examples. This book

is not written only for those who aspire to organizational or political leadership, but also for anyone who wishes to make a difference by exerting leadership for a valued cause.

4. *Our understanding of leadership requires the vantage point of multiple perspectives.* During the twentieth century, leadership came under intense scrutiny as a subject of study, largely because the Industrial Revolution led to large organizations—and large organizations need people to run them. Researchers set about finding out just what kind of leadership was required to make these new enterprises effective.

   The body of research accumulated from this effort over the past ninety years has molded much of what we think about leadership. These perspectives, now labeled the industrial paradigm of leadership, are often presented as the best way to perceive and practice leadership.

   We propose, instead, that, as valuable as it has been, the industrial paradigm is only one way of viewing leadership. It is definitely not the only way to do so.

5. *Studying leadership across a range of human differences is the only way to approach the subject in the twenty-first century.* The study of human differences—those of race, gender, age, ethnicity, religion, and lifestyle, among other factors—affects nearly every discussion about leadership. Simply adding a chapter on diversity considerations at the end of the book would be too much like an afterthought. Leadership in this new millennium is inextricably linked to the spectrum of human differences. Period. Therefore, while we are excited about our new chapter on "Practicing Leadership in a Global and Multicultural Society," we have also incorporated this knowledge throughout the book. We have tried to make a credible start in this ongoing process, but there is much more to do.

6. *Leadership can best be understood through metaphors and described indirectly through paradigms.* Since no single, straightforward definition or view of leadership captures all of its essence, our approach to studying leadership is gathered from a variety of disciplines. In Rost's groundbreaking book, *Leadership for the 21st Century*, the hundreds of definitions he cites show how difficult an entity leadership is to pin down. We follow his example and find that leadership is better understood when we don't come straight at it.

7. *The only leadership is ethical leadership.* Practicing a high standard of ethics and a true appreciation and leveraging of diversity is the core of leadership. Leadership requires leading for the common good toward an authentic and appropriate goal. A leader is a person who values the truth and who always reflects upon the ethical implications of decisions, choosing the decision that is most ethical. A leader also appreciates and values all elements of human difference and facilitates a process whereby followers utilize or leverage qualities and characteristics that they possess.

8. *Good leaders are good followers.* You can't lead well if you can't follow well, and you can't follow well if you can't lead well. All goals that involve two or more people require an interactive process where leadership is shared based on position, situation, and expertise. Skilled leaders know when they need to be in front of a group, part of the group, and behind the group.

9. *Every leader leads differently.* Some may want to begin with the contribution of a specific discipline that they enjoy. Others may wish to begin with the theories that guide us today and tomorrow. Those who wish to "begin with the end in mind" as Covey's seven habits explain, will want to begin with our last chapter "It's Your Turn." Regardless of your approach, our goal is to help you further develop your own view and approach to leadership as you continue your own leadership journey.

10. *Leadership is a verb.* We are committed to the notion that training to *be* a leader is a misguided, though pervasive, form of leadership development. The view that great men and women are the sole practitioners of leadership—what some have dubbed the *John Wayne* view of leadership—is deeply embedded in Western culture.

   The Information Age has begun to show the difficulties with this image of the leader as the lonely-at-the-top, all-knowing hero. In every context, a flood of information makes it impossible for one person to go solo. We need each other's eyes, ears, and insights to better gauge the situation and the necessary actions for exerting leadership.

   In the new paradigms of leadership, leaders and *collaborators* (a term we prefer to *followers*) together *practice leadership*. Leadership is the process by which people work together to achieve mutual goals. We focus, accordingly, on the roles of collaborators as well as on those who practice leadership. Both are vital to twenty-first-century leadership, and we must develop the skills to do both well.

✦ A PREVIEW OF THE PUZZLE

We view the process of developing your own knowledge base and personal approach to leadership as analogous to putting together the pieces of a puzzle. For some, each piece will be of approximately equal size and shape, reflecting an ability to effectively integrate and apply all the subcomponents of leadership as described in this text with no particular personal areas of interest of expertise. For most of us, however, our puzzle will be skewed toward certain characteristics, skills, or ideas, reflecting our personal interests and strengths. For example, some readers may have a particular interest or skill in communication, and the ideas in Chapter 6, which highlights the contributions of the field of communications to our understanding of leadership, may be particularly important to these readers and may form a disproportionate share of their own personal puzzle. Others may particularly respond to the ideas of ethical leadership presented in Chapter 2, or to teaming and leadership, presented in Chapter 10. There is no one right path to being successful and we believe that successful organizations contain leaders who possess a range of skill sets.

Whatever your personal tastes and interests, we encourage you to read each chapter with an open mind and to reflect upon not only how the ideas presented apply to leadership in a general sense, but also how they fit into your own personal "puzzle" of leadership. Are the ideas in each chapter the *corner* pieces of your approach (meaning that they are likely to provide a framework for your work as a leader), or are they pieces in the murky middle whose place will not be determined until the puzzle is near completion?

The book is divided into five sections. Section I is new and was developed by the senior author especially for this textbook. Academics would call it a mega-analysis of leadership literature. The goal of this section is to provide a framework for placing all inputs we get concerning leadership. It is a way to hold the puzzle together. This section is called "Leadership in the Modern World: An Overview."

Section II, "The Core Elements of Effective Leadership," contains one new and one significantly rewritten chapter. Chapter 2, "Ethical Leadership," gives the reader a foundation, a base level understanding that applies to all the chapters, while Chapter 3, "Leadership in a Global and Multicultural Society," presents a context for the rest of the book. All leadership must be viewed based on its cultural and subcultural context. Although each reader will be working to create his or her own personal leadership puzzle, it is the position of these authors that ethics and understanding of our multicultural society are essential components for any leader. A leader who is unethical and/or does not understand or value diversity will never be able to put all the pieces together to be a successful leader.

Section III, "The Disciplinary Roots of Leadership," includes expanded and updated chapters on psychology (Chapters 4 and 5), intelligence, personality, and motivation, communication (Chapter 6), philosophy (Chapter 7), political science (Chapter 8), and management (Chapter 9). A new chapter has been added ("Teaming and Leadership," Chapter 10) to reflect the importance of leading teams, be they project teams, virtual teams, or traditional teams. These chapters provide a framework for understanding how different disciplines approach leadership. It is our belief that each of these disciplines provides valuable contributions to our understanding of leadership and we would argue that completely ignoring any one of these disciplines inevitably leads to an incomplete personal puzzle. This said, it has also been our experience that different readers, based on personal interests, values, and beliefs, will place more or less emphasis on (and thus devote more or fewer puzzle pieces to) each chapter's ideas. The goal is for everyone's personal leadership puzzle to not look the same, and we hope that through reading these chapters you discover which of these disciplines resonates most with you and why.

Section IV, "Current and Future Approaches" (Chapters 11 and 12), gives an overview of the traditional and current popular theories as well as a look at the future and approaches we believe will grow in importance and usage as the twenty-first century continues.

Finally, in Section V we discuss applying leadership. Two very different contexts are presented. First we discuss military science (Chapter 13) and applying leadership in a time-sensitive, highly charged situation. Then in a new chapter, "Environmental Leadership" (Chapter 14), we discuss approaches to leading our world in dealing with an extremely important larger concern. These chapters are meant to set the stage for Chapter 15, "It's Your Turn." This is our final chapter, and it can be used to guide readers through the process of creating their own approach to leadership.

Each chapter has the following features:

- *Leadership Moments:* A mini case to help the reader reflect upon issues that will be raised.
- *Leadership Profiles:* Two to four profiles or mini biographies of well-known (and not very well-known) people or organizations that illustrate the principles being discussed.
- *Leadership Skills* (in some chapters): Specific suggestions for applying the skills as discussed in the chapter.
- *Chapter Summary:* A brief summary of the key points in the chapter (in a few instances where there is a great deal of material covered there are summaries within the chapter).
- *Create Your Own Theory:* A unique feature of the book where readers are guided through the process of using the material in the chapter to create elements of their own approach to leadership that will be pulled together in the final chapter.
- *Key Terms, Questions for Discussion and Review:* Each chapter ends with these useful guides for review and further enquiry.
- A separate *Instructor's Manual, Test Bank,* and set of *Web Cases* are available to the instructor.

Good luck as you approach the puzzle of leadership!

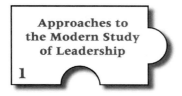

PART I

Leadership in the Modern World: An Overview

CHAPTER 1

Approaches to the Modern Study of Leadership

1

Approaches to the Modern Study of Leadership

■ ■ ■

LEADERSHIP MOMENT

It is the first day of class, and the professor has written the following question on the board: "Who is a leader?" The class is then divided into groups of four, with the instruction that these groups are to talk about whom their ideal leaders are, identify the common denominators between the individuals they select, and report back to the class.

Johannes is first, and he says, "This is easy. Leaders are people who can direct others—like Napoleon or Patton. They don't let other people tell them what to do and they are people that everyone respects, because if you cross them..."

"I agree that leaders are people that others respect," says Judy, "but I think the mark of a great leader is someone who works not for glory but for the betterment of others, like Mother Theresa or Mahatma Gandhi or Nelson Mandela—or even Jesus Christ. Leaders do it for other people— if you're only in it for glory, you're not really a leader."

Maya adds, "I think you both are forgetting about the little guy. Sure, Napoleon and Mandela are leaders who changed the world, but what about people who aren't heads of armies or heads of state? I think leadership is found in everyday acts, like the Columbine teacher (Dave Sanders) who died trying to save his students or the single mom who works three jobs in order to send her children to college. Those are the real leaders."

"I think Pat Tillman is a true leader," says Zach. "He gave up a lucrative career as an NFL football player to fight in Iraq and died serving the country. Johannes, you are our leader. Please give our report to the class."

1. *What should Johannes say?*
2. *Are there any common denominators among these differing ideas on leadership?*
3. *Are all of the group's ideas about leadership valid? Why or why not?*

What is this thing called *leadership?* There are many ways to complete the sentence, "Leadership is..."

If you look in the popular press, you might think leaders are any of the following:

- Quick-change artists
- Quarterbacks
- Referees
- Trapeze artists
- Despots
- Brown nosers
- Servants of the public
- Personal trainers
- Politicians
- Rich people

Let's look at some definition of this seemingly all-encompassing notion of leadership. Each of the following definitions contains kernels of truth about leadership, but certainly not the comprehensive picture:

> Leadership is all about getting people to work together to make things happen that might otherwise not occur or prevent things from happening that ordinarily would take place.
> —Rosenbach & Taylor, 1993

> Leaders are people who perceive what is needed and what is right and how to mobilize people and resources to accomplish mutual goals.
> —Cronin, 1993

> To be a leader for the next century, you must be able to bring out the best in people. You must be able to motivate people… You have to have humility. Humility says, "I don't have to act like a big shot, like I've got all the answers. I can ask you what your answers are, what your ideas are. And I can be open." Openness is really important. So leadership requires a wholeness, and the ability to contain two seemingly contradictory qualities: "power" and "humility."
> —Patricia Aburdene, co-author of *Megatrends 2000* and *Megatrends for Women*

Leaders are listeners. They know how, as Cronin puts it, "to squint with their ears… If we are to have the leaders we need, we will first have to agree upon priorities. In one sense, if we wish to have leaders to follow, we will often have to show them the way."

According to DuBrin, leadership is the ability to inspire confidence and support among the people who are needed to achieve organizational goals (DuBrin,

1995). DuBrin reviewed five other representational definitions of leadership—after noting that as of 1995, approximately 30,000 research articles, periodical articles, and books had been written on the topic in the twentieth century. Those representative definitions include the following:

- Interpersonal influence directed through communication, toward goal attainment
- The influential increment over and above mechanical compliance with directions and orders
- An act that causes others to act or respond in a shared direction
- The art of influencing people by persuasion or example to follow a line of action
- The principal dynamic force that motivates and coordinates the organization in the accomplishment of its objectives

Most definitions include some aspects of hierarchy, influence, and consideration of the interaction between leader and others. Our favorite definition of leadership is "Leadership is an influence relationship among leaders and followers who intend real changes that reflect their shared purposes" (Rost, 1998).

Who is a leader? Again, there are many definitions. Perhaps the most accepted is Nahavandi's definition: "A leader is defined as any person who influences individuals and groups within an organization, helps them in the establishment of goals and guides them towards the achievement of these goals…" (Nahavandi, 2003). In Chapter 12, we will return to this question and share our views on this question.

How do you study leadership? Lots of ways! In reviewing five management texts, for example, we found that they all agree on the fundamental topics to be covered, but the leadership literature varies vastly in approach, style, and content. One of the challenges is finding a way to organize the literature.

We have created a format for categorizing the literature (Figure 1-1) and have attempted to develop a schema where all the modern approaches to leadership can be organized and viewed in relationship to each other. The numbering (1–12) is for convenience, *not* to create any hierarchy. The numbers *do* reflect, in a general sense, the historical popularization of each of the approaches.

✦ TRAIT THEORY AND OTHER PSYCHOLOGICAL APPROACHES

Perhaps the most common view of leadership is to study the traits of a leader and attempt to learn from or imitate these traits. **Trait theory** says that leadership is a function of nature—some are born to lead and inherit the traits that leaders need (the Kennedys, Bushes, Rockefellers, etc.). Others think that leadership is a function of nurture, that leaders must develop as fully as possible the traits they are born with, and that leaders must develop their skills in other areas as well. They need to use diversity principles to ensure that a team has the comprehensive

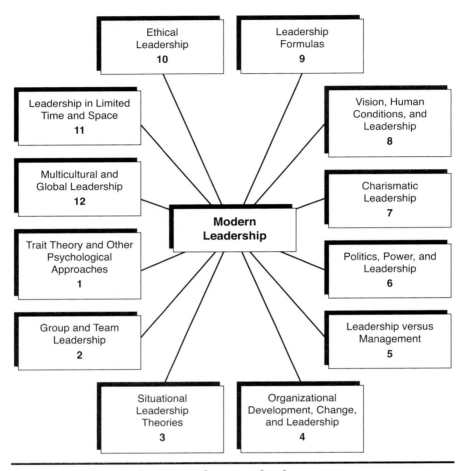

FIGURE 1-1 **Approaches to Modern Leadership**

skill set that is needed. Tools such as the Meyers-Briggs Type Indicator or the Whole Brain Instrument are often helpful in these assessments.

As we demonstrate in Chapters 4 and 5, intelligence, personality, and motivation are often seen as keys to leadership development. You will also notice throughout the text, and especially in Chapters 11 and 12, that many theories are based on some aspect of psychological theory.

✦ GROUP AND TEAM LEADERSHIP

The study of group leadership was an important part of leadership literature. *Group dynamics* courses taught (and still teach) the roles individuals play in groups, such as gatekeepers, process developers, information senders, and so on.

The concept of teams and team building is now central to leadership. We define a team as two or more people who have developed processes to accomplish one or more specific goals (Shriberg, Shriberg, and Kumari, 2005). These teams may be called task forces, committees, quality circles, or project teams, or they may be groups that are central to the organization (such as the board of directors, executive team, or a product launch team). They may be self-directed or they may have a designated leader. They are functional and cross-functional; they may be virtual or face-to-face groups. The art or science of building effective teams is a crucial aspect of leadership. It is difficult to discuss leadership without discussing it as a pluralistic act—the leadership of teams —and viewing the leaders in juxtaposition to each other. These concepts are discussed throughout the book but especially in Chapter 6, Chapter 9, Chapters 11 and 12, and in their own Chapter 10.

✦ SITUATIONAL LEADERSHIP THEORIES

Situational leadership refers to the leader being able to adapt his or her leadership style to the situation at hand. Many modern theorists argue that leadership is the process of balancing the needs of followers, the situation, and the leaders themselves. We believe that there is a fourth group of players—the other stakeholders in an organization who are impacted by the decision that is made. Blanchard's work discusses the need to balance the level of supportive behavior and the level of directive behavior in any given situation (see Chapter 9 [Blanchard 1978, 1999] for a variety of approaches to situational leadership). Although some argue that leaders must have a predictable, constant style, others posit that the situation often dictates the style. Learning when to apply what style is a key to effective leadership.

✦ ORGANIZATIONAL DEVELOPMENT, CHANGE, AND LEADERSHIP

Many see leadership as the process of helping an organization to effectively meet its goal. How is this done? The field and processes of **organizational development** (O.D.) have grown significantly in the last twenty years. The concept of unfreezing an organization, accomplishing the necessary changes, and (some would agree) refreezing them, has become a major area of study. Change theories abound and many recent best sellers describe the process of change. *Good to Great* and *Built to Last* by James Collins (and Jerry Porras) are examples of books that describe the OD and change process. Leadership and change are not synonymous but are often spoken about in the same sentence. Publications giving advice on the OD and change process often top the Best Sellers list. Throughout this text we give profiles of change leaders and discuss organizations that have made significant changes. Original essays by Gordon Barnhart, John Pepper, Stephen Covey, and James Kouzes and Barry Posner discuss the process of change (in Chapters 2, 9, 10, and 11).

✦ LEADERSHIP VERSUS MANAGEMENT

Many leadership texts discuss leadership in relation to management and classical management theory describes leadership as a subset of management. One of the key processes a manager must complete (along with planning, organizing, staffing, evaluating, and continuously improving) is to *lead*. Many leadership theories take the opposite view and see management as a subset of leadership. For example, Gardner lists the ten tasks of leaders and the fourth task is to manage the process.

We believe that management and leadership overlap, but also are different functions. They approach tasks such as developing a work force, completing a project, rewarding participants, and so on, differently. Both approaches are needed.

Leaders and/or managers, often called administrators, leaders, coordinators, project leaders, etc. (their title does not differentiate their approach), can be skilled at both leadership and management, only leadership, only management, or neither. To complete a task or administer an organization successfully, both skills are needed. Chapter 9 is devoted to management in relation to leadership. In this text we agree that the world is overmanaged and underled.

✦ POLITICS, POWER, AND LEADERSHIP

Both leadership and politics can be described as the art and/or science of accomplishing specific goals; the term **politics** implies understanding and resolving human factors involved in decision-making. The field of political science is often seen as *applied leadership* and clearly a good leader must be politically savvy. Power theorists are often divided into **power over** and **power with** approaches.

Power over theorists often discuss authority and responsibility and whether they can be delegated. They discuss using power wisely and appropriately to accomplish goals and objectives.

Power with writers believe in empowering others. In Chapter 12 Rost argues that true leadership is based on influence, not positional power, and that when people are empowered they often are effective. Power grows as it is shared and everyone involved is empowered. Many biographies and autobiographies discuss how a person used power. We view leadership as leading without using power.

In the book, Chapter 8 discusses power and leadership from the top and, along with Chapters 11 and 12, presents a variety of approaches to power sharing and empowering.

✦ CHARISMATIC LEADERSHIP

History is dominated by **charismatic leaders**. How do they become leaders? Why? Who are they? It seems that each generation has its share of charismatic leaders who lead by inspiration—and often by sheer personality. It is said that when the people are in need the leader will come. Some give hope, energy, and bring out the best in people (Mayor Giuliani, Dr. Martin Luther King Jr., President Kennedy), and some bring out the worst in people (Hitler, David

Koresh, Osama Bin Laden). It is important when studying leadership to understand models of charismatic leadership as we discuss in Chapter 6.

◆ VISION, THE HUMAN CONDITION, AND LEADERSHIP

What is the goal of the leader? Does it advance humankind? Is the content (the outcome) the key? Is the vision about a process (the "I have a dream" speech)? Many leadership books and approaches center on a vision of improving some element of the human or organizational condition. Can a leader lead if there is no goal to lead toward? In the last quarter of the twentieth century the field of *visioning* came into vogue. Individuals, organizations, and societies are challenged to set noble goals that enhance the quality of life for all. Leaders that both articulate and move society toward that future are widely admired. This concept is discussed throughout our text and highlighted in Chapters 13 and 14. We urge our readers to create their own vision for themselves in Chapter 15.

◆ LEADERSHIP FORMULAS

Many books, articles, and presentations provide formulas for successful leadership. While clearly there is no one right way, the wisdom of these approaches is often very helpful to people as they develop their own leadership style. Stephen Covey's *Seven Habits of Highly Successful People* has spawned an industry of training and follow-up publications. Maxwell's *21 Indisputable Rules of Success,* Powell's *18 Lessons in Leadership,* as well as Gardner's *10 Functions of Leadership* (see Chapter 12), and Bennis's *4 Major Competencies of Leadership* (see Chapter 12) are a small sampling of the many publications that present an ordered (and, at times, sequential) approach to leadership. The Rule of Three (as discussed in Chapter 13, or as demonstrated in numerous books by Blanchard and others) also illustrates how leadership can be presented by using numbers. This text includes lists in several places, and we do recognize the value of these formula books. Our Web site reviews several of these publications. We challenge our readers to create their own theory—many choose to develop a formula that guides their own approach to practicing leadership.

◆ ETHICAL LEADERSHIP

Kenneth Lay of Enron, Martha Stewart, Al Dunlap of Sunbeam, Dennis Kozlowski of Tyco—all of these corporate leaders have behaved in a manner that has brought disgrace to the image of corporate leaders. Scandals in the Church, governments, and other institutions have also made the public take a hard look at the role and behavior of leaders. Is leadership the opposite of tyranny? What must leaders do to be ethical?

This edition of our book and the newest editions of many leadership books include a chapter on ethics (Chapter 2). Dr. Linda Treviño, a well-known ethicist, develops guidelines and expectations for an ethical leader. As ethics courses are being expanded and developed in all professional endeavors, it appears to us, and we are proud to repeat this fact, that finally we all "got it." *Ethical* leadership is the only leadership. Our text closes with two examples of leadership in action where ethics are stressed—military science and environmental leadership. In our final chapter, we ask the readers to develop their own comprehensive approach to leadership (Chapter 15). We certainly expect that ethics will be central to your theory!

✦ LEADERSHIP IN LIMITED TIME AND SPACE

Most leadership theories and approaches assume the context (the organization) will be continuous. In fact, much of everyone's time is invested with projects that are limited in time—they begin and they end. **Project leadership** requires all the skills and understandings as discussed in this analysis but, in addition, it requires that these skills be applied in limited time. It also adds the skill of *closure*, a carefully planned and executed process where the project ends and everyone involved is made whole and stronger as a result of their involvement. A new literature is emerging on this topic, and Kloppenborg, Shriberg, and Venkatraman's *Project Leadership* is a book that explores the leadership challenges at every stage of a project.

As the microchip has made the world more virtual and the number of people who "lead" others whom they rarely see in person grows, the challenges of **virtual leadership** brought in by the twenty-first century also grows. Kumari created a new chapter on teaming (Chapter 10); two of the main foci of the chapter are leading a project team and leading a virtual team. In this text we view leadership as a continuous, unending, and deeply relationship-oriented phenomenon. We also recognize that time-limited and space-limited (virtual) situations require skilled leadership.

✦ MULTICULTURAL AND GLOBAL LEADERSHIP

Does one lead a 10-year-old in the same manner as one leads an 80-year-old? Do Koreans lead in the same way as the Dutch? Do women lead in the same way as men? Of course not. Indeed, in this world of instantaneous communication and interdependency, leadership cannot and should not be separated from diversity. The Diversity Wheel explored in Chapter 3 presents twenty-eight elements of diversity. The subsets of each of these elements affect the style and expectation of a leader. **Multicultural leadership** is about being able to recognize and appreciate human differences and being inclusive to followers that bring a variety of diversity elements to the table. This text profiles leaders from around the globe whose internal and external dimensions vary vastly. Honoring and leveraging diversity is the focus of Chapter 3, but it, like ethics, is a foundation for all other chapters.

The greatest challenge of our modern era is to lead and follow people who are different in many ways than you are. We argue that all leadership must be based on a respect and understanding of human differences.

The four profiles that follow feature several of the approaches discussed in this chapter. Can you identify them?

MIEP GIES
Hider, Helper

In the Prologue to *Anne Frank Remembered, The Story of the Woman Who Helped to Hide the Frank Family*, Miep Gies wrote:

> I am not a hero. I stand at the end of the long, long line of good Dutch people who did what I did or more—much more—during those dark and terrible times years ago, but always like yesterday in the hearts of those who bear witness. Never a day goes by that I do not think of what happened then.
>
> More than twenty thousand Dutch people helped to hide Jews and others in need of hiding during those years. I willingly did what I could to help. My husband did as well. It was not enough.

Just over five feet tall, this blue-eyed blond was a sickly child in Vienna when WWI began. Sent to the Netherlands in a humanitarian program for hungry Austrian children, Gies was informally adopted by a large and loving Dutch family. Eventually, she came to consider herself a Dutch national. In her early adolescence she kept a diary, much like her future friend Anne Frank was to do.

In Amsterdam, Gies started working for Travies and Co., makers of products for the homemaker. She became friends with the president, a shy man named Otto Frank. Gradually, she and her fiancé became good friends with the entire Frank family.

Gies was given increasing responsibility in the small company, and eventually she became a trusted advisor to Otto. She and her husband, Jan, were among the very few to know the whereabouts of the Franks and the four others hidden above the business address in Amsterdam. Daily she visited the residents of the "Annex," as Anne called it in her diary. She saw to every detail of their lives, growing exhausted with the strain of trying to feed eight people on stolen ration cards for five, a situation made more frantic by the poor conditions in occupied Holland.

She and Jan also sheltered another Jew in their own house for months at a time, although she never told the Franks of this fact, fearing that it would worry them. Jan also took part in the underground resistance.

Despite their careful efforts, the German Secret Service discovered the secret annex, and on August 4, 1945, Miep watched them take away her friends. She was able to save the diary that became a classic tale of courage. Miep notes that she had to be persuaded to write *Anne Frank Remembered*:

> I had to think of the place that Anne Frank holds in history and what her story has come to mean for the many millions of people who have been touched by it. I'm told that every night when the sun goes down,

somewhere in the world the curtain is going up on the stage play made from Anne's diary…Her voice has reached the far edges of the earth.

Gies and her husband hoped for an eventual return of the Franks—in fact, she even went on foot to the Gestapo in a bold attempt to bribe officials for their freedom. She kept the business going despite horrible conditions—no food, no coal, little hope. Many times she bicycled out to the country, evading German guards to beg for food from farmers. She somehow managed to keep the company alive, knowing once again that others depended on her.

After the Germans surrendered, Otto Frank came home from Auschwitz; the rest of the Frank family did not. Miep relinquished the leadership of the business to him. She had been an effective leader in an extremely difficult period, but she knew it was time to step down.

Otto Frank lived with Jan and Miep, coming to consider them family, for seven years until he moved to be near his mother in Switzerland. For long months after the war ended, Mr. Frank, Miep, and Jan waited to hear about Anne and her sister, who had been sent to a work camp at Bergen-Belsen. Finally, a letter from the camp nurse confirmed the worst: both girls had died from typhus. Anne had died only a few weeks before the camp was liberated.

It was only then that Miep turned to Anne's diary. Having left it untouched for over a year, she gave the papers to Mr. Frank, saying, "Here is your daughter Anne's legacy to you."

Miep withdrew totally from the business, feeling that taking care of three men at home—Jan, Otto Frank, and another family friend—was her full-time job.

She has since turned her attention to keeping Anne's memory alive. Working with the Anne Frank Foundation, Miep Gies has traveled throughout the world, telling the story of a young girl whose humanity could not be silenced. Characteristically, she shrugs off praise for her role in the drama:

> My story is the story of very ordinary people during extraordinarily terrible times. Times the like of which I hope with all my heart will never, never come again. It is for all of us ordinary people all over the world to see to it that they do not.

(For more information visit http://teacher.scholastic.com/frank/miep.htm.)

MARTIN LUTHER

A Hammer for Religious Expression

While some leaders enter the world stage quietly, only achieving international acclaim toward the end of their careers, others arrive with all the subtlety of a lightning bolt. Such was the story of Martin Luther, who, by nailing his famous 95 *Theses* to the doors of the Wittenberg Castle Church on October 31, 1517, sparked a religious debate that continues to this day.

"During the Reformation, the Church feared that Martin Luther would hit like an atomic bomb and drive a wedge that would permanently divide West Europe's Christianities," said *Time* magazine senior religion writer David Van Biema in a November 1, 1999, article. And the church's fears were legitimate, for, greatly aided by the recent invention of the printing press, Luther's "heretical" words were printed in several editions within months and spread like wildfire across Europe, inspiring others to challenge the hegemonic church.

The church's response was initially to ignore Luther, but after his writings became more widespread, a papal bull was issued against him; which Luther burned. Luther was called upon to recant his writings, which he refused to do. Instead, he wrote a letter to Pope Leo X in which he apologized personally to the Pope, but continued to denounce what he viewed as the false doctrine and corruption of the Church. Despite his growing popular support, Luther was subsequently excommunicated from the Church and barred from the Empire by Emperor Charles V. However, Luther was squired to safety by friends and continued to write, even after he was ordered to stop publishing. In the meantime, Protestantism continues to spread across Europe. The genie had been let out of the bottle, based in large part on the courage and writings of one man.

And, nearly 500 years later, while the divisions between modern-day Lutherans and the Vatican remain real, in the fall of 1999 an event took place that surely would have been surprising to Martin Luther. The Catholic and Lutheran churches formally made peace with each other.

KING HUSSEIN
A Monarch Turns International Peacemaker

Being a head of state in the treacherous terrain of the Middle East is a significant challenge for even the most savvy of leaders. Jordan's King Hussein, however, was not afforded the luxury of time or experience before assuming leadership of his nation. Born on November 14, 1935, he was only sixteen when he witnessed his grandfather King Abdullah's—who was then King of Jordan—assassination in Jerusalem (the young Hussein's life was saved when a bullet headed for his chest was deflected by a medal that he was wearing). He was named King at age seventeen and formally ascended the throne on his eighteenth birthday. Few at this time expected that this young king would hold his throne, let alone become by the time of his death in 1999 the longest ruling head of state in the world.

Not that Hussein did not have challenges to his rule. Acting decisively, before his twenty-first birthday, this diminutive (he was 5'4") leader had ousted the British army commander he had inherited and fended off a military coup attempt. Over the next forty-three years, he would survive seventeen known assassination attempts, a disastrous war with Israel in 1967 in which Jordan lost much territory (including all of its holdings in Jerusalem), a civil war with the Palestinians in which he sent Yassir Arafat into exile, and a shaky balancing act during the Persian Gulf War between his Western and Middle Eastern allies.

Hussein was never your typical king. He ruled with a firm hand, yet had an extraordinary capacity for forgiveness. Those who plotted to assassinate him were arrested, but not executed, rare in the "eye-for-an-eye" ethos of much of the Middle East. An avid ham radio enthusiast, he was known throughout the world as the friendly voice of "JY1." He also was known to pilot his royal jet and could frequently be seen racing around Aqaba on his motorcycle, queen in tow. Toward the end of his life, he was an active Internet participant, always seeking to connect with the world.

If his legacy were simply consolidating his authority while a teenager and building Jordan up to its current extremely influential role in Middle East, that alone would be the story of an extraordinary leader. However, what transformed King Hussein into a leader for the ages was his ability to become a living symbol of hope for peace in the Middle East. During his rule, his most damaging military defeat was at the hands of Yitzhak Rabin and the Israelis, and his most significant internal threat took place when Yassir Arafat led Palestinians who had been displaced from Israel in a war against Hussein. There were few people in the world more entitled to a personal grudge with both Rabin and Arafat than King Hussein. Yet, Hussein was able to move beyond this, and by the end of his life he counted Rabin and Arafat among his friends.

When Hussein's plane landed in Jordan for the last time, two days before his death, he was greeted by Arafat, who planted a kiss on his forehead. This was not a token gesture, but rather a tribute to a man who worked tirelessly for peace in the Middle East, a man who was credited by President Clinton for saving the groundbreaking Oslo peace accords and who twice left his sickbed at the Mayo Clinic to go to the Wye River meetings of 1998 and push its participants towards peace.

So also did Hussein make peace with Yitzhak Rabin and Israel. In a scene that once seemed impossible, Hussein memorably rushed to the side of the parents of Israeli children who had been killed by a crazed Jordanian soldier and apologized. Having formally made peace with Israel in 1994, he formed a strong friendship with its then president, the former military general Yitzhak Rabin. In a moving tribute at Rabin's funeral in 1995, Hussein eulogized,

> "I had never thought that the moment would come like this when I would grieve the loss of a brother, a colleague, and a friend—a man—a soldier—who met us on the opposite side of the divide. You lived as a soldier, you died as a soldier for peace. I commit before you, before my people in Jordan, before the world, myself to continue to do our utmost to ensure that we leave a similar legacy."

(For more information visit http://www.kinghussein.gov.jo/kinghussein.html.)

NELSON MANDELA
Enduring to Triumph

The saga sounds more like a myth than a historical event: after spending twenty-seven years behind bars for protesting South Africa's oppression of blacks and people of color, Nelson Mandela became the first popularly elected president of South Africa in the nation's first all-race election.

His autobiography, *Long Walk to Freedom*, chronicles his birth to a royal family in the Transkei section of South Africa, his decision to renounce his right to succeed his father as chief of the Tembu in order to study law, and his gradual awakening to the realities of the political situation in his country. Mandela became convinced of the need to join forces with the other people of color—the "coloreds" and the Indians—who were also discriminated against by the government. Deeply influenced by Mahatma Gandhi's teaching and by his example in South Africa, Mandela espoused nonviolence for years, until he determined that armed hostility would be the only way to overcome the oppressor. He set about to help plan armed resistance to the government.

Mandela had complied with countless bans against participating in any meeting or group event. Finally, after the 1960 massacre of thousands of unarmed people protesting the pass laws (limiting travel by blacks and insisting that they submit to checks of their passes), he became a fugitive. He lived underground for eighteen months, donning a variety of disguises to avoid being caught. He was disguised as a chauffeur when he was arrested by security police in 1962. Two years later, Mandela was found guilty of sabotage against the government. He was eventually taken to desolate Robben Island to begin his long imprisonment. In his trial, Mandela summarized the purpose of his wrongdoings:

> I would say that the whole life of any thinking African in this country drives him continuously to a conflict between his conscience on the one hand and the law on the other. This is not a conflict peculiar to this country. The conflict arises for men of conscience, for men who think and who feel deeply in every country...law as it is applied, the law as it has been developed over a long period of history, and especially the law as it is written and designed by the Nationalist government is a law which, in our views, is immoral, unjust, and intolerable. Our consciences dictate that we must protest against it, that we must oppose it and that we must attempt to alter it...men, I think, are not capable of doing nothing, of saying nothing, of not reacting to injustice, of not protesting against oppression, of not striving for the good society and the good life in the ways they see it.

Never losing hope that both he and the people would eventually be free, Mandela somehow survived his time in prison and continued to communicate with the still-banned African National Congress. When South African President F.W. de Klerk announced to Parliament a series of sweeping reforms that signaled the death knell of apartheid, he also announced that the ANC was no longer banned and that political prisoners would be freed.

On February 11, 1990, Mandela walked out of prison to a tumultuous welcome. He delivered his first remarks after the long silence: "Friends, comrades and fellow South Africans. I greet you all in the name of peace, democracy and freedom for all! I stand here before you not as a prophet but as a humble servant of you, the people. Your tireless and heroic sacrifices have made it possible for me to be here today. I therefore place the remaining years of my life in your hands."

He wrote in his autobiography:

> I wanted first of all to tell the people that I was not a messiah, but an ordinary man who had become a leader because of extraordinary circumstances. I wanted immediately to thank the people all over the world who had campaigned for my release…It was vital for me to show my people and the government that I was unbroken and unbowed, and that the struggle was not over for me but beginning anew in a different form. I affirmed that I was 'a loyal and disciplined member of the African National Congress.' I encouraged the people to return to the barricades, to intensify the struggle, and we would walk the last mile together.

In the next few days he reiterated the dream of a nonracial, united, and democratic South Africa based on a one-person, one-vote rule expressing no hatred for whites but instead outrage at the system that turned blacks and whites against each other.

He was under enormous pressure after his release. Knowing that the government wanted nothing more than to see him appear foolish and fallible to the people, Mandela nevertheless had to begin negotiations about the future of the country.

Time and time again, he sought to assure the whites that they were also South Africans and that this was their land, too. "I would not mince words about the horrors of apartheid, but I said, over and over, that we should forget the past and concentrate on building a better future for all."

He set about what he explains is his mission: "One of preaching reconciliation, of binding the wounds of the country, of engendering trust and confidence…At every opportunity I said all South Africans must now unite and join hands and say we are one country, one nation, one people, marching together into the future."

In *Days of Grace*, Arthur Ashe Jr. expressed many people's marvel about Mandela:

> To have spent twenty-seven years in jail for political reasons, to have been deprived of the whole mighty center of one's life, and then to

emerge apparently without a trace of bitterness, alert and ready to lead one's country forward, may be the most extraordinary individual human achievement that I have witnessed in my lifetime. I marvel that he could come out of jail free of bitterness and yet uncompromising in his basic political beliefs; I marvel at his ability to combine an impeccable character, to which virtually everyone attests, with the political wisdom of a Solomon. In jail, I am told his white guards came to have such respect for him that in some ways he was their warden and they the prisoners, more prisoners of apartheid.

(For more information visit http://www.nobel.se/peace/laureates/1993/mandela-bio.html.)

✦ Chapter Summary

This chapter begins by attempting to define leadership, then to categorize and put in context the plethora of literature and approaches to leadership. In a recently completed analysis, Shriberg developed a schema for the twelve elements of leadership. Each is briefly described and references are made to how these elements are presented in the book.

✦ CREATE YOUR OWN THEORY ✦

At the start of this chapter, we put you in the position of having to mediate between four individuals who had differing ideas as to what leadership is and who best embodies it. As is clear by now, we believe that there is no one "correct" model of leadership and it is the challenge of each and every one of us to form our own conceptualization of what leadership means to us. With this in mind, let's return to the opening vignette. Which of the four students do you agree with most? Do you agree with more than one student? None of these students? Why or why not?

We have presented several definitions of leadership. It is now your turn.

1. Before reading the rest of the text, what is your definition of leadership?
2. What is your own style or approach?
3. Which of these elements do you include? Which do you need to add? Why?

✦ Key Terms

charismatic leader

multicultural leadership

organizational development

politics

power over

power with

project leadership

situational leadership

trait theory

virtual leadership

✦ Questions for Discussion and Review

1. Of the definitions of leadership given, which do you prefer? Why?
2. What psychological approach to leadership do you use? Which approaches are less used by you?
3. Name three groups you belong to. Name three teams you belong to. Explain why some are groups and some are teams.
4. Give an example of situational leadership that you experienced.
5. Are change and leadership the same thing?
6. What is the difference between leadership and management?
7. What does the term *politics* mean to you?
8. Who is your favorite charismatic leader? Why is that person charismatic?
9. Name two ethical leaders you admire. Why do you admire them?
10. What is a virtual team?

The Core Elements of Effective Leadership

CHAPTER 2

Ethical Leadership[1]

LEADERSHIP MOMENT

Kelly Smith is confused. As the purchasing manager for a medium-sized manufacturing company, she has just been given the task of choosing a vendor for a $100,000 contract for a production line component. The regular procedure is for the company to ask vendors for proposals and then choose the one that provides the required specifications at least cost. However, this time Kelly has been given, by her boss, the names of two vendors and asked to pick one. On further probing, Kelly finds out that of the two companies being considered, the spouse of a board member owns one and an influential local politician owns the other. Both companies have quoted seemingly competitive rates, but no other proposals have been solicited, so Kelly does not know whether another company would offer better rates. Although nothing has been said to her explicitly, she feels that these two companies have been short listed in order to serve the interests of some senior executives in her company. Choosing a vendor in this manner is a clear violation of the established guidelines. However, her boss has clearly instructed her to go ahead without requesting other proposals. On the one hand, if she ignores his instructions, she will likely be in trouble with senior management. On the other hand, if she does follow instructions, she will earn the goodwill of the parties involved, and there will probably be no immediate harm to her department or her company. However, it will set an undesirable and clearly unethical precedent.

1. *What would you do?*
2. *How would your view change if you were likely to lose your job if you violated the boss's direct order?*
3. *Would your opinion be different if the contract was for $100 million instead of $100,000?*

---

1. This chapter is adapted from chapter 9 in Treviño & Nelson, *Managing Business Ethics,* "Straight Talk About How to Do It Right," John Wiley & Sons, Inc.

It is the position of this text that people cannot be successful leaders if they are not ethical. The last few years have witnessed scandalous behavior in the business community and virtually every other sector of society (religious, government, sports, military, and education). Although some are quick to pin the blame on a few "bad apples," there is generally more to the story than that (Treviño & Youngblood, 1990). "Bad apples" feel free to behave badly when the organization's ethical context does not clearly support doing the right thing. And, sometimes, bad contexts can create bad behavior in people who would not ordinarily engage in it. Note the behavior demonstrated in pictures of prisoner treatment at the Abu Ghraib prison in Iraq. Without a strong ethical context (standards, guidelines, training, etc.) and clear ethical leadership, a number of "normal" American soldiers engaged in horrific behaviors.

It is important to understand that most people, including adults, look to their peers and significant others (such as leaders) for guidance regarding ethically appropriate behavior. The substantial literature and research on cognitive moral development (Kohlberg, 1969) says clearly that most adults are not autonomous moral actors. They look to others for guidance. And, without guidance from leaders, most will follow what their peers do. How many of you have heard people ask their friends, "What would you do in this situation?"

So, leadership is essential to create a strong ethical context in organization, beginning with executive leaders who set the "tone at the top" (Clinard, 1983; Posner & Schmidt, 1992) and the organization's overall ethical culture. From there, messages about what is appropriate and inappropriate are reinforced by leaders at all other levels in the organization through their daily behavior and their implementation of organizational systems.

✦ EXECUTIVE LEADERS CREATE ETHICAL CULTURE

Although known discussions of the central components of leadership date back several thousand years (see Chapter 7), it has been only recently that modern academics have devoted significant attention to what constitutes ethical leadership and how leaders can shape the ethical elements of their organization (Treviño, Hartman & Brown, 2000; Treviño, Brown, & Hartman, 2003). Let's begin by considering executive leadership and how executives create ethical culture. Anthropologists define culture as "a body of learned beliefs, traditions, and guides for behavior shared among members of a society or a group" (Barrett, 1984). This idea of culture also has been used extensively to understand organizations, as well (Deal & Kennedy, 1982).

Ethical culture can be thought of as a subset of the broader organizational culture and includes a number of formal and informal systems that work together to support ethical conduct in the organization. Formal systems include the organization's selection system, formal rules and codes, authority structure, reward system, orientation and training programs, formal decision processes, and so on. Informal systems include norms of daily behavior, heroes, rituals, myths and stories, and the language that is used by organization members.

Leadership is critical to an organization's culture because senior leaders create these systems and structures (Schein, 1985), and everyone looks to their behavior for guidance about how to behave with regard to ethics—and virtually everything else in the organization as well. Often, an organization's founder has a vision for how the organization should operate. He or she may personify the culture's values, providing a model for others to observe and follow and guiding decision making at all organizational levels. Most everyone is familiar with the demise of the auditing firm, Arthur Andersen, which had been one of the United States' premier accounting and consulting firms prior to the Enron scandal. The saddest part of the Andersen story may be that Arthur Andersen, the firm's founder, was a strong ethical leader. Andersen said, "My own mother told me, 'Think straight—talk straight. ...This challenge will never fail anyone in a time of trial and temptation." "Think straight, talk straight" was the mantra for decades at the company. Partners said with pride that integrity mattered more than fees. The story about Andersen's ethics became part of the firm's lore. At the age of twenty-eight, when he was just starting his business, Andersen confronted a railway executive who demanded that his books be approved. Andersen said, "There's not enough money in the city of Chicago to induce me to change that report." Andersen lost the business, but later the railway company filed for bankruptcy and Arthur Andersen became known as a firm one could trust. In the 1930s, Andersen talked about the special responsibility of accountants to the public and the importance of their independence of judgment and action. Andersen's management approach was a top down, "one-firm" concept. No matter where they were in the world, if they were in an Andersen facility, customers knew they would receive the same quality and type of work. Employees were trained in the "Andersen Way," and that way included strong ethics. Training at the St. Charles, Illinois, facility was sacred at Andersen. The professionals it created spoke the same language and shared the same values. They felt part of a very special group that called themselves *Androids.* Andersen died in 1947 but was followed by Leonard Spacek, a leader with similar convictions who ran the firm in the 1950s and 1960s. The company's strong ethical culture continued pretty much through the 1980s. People didn't expect to get rich—rather, they wanted "a good career at a place with a good name." And partners acted in the long-term best interest of the firm. When you talk with retired Andersen veterans, they'll tell you about those years and you can feel the pride they used to feel (Toffler, 2003).

Senior executives are particularly important because employees take their cues from the messages sent by those in formal leadership roles. But, most employees don't know the senior executives of their organization personally. They only know them from afar. Senior executives must develop a reputation for ethical leadership by being visible and in the forefront on ethics issues. Research suggests that such a reputation rests upon dual dimensions: a **moral person dimension** and a **moral manager dimension** (Treviño, Hartman, & Brown, 2000; Treviño, Brown, & Hartman, 2003).

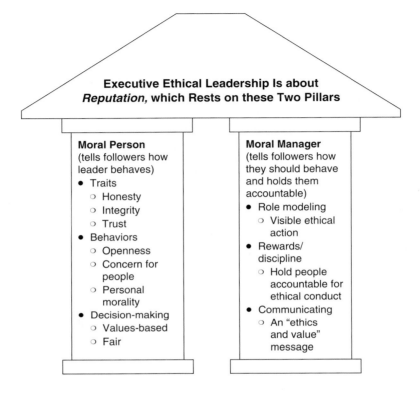

Executive Ethical Leadership Is about
***Reputation,* which Rests on these Two Pillars**

Moral Person
(tells followers how
leader behaves)
- Traits
  - Honesty
  - Integrity
  - Trust
- Behaviors
  - Openness
  - Concern for
    people
  - Personal
    morality
- Decision-making
  - Values-based
  - Fair

Moral Manager
(tells followers how
they should behave
and holds them
accountable)
- Role modeling
  - Visible ethical
    action
- Rewards/
  discipline
  - Hold people
    accountable for
    ethical conduct
- Communicating
  - An "ethics
    and value"
    message

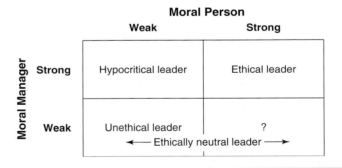

	Moral Person	
	Weak	**Strong**
Strong	Hypocritical leader	Ethical leader
Weak	Unethical leader	?

Moral Manager

◄——— Ethically neutral leader ———►

FIGURE 2-1   Executive Ethical Leader Reputation Matrix

The moral person dimension represents the ethical part of the term *ethical leadership*. As a *moral person*, the executive models personal traits such as integrity, honesty, and trustworthiness, traits that long have been known to characterize effective leaders (Bass, 1990; Kouzes & Posner, 1993; Kouzes & Posner, 1995; Schmidt & Posner, 1982; Posner & Schmidt, 1992). More important than personal traits, however, are visible behaviors. These include doing the right thing, showing concern for people and treating them with dignity and respect, being open, listening, and living a personally moral life. Finally, part of being viewed as a moral person is making decisions in a particular way—decisions that are based on values, fairness, concern for society, and other ethical rules such as the Golden Rule ("Do unto others as you would have them do unto you").

Being a moral person, however, isn't enough to be perceived as an ethical leader. Executives must also act as *moral managers*—they must focus on the leadership part of the term *ethical leadership* by making ethics and values an important part of their leadership agenda and proactively shaping the firm's ethical culture. They do that by conveying the importance of ethical conduct in a variety of ways. The large majority of the messages that employees receive in business are about bottom-line goals. Therefore, senior executives must make ethics a priority if it is to get attention from employees. Moral managers do this by visibly modeling ethical conduct, communicating openly and regularly with employees about ethics and values, and by using the reward system (both rewards and discipline) to hold everyone accountable to the standards regardless of one's level in the organization or the level of productivity. If the organization's top salesperson is caught lying to customers, she must be harshly disciplined.

James Burke, former CEO of Johnson & Johnson, is one of the best-known examples of a highly visible ethical leader. Soon after being appointed CEO in the late 1970s, he challenged his senior managers to revisit and update the company's age-old credo that put caring about customers first in the list of company values. He wasn't willing to have it hanging on the wall unless his senior managers were committed to living it. After much discussion and input from J&J sites around the world, the credo was revised, but its commitment to customers first and foremost remained intact. Less than three years later, in 1982, the Tylenol poisoning crisis occurred in Chicago. The credo was credited with guiding corporate decision makers to make the right choices throughout the crisis.

In that crisis, seven people in the Chicago area died from taking cyanide-laced Tylenol, a painkiller produced by McNeil Labs, a division of Johnson & Johnson. Although the cause was unknown for several weeks, a thorough investigation later proved that the poisonings were the result of external sabotage. Nevertheless, because of the company's clear commitment to customers, the company recalled all 31 million bottles of Tylenol (a retail value of over $100 million) and sent Mailgram messages to more than 500,000 doctors, hospitals, and distributors of Tylenol. It also established a crisis phone line where consumers could call a toll-free 800-number to ask questions about the product. In addition, Burke and other executives were accessible to the press and were interviewed by a variety of media. Johnson & Johnson then offered coupons to entice consumers back to Tylenol and, ultimately, redesigned Tylenol's packaging so that it would be tamper resistant—as it remains today.

Johnson & Johnson's reaction to the Tylenol crisis demonstrated that its credo wasn't hollow. And, by being accessible to the press, its executives displayed concern for consumers by refusing to dodge responsibility or blame any other party for its difficulties. Following the crisis, Burke initiated a regular credo survey process in which employees were asked about the company's performance with regard to the credo—a process that continues to this day (Treviño, Hartman, & Brown, 2000). It was clear to everyone that Burke really cared about the credo and the values it represented.

Unethical Leadership

Unfortunately, unethical leaders can influence the development of an unethical culture just as much as ethical leaders can influence the development of an ethical culture. In terms of the matrix, unethical leaders are weak moral persons and weak moral managers. In interviews with senior executives, Al Dunlap was cited most often as a senior executive with a reputation for **unethical leadership.** Dunlap's reputation for making struggling companies profitable had a down side—one of his strategies was to slash payroll and fire as many employees as possible, a pattern that earned him the nickname "Chainsaw Al". In fact, John Byrne of *BusinessWeek,* wrote a book about Dunlap. According to Byrne, while CEO of Sunbeam, Dunlap was known for emotional abuse of employees—being "condescending, belligerent and disrespectful." "At his worst, he became viciously profane, even violent. Executives said he would throw papers or furniture, bang his hands on his desk, and shout so ferociously that a manager's hair would be blown back by the stream of air that rushed from Dunlap's mouth." Dunlap also demanded that employees make the numbers at all costs, and rewarded them handsomely for doing so. As a result, they felt pressure to use questionable accounting and sales techniques. Dunlap also lied to Wall Street, assuring them that the firm was making its projections and would continue to reach even higher. In the end, Dunlap couldn't cover up the real state of affairs and Sunbeam's board fired him in 1998. But, he left the company crippled (Byrne, 1999). In 2002, Dunlap settled a civil suit filed by the SEC. He paid a $500,000 fine and agreed never to serve again as an officer or director of a public company.

Hypocritical Leadership

Perhaps nothing makes us more cynical than a leader who talks incessantly about integrity and ethical values, but then engages in unethical conduct, encourages others to do so either explicitly or implicitly, rewards only bottom-line results, and fails to discipline misconduct. This leader is strong on the communication aspect of moral management but clearly doesn't "walk the ethical talk." It's a "do as I say, not as I do" approach. Al Dunlap made no pretense about ethics. All that mattered was the bottom line, and he didn't pretend to be a good guy. But, **hypocritical leadership** is all about ethical pretense. The problem is that by putting the spotlight on integrity, the leader actually raises follower expectations and awareness of ethical issues. At the same time, employees realize that they can't trust anything the leader says. That leads to cynicism, and employees are likely to disregard ethical standards themselves if they see the leader doing so.

Jim Bakker stands out as an excellent example of hypocritical leadership. In the late 1970s and early 1980s, Bakker built PTL Ministries into one of the world's biggest religious broadcasting empires. At its peak, Bakker's television ministry reached more than 10 million homes and had 2,000 employees. Bakker, along with his wife Tammy Faye, claimed to be doing "the Lord's work" as he raked in millions of dollars, convincing the faithful to purchase a limited number of lifetime memberships in two hotels he claimed would be built at the PTL's Heritage USA Christian theme park. The problem was that the 25,000 lifetime memberships (promising a free annual family stay for four days and three nights) in the Heritage Grand Hotel morphed into 66,683 memberships. And, instead of the limited 30,000 memberships at the proposed Heritage Towers, PTL sold 68,755 memberships. It would be impossible to provide promised services to this many people given the proposed size of the project. The funds donated for these projects were being tapped to support PTL operating expenses, including huge salaries and bonuses for the Bakkers and others. Eventually, the house of cards collapsed, and PTL filed for bankruptcy in 1987, three months after Bakker resigned in disgrace. The IRS revoked PTL's tax-exempt status, and in 1989, Bakker was convicted on fraud and conspiracy charges. He spent eight years in prison (Tidwell, 1993).

Ethically Neutral Leadership

Many top managers are neither strong ethical leaders nor unethical leaders. They fall into what employees perceive to be an **ethically neutral leadership** zone. They simply don't provide leadership in the crucial area of ethics, and employees aren't sure what the leader thinks about ethics or if she or he cares. On the moral person dimension, the ethically neutral leader is not clearly unethical, but is perceived to be more self-centered than people-oriented. And, on the moral manager dimension, the ethically neutral leader is thought to focus intently on the bottom line without setting complementary ethical goals. There is little or no ethics message coming from the top. But, it turns out that such silence sends an important message. In the context of all the other messages being sent in a highly competitive business environment, employees are likely to interpret silence to mean that the top executive really doesn't care how business goals are met (only that they are met), and they'll act on that message (Treviño, Hartman, & Brown, 2000).

Consider Sandy Weill, chairman of the board and formerly CEO of Citigroup. A 2002 *Fortune* magazine article described the firm as a "blockbuster money machine." But, the article also recounted recent allegations. "Citi helped Enron hide debt; Salomon peddled worthless WorldCom debt; Star analyst Jack Grubman recommended Winstar as it was heading for bankruptcy; Salomon rewarded telecom execs with hot IPOs," and more (Loomis, 2002: 74–75). So, the company is spending lots of time and money playing defense with the media. According to *Fortune*, Weill is contrite and has now "gotten religion," if a bit late. Weill has "told his board that he feels his most important job from now on is to be sure that Citigroup operates at the highest level of ethics and with the utmost integrity" (Loomis, 2002: 76). As a result, new procedures and business standards are being developed. However, the article also cites widespread cynicism about the turnabout, noting that Weill is often "tone deaf" on these issues, and it took a while for Mr. Weill to "get to the party."

At least from the perspective of public perception, Weill seems to exemplify ethically neutral leadership. Being tone deaf on these issues is exactly what ethically neutral leadership is about. Weill's public statement that the "company is too big to micromanage" applies here. He says a CEO relies on "very competent people" and trusts them to do a good job. So, he delegated ethics management to the executives running Citigroup's various businesses. If they thought ethics was important, it got resources and attention. If they didn't, it didn't. And, with corporate rewards focused primarily on the bottom line, there was probably little motivation for managers to attend to such issues. This decentralized approach to ethics management contrasts sharply with John Reed's (the prior CEO's) leadership on ethics issues. Reed encouraged and supported the development of a strong centralized corporate ethics program with global reach. Certainly, Citigroup is much larger, more diverse, and arguably harder to manage now. Nevertheless, if an executive is to be perceived by employees as an ethical leader, a clear ethics message from the top is required—one that is at least as loud as the messages about the bottom line.

Research has found that ethical leadership is critical to employees. In a recent study, unethical behavior was lower, and employees were more committed to their organization, more ethically aware, and more willing to report problems to management in firms that had an ethical culture characterized by top executives who represented high ethical standards, regularly showed that they cared about ethics, and were models of ethical behavior (Treviño, Weaver, Gibson, & Toffler, 1999). But, interestingly, senior executives are often unaware of how important their ethical leadership is. Many believe that being an ethical person who makes ethical decisions should be enough. But it isn't enough. Executives must lead on this issue (be moral managers as well as moral persons) if it is to register with employees. In a highly competitive environment that focuses on the bottom line, employees need to know that the executive leaders in their organization care about ethics as much as they care about bottom line performance. An ethical leader makes it clear that strong bottom line results are expected, but only if they can be delivered in a highly ethical manner.

✦ SUPERVISORS LEAD ON ETHICS EVERY DAY

As important as executives are for setting the ethical tone at the top, designing organizational policies and systems, and modeling appropriate behavior, supervisors are also the ones who actually implement these policies on a day to day basis. They hire, fire, oversee daily work, conduct performance appraisals, and make promotion and compensation decisions, among other activities. And, because most employees work closely with their supervisor, they have many opportunities to observe that supervisor directly in action and to take their cues from his or her behavior. Among the most important cues is how the supervisor treats those he or she is supervising. A supervisor who is an ethical leader is concerned first and foremost about the well-being of his or her people, developing and supporting them in difficult situations.

If you're a leader, it's time to evaluate your own ethical leadership. Would followers say that, as a moral person, your personal/professional behavior is ethical (honest, fair, and trustworthy)? Would they say that you think of other people's needs above your own, and that you take good care of the people who work for you? Would they say that you make good and fair decisions based on ethical principles and values? Would they say that, as a *moral manager,* you communicate loudly and clearly that ethics is as important as bottom-line performance? Do people know that you'll put your money where your mouth is? Have you shown that you would be willing to walk away from business in order to live your principles? Finally, would they say that you hold yourself and everyone else accountable by rewarding ethical performance and disciplining unethical performance even if that means losing business or disciplining a high-level employee or high performer?

Interestingly, many people believe that ethical leadership is mostly about vision and values. But, both of these are highly abstract and future oriented. Research suggests that ethical leadership is more concrete and more about the "here and now." Vision and values set a general direction and tone, but in today's complex and competitive business environment, people need concrete evidence that their leader is a person of integrity who cares about ethics at least as much as bottom-line performance. Employees learn this by observing how leaders behave toward them and others, how leaders make decisions, and whether leaders set explicit ethical standards and take concrete action to reinforce those standards every day.

✦ LEADERSHIP SKILLS ✦
A Guide for Ethical Decision Making

We often find ourselves in ethical binds, at work and in our personal lives. So how should we go about dealing with a situation that calls for an ethical decision to be made? The first step, of course, is to make sure you have all the facts. This might not be as easy as it sounds, but it is vital to the process. Once all the information has been collected, it must be analyzed to determine the appropriate course of action. Several philosophical theories exist that can help serve as a framework for making a morally correct choice. Five of the more popular ethical theories are outlined as follows:

1. *The rights theory.* The main proponent of the **rights theory** was the eighteenth-century philosopher Immanuel Kant. This approach says that in making a decision the basic moral rights of all involved must be protected. Some of the rights that must be considered are:

   a. The right to the truth about things that impact us

   b. The right to privacy (as long as others' rights are not violated)

    c. The right to be safe from harm or injury (unless the risk has been taken on knowingly)

    d. The right to what has been promised as part of a contract or agreement

2. *The common good theory.* One of the oldest approaches to ethics and states is the **common good theory,** which states that the good of an individual is inseparable from the good of the larger society. Therefore, an ethical decision is one that benefits the most people in society and is made keeping in mind its impact on the community.

3. *The fairness theory.* The **fairness theory** emphasizes that an ethical action treats everyone equally, without showing either favoritism or discrimination against anyone. Before making a decision, the fairness of the consequences must be determined.

4. *The utilitarian approach.* This approach is most widely associated with John Stuart Mill. The **utilitarian approach** asks that all the available alternatives be evaluated and the choice be made by picking the option that causes the greatest good (or the least harm) to the greatest number of people.

5. *The virtue ethics approach.* Aristotle was one of the main proponents of this approach. The **virtue ethics approach** says that when making a decision, we must choose the alternative that builds desirable character traits within us. According to this theory, an action is ethical if it builds within a person virtuous traits such as honesty, selflessness, courage, and so on.

Each of these theories can serve as a backdrop for making a decision. Asking yourself whether a decision, for example, violates the rights of any affected parties may be a good starting point to arrive at an ethically sound decision. Which of these approaches best fit with your personal model of ethical leadership, and in which situations might you see yourself applying each of these theories?

More often than not, leading ethical conduct is about courage. It is about being able to leave behind a sheltered existence to stand up for a cause, about being able to effect change. Is ethically neutral leadership acceptable, or is it the leader's responsibility to lead a paradigm shift? The following essay by Gordon Barnhart talks about leading change and the courage needed to accomplish it.

THE HERO'S JOURNEY
by Gordon Barnhart

The heroic journey is the story of the change process in its healthiest form. The classic heroic journey begins with crossing a threshold, leaving a known world or comfort zone. After crossing that threshold, we face tests and trials that usually require new or altered ways of perceiving, thinking, and acting. As Alice found in *Alice in Wonderland,* things often aren't what they seem. What worked before is no longer effective, and can even be counterproductive or dangerous.

Many journeys are failures because we never really leave the known world. Because we never truly let go, we can never really discover the new truths and the revelations that are possible. Our trials may be physical, intellectual, emotional, or spiritual, and consequently, our changes may be in those same areas. We may face tests in dealing with mistakes and failures; avoiding the seductive lures of taking the easy way out; dealing with uncertainty, doubt, and perhaps despair; and finding sources of energy and renewal along the way.

Few, if any, of the heroes who do cross the threshold must face the trials and tests alone, even though the heroic journey is ultimately an individual one. Almost every journey features helpers of various sorts who can provide direction, tools, nourishment, encouragement, and coaching in coping in the new environment.

Healers will also be present to help overcome the inevitable injuries that befall us on our journeys. As the tests, the help and healing may take the form of physical, emotional, intellectual, or spiritual help. Although the roles of helpers and healers may vary, they will almost always be present in some form. Our challenge is to see them and use their help on the journey.

We may also find companions for part of the journey, just as we're likely to encounter other characters, including tricksters, jokers, allies, enemies, and opponents.

Those of us who successfully meet the challenges of the journey will arrive at the final phase, which is some form of return or completion. We "return" with the gifts that we have discovered, whether they are new truths, new abilities, new technologies, or new opportunities.

The return may be the most difficult part of all because a hero's return may evoke changes that the rest of the "kingdom" does not appreciate. The hero's changes will alter relationships, requiring changes in others that may ripple in many directions and for long distances. The gifts of the hero can easily threaten the status quo.

Sometimes heroes are welcomed and celebrated; sometimes they are ignored. Sometimes they are shunned, reviled, or attacked (even crucified). The reactions hold true in families, organizations, corporations, or communities—regardless of size.

We face major challenges in beginning the journey and crossing the threshold, traversing the unknown and facing the trials and tests found there, and in dealing with the impact of our return.

The hero's journey requires three forms of courage, each more challenging than it first appears:

- The courage to see and speak the truth
- The courage to create and affirm a vision of the desired state
- The courage to persevere, to "hold the course"

Although ethics is clearly important for supervisors, you do not need to be in a formal leadership role for your ethics to have an impact on the world. We recommend that as you read through the different chapters in this text, you continually think about how ethics apply to your daily life and the type of ethical leader you either already are or are seeking to become. The next section provides an example of a guide for ethical decision making that can help you in this journey, followed by an example of three individuals—Roger Boisjoly, Sherron Watkins, and Rosa Parks—who took a strong ethical stand at great professional and personal risk.

ROGER BOISJOLY
The Man Who Tried to Stop the *Challenger*

Roger Boisjoly was a technical troubleshooter at Morton Thiokol Inc. (MTI), a company that manufactured rocket boosters for the National Aeronautics and Space Administration (NASA) when the space shuttle *Challenger* disaster shocked the world and changed his life forever. With more than twenty-five years of experience in the industry, he took very seriously his professional responsibility to make well-informed, fact-based decisions in any projects he undertook. His commitment to voicing the truth before and immediately after the *Challenger* exploded in January 1986 both brought him recognition as a person of ethical courage—and eventually cost him his career.

In January 1985, Boisjoly was involved in a project to improve the performance of the O-rings that served as connectors between segments of MTI's rocket boosters. He found that the seal had allowed hot gas to pass through. In April of the same year, an examination of seals from another rocket again showed that the seals were faulty—the primary seal was completely broken and the secondary seal had also suffered some damage. Boisjoly recognized that the O-rings would not withstand severe cold, but the problem could be corrected if the diameter was increased. However, the management at MTI ignored his memo pointing out the weakness of the seal, and the engineering team watched helplessly as no action was taken to correct the potentially fatal design flaw.

The rules stated that a launch could only take place if both NASA and the contractors gave the go-ahead. So on January 28, 1986, when cold weather conditions were threatening to test the limits of the seals, Boisjoly and other MTI engineers decided that the launch was not a good idea. NASA was prepared to cancel on MTI's recommendation; however, MTI management decided to go ahead because they did not want their relationship with NASA to be in jeopardy. Within seconds of takeoff, Boisjoly and others watched in silent horror as the shuttle exploded into flames, taking with it seven innocent lives and billions of dollars in investment.

Boisjoly had spent one whole year trying his best to be heard, risking his job at times, but he failed to stop the launch. Since the *Challenger* disaster, the final decision to launch rests with the astronauts, and two launches have been stopped. The American Association for Advancement of Sciences recognized Boisjoly's persistence before and immediately following the crash and awarded him the Prize for Scientific Freedom and Responsibility. He subsequently made a career for himself as a forensic engineer. He also travels around the country, sharing his story through lectures and workshops, driving home the importance of ethical behavior and professional responsibility. He often begins his lectures with a video of the shuttle taking off and the shocked faces of the ground crew as their colleagues went down in a ball of fire. Emphasizing that the accident was a result of the combination of poor design, bad weather, and management apathy, he says, "Your first responsibility is to others. Always tell the customer what they need to hear, not what they want to hear. And ask yourself, would you allow a family member to use the product or process with no reservations?"

SHERRON WATKINS
The Whistle-Blower at Enron

Although most adults take their cues for moral behavior from their peers, there are those rare free thinkers who set high standards for themselves regardless of the behavior of those around them. Sherron Watkins is one such person.

In 2001, Sherron Watkins was just another Enron employee who had decided to turn in her high-profile responsibilities and take up a back-office position in order to spend more time with her family. Her decision started a chain of events that finally led to Enron's fall and to her being named one of *Time* magazine's Persons of the Year for her courageous role in blowing the whistle on unethical practices at Enron.

Several times during her career with Enron, Ms. Watkins and other employees had seen warning signs indicating that Enron's accounting practices were going beyond just creative to highly aggressive. In essence, Enron was borrowing heavily and disguising its debts as revenues. Its debt to equity ratio was an astounding 250 percent, and no one, including the bankers and the auditors, was batting an eyelid. When she realized that the firm was excessively over-leveraged, Watkins decided that it was time to act. Her first reaction was to start looking for another job, while preparing to warn incoming CEO Ken Lay of the mess that had been made by his predecessor, Jeff Skilling. Jeff Skilling had resigned a few days after Enron's stock price fell dramatically, and Watkins sent a memo to Ken Lay warning him of the potential disaster. From then on, events unfolded rapidly—the memo made its way to the media, Enron was forced to take a hit of $700 million to its pretax profits, it fired several thousand employees, and filed for bankruptcy in December 2001.

For Watkins, the decision to speak up was not an easy one. She was surrounded by colleagues who, though aware of what went on, had remained silent for two main reasons. The first reason is what she describes as the "frog-in-boiling-water" syndrome, where employees tolerate unethical practices because the gradual increase in the magnitude lessens the impact of such unethical practices on the conscience. The second reason is that employees draw their cues about acceptable practices from the top management's actions. In Enron's case, there had been continuing instances of senior executives indulging in unethical practices (from using the corporate jet for personal trips to paying themselves huge bonuses while laying off thousands of employees with meager severance packages). Not only did Watkins lack the support of her peers, but she was also perilously close to losing her job, as she found out when she came across a memo from one of Enron's external lawyers suggesting that "the employee who made the sensitive report" be terminated because Texas law provided no protection to whistle-blowers at the time! The knowledge that the company she was trying to save had considered terminating her was, to Watkins, much harder to come to terms with than the threats to her physical safety and her demotion from her plush executive suite to a tiny, shabby little office.

Watkins's commitment to workplace ethics has earned her numerous accolades. She was the recipient of the Court TV Scales of Justice Award and its Everyday Hero's Award, and the Women Mean Business Award from the Business and Professional Women/USA Organization. Barbara Walters included her as one of the 10 Most Fascinating People of 2002. Watkins credits her courage to her small town upbringing. She says growing up in a small town instilled in her the belief that she could make a difference if she really wanted to. And make a difference she did.

ROSA PARKS

A Time to Sit

Rosa McCauley Parks was forty-two that afternoon in Montgomery, Alabama. The soft-spoken woman took the bus every day to her job as a seamstress. She fumed with the injustice and indignity of the bus company and its drivers. Once before, bus driver James Blake had tested her spirit: he let her enter the front door to pay, but then insisted she follow the custom in which blacks then got off and reentered through the back door to claim a seat. This time, when she had paid and moved outside to the rear door, he pulled away before she could reenter. It was an insult that black people faced all the time in Montgomery.

On the next occasion, she was ready for Mr. Blake. He ordered her to leave her seat so a white person could sit, but Parks calmly said no. He insisted, in louder and louder terms. "No," came her reply, just as firmly. It wasn't simply that she was tired. Yes, she was weary from working, but she was more tired of the treatment she and her fellow blacks had to put up with.

What many people don't know is that Rosa Parks was sophisticated about her rights. For twelve years she had been secretary of the local NAACP, watching and learning as the group took on ever more ambitious goals. In addition, shortly before her famous act of resistance, she had participated in a training session at the Highlander School in Tennessee, where blacks and whites met to encourage each other and learn how to organize opposition to injustice. She was much more than a symbol of resistance and protest; but she was an awfully dignified symbol.

Throughout the eleven-month bus boycott that Parks's resistance prompted, she and her husband endured hate calls, death threats, and eventually, the loss of both of their jobs before segregation in public transportation was struck down by the U.S. Supreme Court in 1956. The Parks moved to Detroit, where Rosa took care of her ailing mother and husband.

Rosa Parks has continued to be active in civil rights, resisting many people's attempts to see her only as a symbol and not as a woman with definite views and convictions. In addition to winning a seat on the board of the Detroit NAACP, she founded the Institute for Self Development, to encourage young people to work for change and to grow as people.

(For more information visit http://www.time.com/time/time100/heroes/profile/parks01.html.)

✦ Chapter Summary

People usually take cues for ethical behavior from the world around them. Therefore, it is critical for leaders not only to model ethical behaviors in their own lives but also to be *perceived* as ethical by those members of their organization who only see them from a distance. An important part of promoting this perception is sending a strong message that ethics are the organization's highest priority. Just as ethical leaders can cultivate an ethical culture, unethical leaders can create and promote an unethical climate throughout the organization. While some unethical leaders make no pretense of what they are, there are others who talk about integrity but practice and encourage unethical behavior. Such hypocritical leaders create a culture of mistrust and cynicism. In addition to ethical, unethical, and hypocritical leaders, there is a fourth category of ethically neutral leaders. These leaders do not take a stand one way or another on ethics, focusing instead on bottom lines. This lack of expression on so important an issue often conveys the message to employees that the end always justifies the means. It is obvious, therefore, that embodying a commitment to ethics through one's actions is paramount in order to be considered an ethical leader.

✦ CREATE YOUR OWN THEORY ✦

We've seen in this chapter that sometimes not taking a stand on an issue can set as bad an example as actually being the perpetrator of unethical behavior. What does this mean for your own leadership style?

In the opening leadership moment, Kelly will face no visibly negative consequences if she remains ethically neutral and does not actively protest.

Many of us face this situation in our careers, where unethical behavior filters down from the top of the organization. Sometimes, we do nothing, feeling less responsible if the origin of the behavior is somewhere higher up. Other times, the dollar value of the transaction makes an impact on our actions. Is your reaction to unethical behavior the same in all situations, or does it differ depending on circumstances? What criteria do you use to determine whether the line has been crossed?

◆ Key Terms

common good theory

ethical culture

ethically neutral leadership

fairness theory

hypocritical leadership

moral manager dimension

moral person dimension

rights theory

unethical leadership

utilitarianism theory

virtue ethics theory

◆ Questions for Discussion and Review

1. Why is it important for leaders to demonstrate ethical conduct?
2. What impact can a leader's position on ethics have on the culture of an organization?
3. Describe the dimensions of building a reputation for ethical behavior.
4. What is meant by the terms *hypocritical leadership* and *ethically neutral leadership*?
5. How does the rights theory compare with the fairness theory?
6. How does the common good theory compare with the utilitarianism theory?
7. What theory of ethics, in your opinion, prevails at the United Nations?

CHAPTER 3

Leadership in a Global and Multicultural Society[1]

For five years, you have been the president and CEO of a successful Midwestern U.S. utility company that merged with four other regional utility providers to support their ability to weather the financial constraints of deregulation and the resulting competition. At the start of the merger, you are named CEO of the newly consolidated organization. You now have former competitors and counterparts reporting to you, and are faced with the task of creating a shared vision for these individuals and the very different branches of the organization they lead. Your business units, though all located within a 100-mile radius, represent significant diversity in their organizational cultures, physical locations, workforce composition, customer populations, and types of services they deliver. Additionally, the utility industry is experiencing significant technology updates and rising costs resulting in reductions in revenue, and the communities you serve are experiencing significant waves of immigration of limited or non-English speaking Africans and Latinos. How can you address these issues to ensure the current and future success of your organization?

1. *What challenges would you anticipate in creating a shared vision for this new organization?*

2. *What internal and external environmental factors should you consider in carving out a multicultural leadership path that will support the success of your organization?*

3. *How might you need to work differently to cultivate the organizational support within the different business units that is necessary to ensure the success of your multicultural leadership effort?*

---

1. This chapter is adapted from Chapter 3, "Cultural Anthropology," written by Megan L. Clough, and Chapter 8, "Practicing Leadership in a Multicultural Society," written by Ann Harbison, Steven Reudisili, Arthur Shriberg from *Practicing Leadership: Principles and Applications*, John Wiley & Sons, Inc. (2002).

Whether you lead a not-for-profit healthcare system in the midwestern United States or you are a college student developing your professional and/or personal path, you are undoubtedly a part of our world's increasingly interconnected global economy and multicultural societies. The challenges brought on by this dynamic require different responses from the various players in our society: companies must strategize about how they will compete in international markets; government agencies must debate over how they will effectively serve growing minority and immigrant populations; hospitals and health organizations must consider the patient care implications introduced by different religious beliefs and practices; managers and leaders must understand how to attract, motivate, and retain Baby Boomer, Generation X, and Millenial talent; and individuals with self-questioning and leadership skills must learn to thrive in the increasingly multicultural world.

In this text, it is argued that while different leaders have different skills and talents, there are two core frames in which all leaders must have a solid grounding. The first frame, *ethics,* was discussed in the previous chapter. This chapter describes the second frame, which is the ability to lead in a multicultural society and global economy. Although this chapter focuses on this dimension primarily from an organizational perspective, we believe that one does not have to be a captain of industry to be a successful multicultural leader.

While individual leaders, particularly charismatic leaders, are often the public face of an organization, it is the constituencies surrounding leaders who actuate their power and influence. Therefore, knowing whom one is leading and how that population is evolving is an absolute imperative for success in the twenty-first century. This chapter explores the implications of leading in an evolving multicultural society within the United States and the enormous challenges and opportunities that accompany being a leader of a global business or organization.

✦ IMPORTANCE OF MULTICULTURAL LEADERSHIP

You may be a brand manager with a U.S.-based multinational company who is developing products and media to tap into the growing purchasing power of the Latino population. You may be a resident advisor on a college campus responsible for a building where students from eleven countries live. You may be a human resources executive challenged with developing strategies to reduce employee turnover by improving your company's ability to attract, develop, and retain Generation X talent. Irrespective of the industry, success in each of these situations is important to the organizations' well-being, and the successful outcome requires leaders to have insight and knowledge about a group other than his or her own. In the 1990s, consulting firm KPMG utilized the slogan "think globally, act locally" in its promotional ads. Increasingly, this is exactly the approach that leaders must take to be successful in today's multicultural and global marketplace.

Successful leadership in an increasingly multicultural society requires **cultural competency,** the ability of individuals and organizations to function appropriately and effectively in cross-cultural situations or with diverse populations, as well as technical competency. Therefore, leaders must cultivate organizational cultures that are culturally competent in order to effectively mobilize their constituencies.

Two of the most common terms used when discussing **multicultural leadership** are *culture* and *diversity*. These words are, at times, used (or, more accurately, misused) interchangeably and are generally not well understood. The following two sections provide definitions of these terms, along with examples of their application.

Culture and Learned Behaviors

The definition of **culture** that we use as a working definition in this chapter comes from anthropology. It is, "Culture is *elements of learned behaviors* and meaning systems common to a human society." Let's explore **learned behaviors.**

Every day we learn social lessons and behaviors. In fact, we can't get away from them. How we choose to sleep, bathe, and eat all reflect these social lessons and ultimately are our culture. For example, in Japan most people sleep on futons, whereas in the United States most people sleep on mattresses. In addition, Japanese bathing methods are different from the showers people take in the United States, and so is the food. So if you are Japanese, you learn one set of standard behaviors, whereas if you are American it is likely that you will learn a different set. These behaviors describe and contribute to our culture.

We learn our culture by mimicking the behaviors of those who teach us when we are children. And this is one link to leadership. What does being a leader mean to you? Where do you get the answers that pop into your head as we consider that question? Can you see your father or mother modeling or describing their sense of leadership? Your teacher? Television?

In large part, our culture forms our definition and behaviors for leadership. For instance, when we choose to be a leader, we typically express this by molding our behaviors to act according to how we were taught.

Let's explore two different lessons on leadership and examine how they ultimately translated into differing behaviors. During World War II, Japanese fighter pilots called *Kamikaze* were taught that honorable leaders give their lives so that others might survive. In enacting this type of leadership, *Kamikaze* pilots were specific. Do you know what they did? These pilots would dive their booby-trapped planes into enemy territory. However, rather than exiting their planes, the pilots would stay in them and crash. They would give their lives so that their country could win in war. In Japanese culture, these pilots were considered brave and became legends.

By contrast, in the United States fighter pilots were taught that honor involved dedication to staying alive so they could continue to help their platoon. As a result, U.S. fighter pilots always evacuated if their plane went into a dive. Committing suicide would have been considered weak and dishonorable.

What has been described thus far in this section has referred to learned behaviors, described in Chapter 4 as *nurture*. However, *nature*, responsible for those characteristics present at birth, also plays a role in culture. Specifically, our behaviors are determined in part by our physical capabilities. For instance, how we walk is determined by the fact that we have two legs. How we talk is determined by the fact that we have a mouth with vocal chords. So, though there is great variety in behaviors across the world, in at least one way our cultures are limited and commonly shaped.

Multiculturalism and Diversity—What Is the Connection?

Diversity is often described as differences in culture. We often think of culture in terms of nationality and ethnicity. However, because culture refers to groups with shared identity and history, it can also refer to other dimensions of our social identity. These dimensions can include gender, religion, region of the country in which we live, socioeconomic position, or generation. For example, you are a part of a culture based on your gender—every society has differences in the ways males and females are socialized. Therefore, leaders aspiring to be effective in multicultural environments must develop an awareness of the different dimensions of culture that are and will be most central to their different constituencies of customers or followers.

Gardenswartz and Rowe (1994), as seen in Figure 3.1, provide an excellent tool, the diversity wheel, for illustrating the multiple dimensions of diversity that make up each of us as individuals.

The *diversity wheel* comprises four circles. The first circle represents our personality—the internal aspects of our character and temperament that uniquely define us. The second circle on the kaleidoscope represents our physical attributes, such as gender, race, and ethnicity, which are largely visible to others. The third circle represents our social characteristics such as marital status, educational background, economic status, religion, and geography. Finally, the outer circle represents the organizational aspects of our identity—our position within a work system, seniority, and formal authority. All individuals are represented by the diversity wheel, and so too does each individual possess a complex, multicultural identity based on each of the four circles. This includes white males, often not thought to be included in topics of diversity.

The diversity wheel is valuable in that it can remind multicultural leaders that even if their constituencies look physically similar, they may very well represent diverse cultures, even within the United States. Understanding how dimensions of diversity at each level affect attitudes, behaviors, and motivations can be tremendously valuable to leaders when they are leading across cultures.

Challenges to Leading Diversity

A primary reason that being an inclusive leader is challenging relates to our inherent dislike for uncertainty and change. While we learn thoughts and behaviors in a somewhat sterile way, we become emotionally and otherwise attached to our cultural lessons and beliefs. As a result, we often want to preserve and sustain them more than we want to learn other thoughts and behaviors.

In many instances, there are incentives for maintaining our cultures as they are. For example, in organizations and politics, power is frequently granted to individuals who exhibit particular thoughts and behaviors, and we risk losing

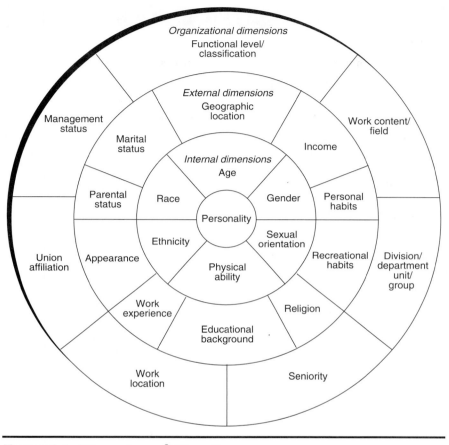

FIGURE 3-1 Dimensions of Diversity
SOURCE: Gardenswartz, L., and A. Rowe (1994).

power if we adopt alternative perspectives and behaviors. This need for self-preservation is an important consideration in identifying challenges to establishing an inclusive leadership style.

Successful multicultural leaders have taken steps to understand how their own cultures shape their view of the world and leverage their understanding of other cultural views, or cultural competency, to support their effectiveness. This development process, however, often does not occur, since raising their emotional and intellectual understanding requires leaders to assume the risk of adopting alternative perspectives and behaviors, which they may not be prepared to do. As a result, leaders frequently attempt to approach multicultural leadership efforts as they would other business issues, and skip the personal development and introspection. Failure to take this critical step may result in diversity or multicultural efforts that fail because the leadership is unprepared, individually and organizationally.

◆ CREATE YOUR OWN THEORY ◆

Viewing the Diversity Wheel from a Developmental Framework

One of the many ways that the diversity wheel depicted in Figure 3-1 can be viewed is through the lens of time. That is, for many people, different dimensions of the wheel are more or less salient at different points in their life. For example, the internal dimension of age is often very important to children and adolescents (e.g., the three-year-old who corrects you and says that she is three *and a half* when you say that she is three, or the fifteen year old anxiously awaiting his sixteenth birthday so that he can get his driver's license), often then becomes somewhat less important during middle adulthood, but may then become increasingly important as one approaches and enters retirement. Similarly, while your typical five-year-old may not think a lot about his or her appearance or geographic location, these things may become very important later in life.

We encourage you to view the diversity wheel and determine which dimensions were most important to you at different stages in your life. Start with age five, then increase by multiples of five until you reach your current age. How have things changed? Are there some dimensions that have always been central to your personal identity and others that have been more or less important at different points? Now project five and ten years into your future. What dimensions do you see as continuing to be central to your personal identity, and what dimensions may become more or less important with time?

According to diversity management pioneer Merlin Pope, the founder of one of the nation's oldest diversity management consulting firms, Pope & Associates (www.popeandassociates.com), "Diversity can be positive, it can be negative, but is never neutral." With that in mind, multicultural leadership, whether done well, not well, or not at all, significantly influences a number of aspects of an organization and its performance. This is true whether it's a small physician's practice or a large multinational retailer, or a heavily regulated government agency. Savvy leaders recognize effective diversity management as core to their business's success and build their diversity or multicultural efforts to support strategic objectives.

◆ CREATING EFFECTIVE WORKFORCE DIVERSITY EFFORTS

Today's increasingly global marketplace has produced an environment of competition that requires organizations to continually operate at their greatest levels of efficiency to achieve and maintain success. When you consider the factors that impact organizational efficiency in a global economy, what do you find? In general, you find a more ambiguous and less predictable reality that requires leaders to employ a more flexible approach that will allow their organizations to keep up with the pace of their environments' change. Compound this with the reality of increasing multicultural populations across the United States and in the workplace, and the challenge of managing those differences while capturing multicultural populations as customers who represent growing purchasing power, and you have the business case for a comprehensive **workforce diversity effort.** Workforce diversity focuses on the composition of the workforce and what is needed to build, develop, retain, and maximize its capabilities in support of organizational objectives. To do this in a manner that yields a return on the investment requires a comprehensive effort, as opposed to the fragmented approach many organizations often take. Effectively leading such an effort requires cultural competency.

Consider this example: The litigation manager of an east coast U.S. health care system recognized that a lot of her company's litigation stemmed from managers' and employees' inability to meet the unique needs of their diversified patient population. She took this information to the organization's CEO, and the CEO determined that it was becoming increasingly important for the organization to employ a workforce that would understand the unique needs of its customer population, which was increasingly African American and Hispanic, and established the goal of attaining a workforce that mirrored the racial and ethnic composition of the organization's customer base as part of her three year strategic plan. To meet this objective, the organization created reports and databases to track the racial, ethnic, gender, and generational representation of its workforce across all levels and required managers to create action plans to accomplish their goals of appropriate representation among their staffs. Similarly, the organization broadened its recruitment sources to reach a more diverse base of candidates for employment. The president felt confident that she was taking all of the necessary steps to attain the goal, yet at the end of three years, the organization saw a decline, not an increase, in its African American and Hispanic workforce representation. Desperate to understand what went wrong, the president hired an external consultant to assess the factors that prohibited her company from meeting the goal. The assessment recognized the following factors:

- Hiring of multicultural candidates had increased by up to 20 percent across the organization, with the majority of placements occurring in entry-level positions.
- Turnover, voluntary and involuntary, among multicultural employees, however, had increased by up to 25 percent.
- Organizational data indicated that multicultural employees were more likely to receive corrective action.
- Organizational data indicated that multicultural employees were more likely to receive lower performance evaluations.

- Organizational data also indicated that multicultural employees were less likely to receive promotions.
- Organizational surveys indicated that multicultural employees reported feeling less valued.
- Organizational surveys also indicated that multicultural employees reported feeling less able to bring their whole selves to work.
- An external marketing survey indicated that, generally, multicultural customers viewed their encounters with the organization less positively than their majority counterparts.
- The external marketing survey also indicated that multicultural residents of the community, in general, did not view the organization as an employment option.

The assessment's findings, though painful to receive, were eye opening and helped the leadership team to identify for themselves that cultural factors requiring consideration exist above and below the waterline. If you consider the **iceberg view of culture** (depicted visually in Figure 3-2), factors above the waterline include the external, explicit, and observable aspects of a culture. These are important, yet it's often the significant, yet out-of-view, factors that exist below the waterline that go unaddressed by workforce diversity efforts and create the most confusion and misunderstanding. The factors include internal, implicit, and invisible cultural factors. To conceptualize these factors, leaders must ask, "What are the values, beliefs, and assumptions that this population holds that manifest themselves in the visible artifacts that I can observe? What is the political and religious history of this culture that shapes its world view?" Through this type of inquiry, a leader can begin to understand the cultural influences that shape a person's or group's motivation, work behaviors, reward preferences, and communication styles.

How did this organization proceed? The president built consensus among her team that the cultural factors above *and* below the waterline were critical success factors for their organization, and developed a comprehensive delivery

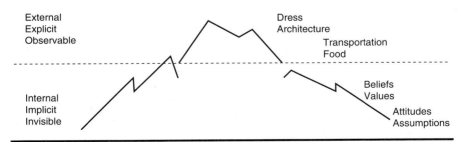

FIGURE 3-2 The Culture Iceberg

effort and strategic plan for proactively managing these factors. Applying the iceberg view of culture, their approach had six phases:

1. Conducting a thorough assessment of areas such as needs, resources, and capabilities across multiple constituencies
2. Identifying goals
3. Developing strategies and tactical steps to meet these goals
4. Implementing these strategies
5. Monitoring and evaluating progress
6. Adjusting their strategies to better support the organization

Not surprisingly, the organization has experienced great success as a result of their workforce diversity efforts. It has seen significant improvement in a number of organizational performance markers, including employee retention, regional market share, patient satisfaction, employee productivity, and a reduction in negative clinical outcomes. Each of these steps has significantly contributed to their improved bottom line. It is critically important to note that to attain this degree of success, the leadership team had to assume a great deal of risk associated with such an approach.

✦ BECOMING A GREAT MULTICULTURAL LEADER— A JOURNEY, NOT A DESTINATION

What characteristics and behaviors make for an effective multicultural leader? As stated earlier in the chapter, a leader's willingness to assume the risk of potentially losing power as a result of adopting behaviors different from those that brought success or would differentiate the leader from peers is paramount to attaining success in leading a comprehensive diversity effort.

Once risk is assumed, leaders need to build **social capital,** a term used by economists and sociologists to refer to the value of interpersonal connections in solidifying a relationship, organizational culture, or business deal. *Financial capital* is a term more familiar to most, and refers to the monetary backing that an individual or business has that increases net worth and the ability to pursue wealth-expanding endeavors. Similarly, social capital conveys the notion that strong relationships have a tremendous value of goodwill. Although the goodwill earned from relationships is hard to quantify, it is often as valuable as a hard asset. For example, the value you receive from a close mentoring relationship may benefit you as much as a graduate degree or certification as it relates to your pursuit of your goals. (Recent accounting practices have recognized goodwill as a quantifiable asset in an organization's books.)

Great multicultural leaders are able to generate this goodwill across cultures and inspire strong interpersonal relationships, not only between people very much like themselves, but also among people who may be quite different from them. As U.S. communities grow more diverse and globalization escalates across industries, this trait will grow increasingly important to leadership success.

In addition to building social capital, leaders who wish to be successful in multicultural environments must establish **multicultural literacy**. Robert Rosen, who authored the book *Global Literacies*, (1999) states that learning how to lead effectively in a multicultural world is a process similar to learning to read. As such, it is often difficult and doesn't come all at once. Ultimately, however, those skills will open up numerous opportunities, both personal and professional. Multicultural literacy is defined as the skills, insights, and attitudes that allow one to learn from diverse individuals and places on a continuous basis. The first step in becoming multiculturally literate is to increase your recognition of your own cultural influences and biases. By acknowledging the customs, attitudes, and values that our own culture promotes, we can more easily accept different cultures' central characteristics. You can remain comfortable in your culture, while still being able to fully engage with cultures different from your own. As with becoming literate in a new language, you do not forget or diminish the knowledge you have of your first language. As a leader, becoming literate in another culture enhances your opportunity for success in all endeavors, personal and professional.

Great multicultural leaders create environments in their organizations where they encourage teaching and learning around them, to support others in their own multicultural journeys. They assist others on a one-on-one basis, but they also consider the organizational structures, policies, and practices that would enhance the overall organizational culture. Multicultural leaders consider the impact of organizational culture and make sure their organizations uphold teaching and learning from one another as a central core value.

Multicultural leaders must serve as **champions** of their organization's diversity efforts, weaving messages and **real symbols** of support into all that they do. This is critically important to establishing a foundation of support necessary for a successful diversity effort, as other leaders and individuals in the organization will need to see the support necessary to sustain them beyond the tendency to avoid the risk associated with embarking upon a diversity effort. Similarly, it is important that leaders display real symbols of their support by committing enough human and fiscal resources to do the work associated with establishing a diversity effort. Without those symbols, the words of support appear to be only lip service, and fail to elicit the support of the rest of the organization.

As leaders communicate about their diversity efforts to internal and external constituencies, one of the most important actions they can take is to convey realistic expectations for the effort, with respect to time and the objectives it will support. For organizations, embarking upon a comprehensive diversity effort will require significant organizational transformation and development of a supportive organizational culture. In most cases, this requires five to ten years to accomplish. Similarly, it requires that accountability for the effort is established, appropriately, for all leaders and individuals within the organization. Such a transition requires tremendous leadership to be attained, and cannot be facilitated by just a few individuals.

✦ COMMUNITY CONTEXT—A CRITICAL IMPORTANT LEADERSHIP CONSIDERATION

As leaders prepare to embark upon a diversity effort, one important external factor to assess is the climate with their community and business community. This type of assessment will, by identifying formal and informal practices and behavioral norms, provide leaders with a sense of what degree of change is likely to be tolerated within the community, which is valuable in calculating the degree of risk they are willing to assume with their diversity efforts. In addition to helping to calculate risk, such an assessment can reveal areas of opportunity for strategic community relationship development, as well as other business, revenue stream, and marketing development opportunities.

✦ LEVERAGING MULTICULTURAL LEADERSHIP ACROSS ALL FUNCTIONS TO SUPPORT BETTER BOTTOM-LINE RESULTS

We have already explored how an effective workforce diversity effort can support improved organizational performance in times of rapid change and financial strain. As the United States grows increasingly multicultural and numerous industries continue to join the global marketplace, there exists significant opportunity to further enhance organizational performance by leveraging diversity in areas such as product or service development, marketing, service and supply chain, and community relations and outreach.

✦ LEADERSHIP SKILLS ✦
WOMEN AND LEADERSHIP

In speaking of leadership in diverse groups, the role of women, the largest demographic group, cannot be ignored. Do men and women lead differently? Do they face different challenges in leadership? While the controversy continues on whether the female biology has an impact on women's ability to lead, the fact remains that even today there is a distinct wage disparity between men and women and not enough representation of women at the top in business organizations. Why does this disparity exist? According to Northouse (2004), there are several factors that create barriers to women's success as business leaders.

- **Organizational factors.** Several studies have reported that organizations often expect higher standards of performance from women. In addition, many organizations have rigid, inhospitable cultures where ambitious women are seen as being against the norm and women of color, in particular, are made to feel that they will not fit in. The fact that there are more men in senior leadership positions and that these men often tend to promote their own kind (other men) translates into a cycle of unfavorable treatment for women trying to get to the top. Also, more often than not, male peers and superiors are inclined to avoid taking an active stance to ensure fair treatment of their female counterparts. In a 1994 study, Ohlott et al. reported that the challenges faced by women leaders were in the nature of lack of support and resources, while challenges faced by their male counterparts were characterized by higher stakes, breadth, and external interface. This difference in the nature of developmental opportunities is another organizational factor that creates difficulties for women.

- **Interpersonal factors.** Gender-related prejudices and stereotyping have a profound effect on the success rate of women in the workplace. Several leadership traits are seen as being masculine, and women are viewed as being less capable and desirous of dealing with a challenge than men. In addition, women often find themselves excluded from informal networks and lack mentoring from white males in the organization.

- **Personal factors**. Women face an added pressure with regard to their nonwork obligations. They are often seen, and indeed often see themselves, as being primarily responsible for household and familial duties. Although some women overcome this obstacle with the assistance of supportive family members or by hiring outside help, others are unable to balance the conflicting roles at work and at home.

Not all women face all these obstacles, and not all of these behaviors are conscious. Nonetheless, parity between men and women in leadership positions can only occur if these barriers are recognized and effectively addressed.

✦ LEADING ACROSS DIFFERENT CULTURAL WORLD VIEWS

Leading and managing globally requires not only a heightened sense of your own cultural beliefs and values, but an understanding of the beliefs and values held by members of other cultural groups, and an ability to balance all to support your desired outcome. This section introduces a tool that can help you interface with people who have different thoughts, behaviors, habits, and characteristics. Industrial sociologist Edwin Nichols researched ways to help individuals make sense of the variety of cultures in the world. Let's examine his research so that we can use it as a tool in becoming the best leaders we can be.

Nichols proposes that four worldviews can clarify the diversity in the world. Also, he has developed a tool for self-assessing our thoughts along eleven aspects of culture, which is depicted in Figure 3-3.

Nichols' premise in designing this tool was that thoughts are the layer of meaning that most significantly distinguishes cultures from each other. He realized that two cultures might act differently, but at their core have similar

My Cultural Patterns

1. Relationships, family, and friends	Nuclear ————	Extended
2. Time and time consciousness	Fixed ————	Fluid
3. Food and eating habits	Necessity ————	Experience
4. Beliefs and attitudes	Egalitarian ————	Hierarchical
5. Dress and appearance	Informal ————	Formal
6. Communication and language	Explicit/Direct ————	Implicit/Indirect
7. Sense of self and space	Distant ————	Close
8. Mental processes and learning styles	Linear ————	Lateral
9. Work habits and practices	Task ————	Relationship
10. Values and norms	Individual ————	Group
11. Emotions	Controlled ————	Expressive

FIGURE 3-3   Eleven Aspects of Cultural Patterns

SOURCE: Adapted from Gardenswartz and Rowe, *Managing Diversity: A Complete Desk Reference and Planning Guide.* Homewood, Ill.: Business One Irwin (1993).

thoughts. Understanding the differing thoughts is the first step in understanding cross-cultural difference.

Nichols' four worldviews are charted in Figure 3-4 with a personal interpretation added. To simplify a complex theory, a hiking analogy is used to illustrate the differing cultural thoughts among the four worldviews Nichols has identified. As you look at your self-assessment along the eleven aspects of culture, where do you fall? Which worldview do you believe you resemble most? Which worldview do you believe best represents your organization's culture? How does this impact your likelihood for success as a leader in this organization? How might you successfully interface with someone from a different worldview?

The two profiles that follow are examples of people that have been successful in bringing together ethnically, socially, physically diverse populations to achieve a common goal. A. G. Lafley is the man behind a very successful effort

World View	Desired Tool	Thought
Member–Object	Good equipment (pack, clothes, food, etc.)	Obtaining identified objects will contribute most to my success.
Member–Member	A friend to take on a trip	Developing camaraderie with other people will contribute most to my success.
Member–Group	A group of people to join me	Being a part of collective, harmonious groups will contribute most to my success.
Member–Great Spirit	A connection with nature to help me	A connection with nature will contribute most to my success.

FIGURE 3-4   Edwin Nichols' Four World View

to leverage diversity at the corporate giant Procter & Gamble. Multicultural leadership is not limited to business situations but can be seen in social situations as well, as can be seen in our second profile, that of Abdul Sattar Edhi. Edhi is a pioneer of social change, and a leader who has been able to serve the needs of a variety of diverse groups through a deep understanding of his own values and beliefs. He has spent most of his life working to better the lives of the needy and destitute in Pakistan and other third-world countries through his charitable organization, the Edhi Foundation, which is the largest welfare organization in Pakistan and the first of its kind in South Asia.

A. G. LAFLEY
Resurrecting Procter & Gamble

Alan George Lafley joined Procter & Gamble in 1977 as assistant brand manager for Joy dishwashing soap. After several successful years at P&G, he was promoted from head of North America to CEO in the year 2000 when his predecessor, Durk Jager, resigned. As CEO, Lafley recognized that Procter & Gamble, a company that markets about 300 brands to consumers in over 140 countries, needed to actively focus on addressing the needs of its very diverse stakeholder base. His commitment to P&G's diversity efforts has brought recognition to the organization both internally and externally.

Top management support and accountability are key elements of Lafley's diversity program. Leadership support is communicated to employees on a regular basis through the Web site, annual diversity letter, and periodic business updates. To foster accountability, diversity strategies are incorporated into the business plans and results are tracked. Senior executives conduct annual diversity reviews focusing on hiring, representation, promotions, and separations. In addition, a well-laid-out succession planning process ensures that women and minorities are given the growth and development opportunities they deserve.

P&G has actively begun recruiting people with disabilities and providing them with all the support they need to become successful at the company. A People With Disabilities Task Force reaches out to college campuses and local agencies to recruit skilled candidates that are often overlooked by other companies because of their disabilities. P&G's commercials are close captioned and feature a diverse cross-section of actors.

Diversity-training programs and support groups ensure increased awareness and understanding among employees.

As a result of its concentrated efforts to promote inclusion, P&G has been awarded the 2001 Inclusion Network Award and was ranked in the Top 50 for Careers and the Disabled (Winter 2000/2001). Lafley's focus on leveraging diversity is strongly driven by his belief in the business need of such efforts. He treats diversity as a business strategy rather than a *feel-good* initiative. Under his guidance, P&G has taken the diversity efforts further than just internal initiatives—the powerful corporation uses its influence with vendors to encourage them to be more inclusive.

Lafley's message to his company's workforce is clear: "All the data I've seen in 30 years of being in business—and all of my personal experience at Procter & Gamble over the last 23 years—convince me that a diverse organization will out-think, out-innovate, and out-perform a homogeneous organization every single time."

(For more information on P&G's inclusion efforts visit http://www.pginclusion.com/cgi-bin /commit.cgi.)

ABDUL SATTAR EDHI
Leading Social Change across Cultures

Edhi was born in 1931 into a Muslim family in a small village in western India. When Edhi was eleven, his mother suffered a paralytic attack and, later, severe mental illness. The young boy spent the next few years taking care of her every need, even cleaning her and changing her. When she finally died a few years later, Edhi was devastated. But watching his mother's helplessness for all those years had cultivated in him a deep sense of compassion for the suffering of others. He vowed to do his bit to alleviate the misery of the poverty-stricken masses.

Edhi's family, like thousands of other Muslim families at the time, migrated to the newly created Pakistan in 1947 when British colonial rule ended in India. Living in the city of Karachi, Pakistan, Edhi had to earn his living as a street peddler and later began selling cloth in Karachi's wholesale market. Even while his own livelihood was a struggle, he continued to think about helping others and soon established a charitable dispensary along with some other members of his community. After a series of ideological differences with his conservative colleagues, he started his own philanthropic organization, the Edhi Foundation. Starting out with an old van that served as an ambulance, Edhi was eventually able to solicit enough donations to start an emergency outpatient clinic and a dispensary for women and children that also contained a training center for nurses. As donations continued to flow in recognition of his work, he expanded the scope of the services to include assistance for battered women, runaways, the mentally challenged, drug addicts, and other disadvantaged groups.

With a fleet of more than 400 ambulances, including air ambulances that provide quick access to remote areas, the foundation's workers and volunteers are the first on the scene of any major crisis in the country. They even go to places that government agencies do not serve. The activities of the foundation are not limited to any one country or group. The foundation has offices in several countries and has provided aid to earthquake victims in Armenia, the victims of the

Gulf War, and refugees and victims of natural disaster in several other countries, including Egypt, Lebanon, Somalia, India, Japan, and Romania. The Foundation's 250 centers across Pakistan are home to more than 6,000 destitute people, and more than a million people benefit annually from its health care and other services. The foundation is never closed for holidays, and Edhi himself has never taken a day off.

Edhi is a strong supporter of women's rights, including their right to work. Many of the foundation's workers are women, several of whom started out as victims seeking help from the foundation and were later trained to take on jobs at the various centers. Empowering women in a conservative society that has traditionally held rigid beliefs about women's roles has not been an easy task. The women that volunteer at the Edhi Foundation's centers for abused women are directed to keep their identity confidential to promote their safety.

The foundation is unique in its society because it is funded solely by charitable donations from individuals and business organizations and not by the government. In fact, Edhi once turned down a hefty amount sent to him by one of the high-ranking government leaders as a token of appreciation for his work. Edhi's active rejection of government aid and stubborn adherence to the principle of self-help not only saves the government huge sums of money every year, but also helps to change the notion of dependence on government and foreign aid for running a successful charity.

The Edhi Foundation is a distinctive example of what an ordinary person can do to help others in need, transcending religious and social barriers with the single purpose of serving humanity. Edhi and his wife, Bilquis, and their children work tirelessly for the foundation and draw no salary, their only source of income being some investments made years ago. Over the last four decades, Edhi has managed to bring about a quiet revolution in the way Pakistani society views welfare services and in the way the rest of the world views the ability of third-world countries to deal with these issues. When he started out, most people cringed at the sight of the destitute and disabled. Now, more and more people are getting involved and queuing up to offer money, food, and their services to the foundation. Edhi begins his day with his morning prayers and spends the rest of it actively contributing in every possible way, feeding the hungry, bathing the handicapped, and even cleaning unclaimed corpses for burial. Edhi says that his religion has reinforced in him the values that he practices. In his own words: "Islam instructed a way of life that emphasized the essential qualities of self-help and compassion, it instructed all the crucial attitudes that I had discovered as solutions and all were missing in application. Islam was a complete program for human uplift, but its instructions were either unheeded or distorted, meanings and interpretations were usurped, self-help and labor considered shameful, its people strayed like lost sheep."

When Edhi was a little boy, his mother used to give him two coins every day, one was for his personal use and the other, she said, was for him to give to someone less fortunate than himself. It is a lesson he carries with him until today.

◆ Chapter Summary

Be it a leader of an international conglomerate or an individual seeking to make a difference in his or her family or community, a leader's effectiveness depends primarily on his or her ability to mobilize others, setting a vision and directing a group to work toward a common goal. To do that, a leader must authentically understand the needs, attitudes, and desires of those he or she is leading. When people lead others very much like themselves, this may be a fairly natural and effortless process. But when they lead others who differ in many ways, their ability to understand those differences is paramount. This is both the challenge and the opportunity of multicultural leadership.

◆ CREATE YOUR OWN THEORY ◆

Choose a leader in your community or school whom you admire. Thinking about all of the constituencies that person must consider, identify what cultures are represented. Don't limit your list to ethnic, regional, or national cultures. Consider also gender, age, education, religion, and economic status, among others. What approach would you recommend this leader take in preparing himself or herself to provide the best leadership to the entire group? What reasons for striving to become a multicultural leader would you give him or her? What strategies do you have for yourself for increasing your multicultural literacy as a leader?

Now think back to our opening Leadership Moment. How might you approach this situation? What characterizes your multicultural leader, and which of these characteristics do you possess? Where do your multicultural skills fall short, and how can you address this?

◆ Key Terms

champions	multicultural leadership
cultural competency	multicultural literacy
culture	real symbols
diversity	social capital
iceberg view of culture	workforce diversity effort
learned behaviors	

◆ Questions for Discussion and Review

1. Why is multicultural leadership even more critical today than it was ten years ago? What conditions do you think will perpetuate the need for effective multicultural leadership?

2. What is cultural competency? Identify an example from your organization when you have seen a demonstration of cultural competency or lack thereof.

3. What are some of the explicit (visible) characteristics of your own culture? Name some of the implicit characteristics.

4. How do leaders establish social capital? Why is this important in global and multicultural leadership?

5. Name four of the eleven cultural patterns, and identify how they may be exercised differently in one country versus another.

6. If your organization were starting a diversity effort, who should be identified as champions to best support its success? What would constitute the necessary real symbols to convey importance to others?

The Disciplinary
Roots of Leadership

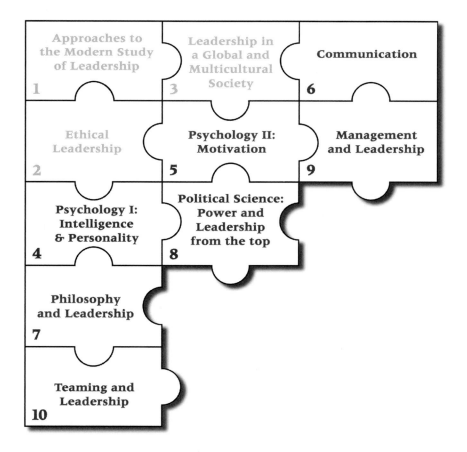

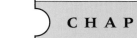

C H A P T E R   4

Psychology I:
Intelligence and Personality

■-■-■

LEADERSHIP MOMENT

Wally Walker was once the rising star of Winkler's Widgets, Inc. Nobody else in the company could understand as well as Wally the workings of a particularly complex widget, the Widgetmaster 2000. Always coming up with ideas for ways of improving the Widgetmaster 2000, he was the acknowledged expert, sought out whenever anyone had any questions related to this product. Unfortunately for Wally, upper management decided six months ago to discontinue Widgetmaster 2000 production and reassigned Wally to a different department. Since this time, Wally has changed noticeably. Although intellectually more than capable of handling his new duties, Wally isn't thrilled about the new product and realizes that dozens of other employees know more about it than he does. He says he no longer feels needed at work and, as a result, he has started to come in later and leave earlier.

Upper management has started to notice this change. As Wally's immediate supervisor, you have been instructed by your boss that unless that "lazy Wally" starts to turn things around, he will be fired.

1.   What would you do?

2.   Do you think it is possible for adults like Wally to adapt to such a dramatic work change? Why or why not?

3.   What assumptions has your boss made about Wally's abilities?

4.   What steps might you take to motivate Wally to pursue his new job with his old vigor?

5.   What ethical and diversity components have the potential to be relevant to your work with Wally?

When one examines the great leaders of today and yesterday, one cannot help but be awed by the sheer range of backgrounds from which these leaders emerge. Consider the U.S. presidents (discussed in greater detail in Chapter 8). Some, like Thomas Jefferson, were of "noble" birth and had a meteoric rise to prominence. Others, such as Abraham Lincoln and Bill Clinton, came from extremely humble beginnings and slowly fought their way to the top.

It is also astonishing to examine the ability of leaders to inspire those who follow them. How did Moses convince the ancient Hebrews to rise up, rebel against incredible odds, and follow him to the Red Sea? How did Franklin Delano Roosevelt (see his Leadership Profile in Chapter 8) inspire hope in millions of Americans faced with the worst depression in history and an upcoming world war? An examination of psychology does not provide all the answers to these questions (only you can do that), but in this chapter and the next we will look at three central components of the intersection of psychology and leadership—intelligence, personality, and motivation. We address the age-old question of whether great leaders are born or made (the answer may surprise you) and consider some of the many theories about motivating others.

✦ INTELLIGENCE

What is **intelligence**? Ask twenty people this question and you will likely receive twenty different answers (or maybe more). Some responses that this author has heard when he has posed this question in college courses include "book smart," "ability to understand what to do without being told," and "ability to pick things up easily." The brain is an extremely complex structure, and to think of an individual as either entirely intelligent or unintelligent is not likely to be a useful distinction for you to make as a leader. More helpful would be to make the following two assumptions: (1) each individual has a particular set of intellectual strengths and weaknesses and (2) situations often dictate performance more than global ability. For example, if you have an employee who is happier and more productive in interpersonal tasks, it would not make sense to have this person work exclusively on individual tasks at a cubicle cut off from most of the other employees. Similarly, if you have a friend who is very bright in other ways but is not particularly detail-oriented, he or she may not be the person you ask to help plan a large party. Finally, have you ever observed a well-educated college professor grapple for ten minutes with a computer problem that your typical twelve-year-old could solve in ten seconds? Clearly, our intellectual abilities are not dispersed equally among all tasks.

Throughout the centuries, there has been no shortage of attempts to break down the almost impossibly large construct of *intelligence* into numerous subcomponents. What follows is a description of four of the most prominent models of intelligence—the psychometric model, Howard Gardner's Multiple Intelligences Model, Daniel Goleman's theory of emotional intelligence, and Robert Sternberg's triarchic theory.

Psychometric Model

When one talks about someone's **IQ** (which stands for *intelligence quotient*), one typically is talking about that person's score on a standardized test designed to measure intelligence. Don't believe Web sites or TV shows that claim they can tell you your IQ in thirty minutes! In fact, don't believe anyone who states that he can determine something as complex as one's intelligence in thirty minutes. IQ tests are only valid when done by trained professionals, and even then they are of limited generalizability. These tests take a number of forms and are typically administered in a school setting or at a private clinic or hospital.

The first modern intelligence test was created by two Frenchmen, Alfred Binet and Theodore Simon, approximately one hundred years ago. The impetus for this test was the recognition by the Minister of Public Instruction in Paris that some schoolchildren were not learning through traditional means. It was decided that a test was needed to help classify students who were mentally retarded. The original Binet-Simon (1905) test had thirty items and no method for scoring the test. The test was expanded to 58 items in 1908, and it was in this version that the concept of a person's overall mental level (now known as IQ) was introduced.

Although Binet's goal was to promote improved education for children who were having difficulty learning in a standard classroom, in the United States, intelligence testing was often utilized for a less noble purpose. In an era of massive immigration, there was a prejudice that those entering the United States were less intelligent that those already living in the United States. By 1911, intelligence testers, led by Henry H. Goddard, were calling for widespread intelligence testing of immigrants at Ellis Island in order to identify those who were intellectually deficient. Using the English translation of the revised Binet-Simon scales, Goddard and others began producing results that, to the uninformed, seemed to confirm the stereotype of the ignorant foreigner. For example, in one case Goddard's assistants reported that 83 percent of the Jews, 80 percent of the Hungarians, 79 percent of the Italians, and 87 percent of the Russians were "feebleminded." Reports like these fed into the notion that certain subgroups are more intelligent than others. They also beg the question of how you think *you* might perform if you were given a translated intelligence test right after you had just spent weeks sailing across the ocean into a strange land.

While terms such as *idiot, imbecile, feebleminded,* and *moron* (all classifications at one time used in the United States to label persons based on their performance on intelligence tests) thankfully are no longer used by professionals who administer IQ tests, there continues to be a misperception that one number or score can adequately label a person. Within the field of psychology, this number is often referred to as *g*, and the concepts behind *g* have their origins in psychometrics and the work of Charles Spearman. Spearman proposed that intelligence can be divided into two factors: *s*, which are specific subfactors of intelligence, and *g*, which can be thought of as general intelligence. In this model, someone with a high *g* would be expected to do well on all intellectual tasks, while uneven abilities are attributed to different *s* levels on specific tasks.

Many IQ tests in use today reflect this dichotomy, with scores often presented both in global format and broken down into specific subareas, all computed statistically. For example, the *Weschler Intelligence Scale for Children*, 4th edition, one of the most commonly used IQ tests in schools, provides four *s* scores (in the areas of verbal comprehension, perceptual reasoning, working memory, and processing speed) and one *g* score (full-scale intelligence quotient).

Thus, from a **psychometric perspective,** intelligence is something that can be measured quantitatively, and these numbers can be used to make meaningful statements about a person's abilities, either in terms of specific *s* factors (e.g., "your working memory skills are above average") or in terms of overall abilities (e.g., "your full-scale IQ falls in the average range"). Not all tests use *g*, and tests vary widely in terms of the specific subareas of intelligence that they measure, but the common denominator of this approach is the use of psychometrically derived test scores to come to conclusions about intelligence.

Gardner's Multiple Intelligence Model

In contrast to the psychometric model, where tests are generally administered in an office and where the results of these tests often lead to a global interpretation (e.g., "Bob's IQ is in the 55th percentile"), Howard Gardner, in his classic (1983) *Frames of Mind: The Theory of Multiple Intelligences*, sought to promote a more naturalistic view of intelligence, focused on real-world skills. In his original model, he divided intelligence into seven different areas:

1. *Musical intelligence:* the ability to understand and create music
2. *Bodily-kinesthetic intelligence:* the ability to use one's body in a skilled way, for self-expression or toward a goal
3. *Spatial intelligence:* the ability to "think in pictures," to perceive the visual world accurately, and recreate (or alter) it in the mind or on paper
4. *Interpersonal intelligence:* ability to perceive and understand other individuals—their moods, desires, and motivations
5. *Intrapersonal intelligence:* an understanding of one's own emotions
6. *Linguistic intelligence:* a sensitivity to the meaning and order of words
7. *Logical-mathematic intelligence:* ability in mathematics and other complex logical systems

Later, Gardner added an eighth form of intelligence, *naturalistic intelligence,* which is the ability to recognize and classify plants, minerals, and animals, including rocks and grass and all variety of flora and fauna. Each of **Gardner's eight forms of intelligence** is of approximately equal importance, yet he notes that in U.S. society two of these forms—linguistic intelligence and logical-mathematic intelligence—tend to be given higher value in schools. As evidence, he states that if you do well in language and logic, you are likely to do well on IQ tests and on college-entry tests such as the SAT and ACT.

◆ **CREATE YOUR OWN THEORY** ◆

A Self-Look at Gardner's Multiple Intelligence Model

Gardner divides intelligence into eight distinct areas, each of approximately equal importance. In reviewing his list, which of Gardner's eight intelligences is your greatest strength and which is your weakest area? How does this relate to your ability to succeed across a variety of tasks? Does possessing a weakness mean that you are less intelligent overall than someone who has a strength in your area of weakness? Are there any areas in which you excel that do not fit into his eight categories of intelligence?

Goleman's Theory of Emotional Intelligence

We have all met leaders who are extremely bright, but fail to inspire, motivate, or empathize with others. Although most successful leaders would likely score quite well on an IQ test, there are wide discrepancies when it comes to emotional capabilities. The ability to fully understand oneself and to relate well with others is known as **emotional intelligence** (EI). There are clear distinctions between rational knowledge-based intelligence and emotional intelligence. In fact, many studies have shown that when it comes to successful leadership, emotional intelligence is even *more* important than innate/rational intelligence. But exactly what are the defining features of a leader who is emotionally intelligent?

Perhaps the name most widely associated with emotional intelligence is Daniel Goleman. In his groundbreaking book, *Emotional Intelligence: Why It Can Matter More Than IQ* (1995), he stated that emotional intelligence can be taught and includes the ability to do the following:

- Motivate oneself and persist despite frustrations
- Regulate one's own moods
- Empathize
- Delay gratification
- Handle stress well
- Have verbal and nonverbal skills in sync
- Have self/other acceptance/tolerance
- Promote group harmony

Goleman has argued that emotional intelligence subsumes most of what is not measured by traditional IQ tests. Goleman's critics argue that his claims about emotional intelligence go beyond the actual data he has obtained to support these claims. Regardless of one's personal opinion about whether intelligence can be divided into that which is measured on traditional IQ tests and emotional intelligence, in this view of the author there can be no disputing that intelligence is more than what is measured by a traditional IQ test. It also is indisputable that some people, regardless of whether it can be accurately measured, have high *emotional intelligence* and others do not.

Recently, Goleman and his colleagues have written on the relationship between emotional intelligence and leadership. In their work *Primal Leadership: Realizing the Power of Emotional Intelligence*, Goleman, Boyatzis, and McKee (2002) assert that there are eighteen different leadership competencies that fall within four domains of emotional intelligence. Table 4-1 lists these domains and competencies in both narrative and list form. How many of these emotional intelligence traits do you possess, and how do these enhance your ability to be an effective leader?

Sternberg's Triarchic Theory

Robert Sternberg's **triarchic theory of intelligence** has its origins in the examination of test performance. Through observing adults complete an intelligence test, Sternberg devised a three-part theory to describe intellectual processes conducive to success on this test. *Componential subtheory* relates to one's ability to solve problems using internal mechanisms. *Experiential subtheory* considers how familiar a person was with the test content. Finally, *contextual subtheory* relates to the relevance of the test content to the individual taking the test.

Here are some examples that illustrate the distinction between these three subtheories. Many of us know people who seem to test above or below their abilities on standardized tests (think of the class valedictorian who scores below an average student on the SAT). Those who score above expectations likely have high componential abilities—they are able to use effective problem solving strategies. Similarly, take two persons of approximately equal intelligence and ask them to answer sports trivia questions. If one of those persons follows sports closely (and thus has high experiential knowledge) and the other does not, the sports fan is likely to do better on that task. Finally, contextual theory acknowledges that different people and different cultures have different values. Therefore, if you take two persons of equal intelligence, one raised in a highly competitive society and the other raised in a setting where cooperation is valued over competition, and then place these two people in a competitive situation, the advantage would go to the person raised in the competitive society.

In Sternberg's writings on leadership, intelligence is not viewed as an overall measurement (as in the concept of g), nor is intelligence seen as a series of discrete skills, as in Gardner's multiple intelligence model. Instead, Sternberg equates intelligence with success. Specifically, in his theory of successful intelligence, he states that people achieve success by recognizing and capitalizing on their personal strengths and by recognizing and either correcting or compensating for their weaknesses. Thus, successful leaders in this model possess the intellectual skill of knowing how to put themselves in the best position to succeed, be that by changing environments or by modifying the environment they are in to bring out their talents.

TABLE 4-1   **Emotional Intelligence and Leadership Competencies**

Emotional Intelligence Domain	*Leadership Competencies*
Self-Awareness: A leader must have an accurate self-assessment of his or her strengths and weaknesses. A leader is self-confident, aware of how his or her feelings affect his or her job performance, and welcomes constructive criticism.	• Emotional self-awareness • Accurate self-awareness • Self-confidence
Self-Management: An emotionally intelligent leader has good self-control, is genuine, adaptable, and achievement-oriented. Such a leader stays calm and clear-headed under crisis situations, admits mistakes, and confronts unethical behavior in others, is flexible in thinking, and has high personal standards and a commitment to life-long learning.	• Self-control • Transparency • Adaptability • Achievement • Initiative • Optimism
Social Awareness: Leaders with emotional intelligence are empathetic and can sense the unspoken emotions in groups. They are keenly aware of and are able to navigate through organizational hierarchies and foster an open communication environment. Emotions have a contagious quality to them. As a leader, people pay attention to how you react to setbacks. Whether you are optimistic, energetic, angry, or rude, your reactions will trickle down to all members of the group.	• Empathy • Organizational awareness • Service
Relationship Management: Emotionally intelligent leaders are able to inspire people and help mobilize a shared mission. They are persuasive and engaging public speakers and enjoy cultivating other people's strengths and interests. Such leaders are a catalyst for change and are skilled at finding practical ways to overcome problems. Teamwork, collaboration, conflict management, and spending time forging close relationships outside of work to promote group harmony are of utmost importance to an emotionally intelligent leader.	• Inspiration • Influence • Developing others • Change catalyst • Conflict management • Teamwork and collaboration

SOURCE: Adapted from Goleman, Boyatzis, & McKee, 2002

LEARNING DISABLED OR WORLD-RENOWNED GENIUS?
The Multiple Dimensions of Intelligence

The prospects did not look good for a young Albert Einstein. It is believed that the internationally acclaimed physicist did not speak until age three, and that by age nine he still spoke hesitantly, prompting his parents to believe that his intelligence was below average. As a teenager, Einstein failed an examination that would have allowed him to pursue a course of studies in electrical engineering, and he was turned down for several positions at universities. It was only while working as a patent worker and writing on theoretical physics in his spare time that Einstein first became widely known in academic circles.

Although it is not clear whether Einstein had a learning disability (many suspect he had), his story is a common one: intellectual talent may not have been apparent in childhood, but the person went on to become recognized as a leader in his field. For example, George Washington, the first president of the United States, could not spell and had poor grammar usage. What follows is a partial listing, created by the Tampa Mayor's Alliance For Persons With Disabilities in 1999 of famous persons known or believed to have had one or more learning disabilities:

- Hans Christian Anderson, children's author
- Alexander Graham Bell, inventor of the telephone
- Cher, musician/actress
- Tom Cruise, actor
- Leonardo DaVinci, artist
- Walt Disney, cartoonist, producer
- Dwight D. Eisenhower, U.S. president
- Whoopi Goldberg, actress/comedian
- Thomas Jefferson, U.S. president
- Magic Johnson, professional basketball player, successful businessman
- John F. Kennedy, U.S. president
- John Lennon, musician
- George Patton, general
- Charles Schwab, founder of Charles Schwab Corporation, a brokerage firm
- Woodrow Wilson, U.S. president
- Wilbur Wright, invented and built the first successful airplane with his brother Orville

(For a full listing, view its Web site at www.tampagov.net/dept_Mayor/Mayors_Alliance/famous_persons/index.asp.)

✦ PERSONALITY

Psychology is the study of human behavior. Human behavior is, of course, a broad area, the scope of which is well beyond that of this text. What, then, are the most salient aspects of human behavior that apply to leadership? Certainly, one important aspect of human behavior is how it forms what we call individual personalities. We'll define **personality** as how people affect others and understand themselves.

In Chapter 7, we discuss some of the great thinkers such as Plato and Thomas Aquinas in terms of their perspective on what contributes to a great leader. Only within the past 150 years, however, has there been significant research that examines personality development over the course of the entire life span. Driven by Darwin's theory of evolution, early personality theorists such as Freud were generally biologists and physicians who sought to understand personality development through the study of physiology. One of the earliest questions that theorists addressed was one that is still debated today: Are great men (in the nineteenth century, these discussions were about men only) born, or are they made?

Are Leaders Born, or Are They Made?

In 1869, Sir Francis Galton was among the first to assert that those qualities that make great leaders are biologically inherited. This is a notion that continues to be hotly disputed in psychology—primarily through what is known as the **nature/nurture debate.** The *nature* side of this equation is that individual personality is based largely on genetics. One either has the biological material to be a leader or one does not. The *nurture* position of this debate, by contrast, states that whether somebody becomes a leader is based less on physiology than on real-life experience. Thus, in a case where two individuals are born with similar physiology (such as identical twins), one twin may develop into a great leader while the other may not, depending on life circumstances.

On the *nature* side, some, like Galton and others, would assert that some individuals are simply natural leaders. History is littered with the exploits of these men and women, and they are commonly depicted in television shows and movies. Although the fundamental characteristics ascribed to these types of leaders vary, typically the characteristics of great leaders were thought to include the following:

- Intelligence, including judgment and verbal ability
- A record of achievement in school and athletics
- Emotional stability and maturity
- Strong achievement drive, persistence, and dependability
- People skills and social flexibility
- Drive to find status and socioeconomic position

Perhaps you can add a few more characteristics to this list.

But were these traits present at birth? Those who have spent time around infants can attest to the fact that, from very early ages, one can often see stark differences between the personalities of young children, even children from the same family. Some babies are easily soothed, for example, while others seem to cry and cry. Clearly, children are born with different personalities, and it is reasonable to assume that some personalities are more conducive to developing leadership than others.

Sigmund Freud did not write about personality development in terms of leadership, but he became the most widely known personality theorist and a major articulator of a viewpoint that leaned more heavily toward the nature side. A biologist by training, Freud postulated that one's personality was formed based on one's ability during childhood to adapt to a world filled with conflict. Children were viewed as passive recipients of stimulation, and maladaptive personality development was attributed to bad mothering. Thus, from this perspective, one's core personality is formed very early on and is created via one's physiological responses to external stimulation. Because the source of personality is so deeply rooted in physiology and early childhood experiences, the classic Freudian framework views treatment as a long process that may require the analyst to assume parental roles in order to recreate the scene of developmental roadblocks.

At the other end—the nurture end—of the continuum are those who follow in the tradition of John Locke, who viewed the infant's mind as a ***tabula rasa*** (blank slate), amenable to all sorts of influences depending on the environment in which one is raised. Among the leading proponents in the United States of the nurture perspective were John Watson (featured in the profile at the end of the chapter) and, later, B. F. Skinner. Skinner began by studying reinforcement mechanisms in animals. He discovered that when he rewarded animals for certain behaviors, those behaviors increased. A human application of this process can be observed in families where children are required to perform chores in order to receive their allowance. Through the work of Watson, Skinner, and many others, the notion of biological determinism began to be challenged. The argument was that childrens' (and, to a certain extent, adults') personalities were not fixed in infancy, but rather, reflected the experiences they encountered throughout their lives. Thus, a child of an alcoholic might not necessarily grow up to abuse alcohol as an adult if raised in an environment where alcohol is not present.

It is now very rare to find an individual who believes in a strictly nature or a strictly nurture perspective. This is due to a number of factors, most notably studies of monozygotic (identical) twins and of children who have been raised in adoptive or foster homes. Accumulating evidence supports the position that both physiology and environmental influences play important roles in human development. For example, in comparing prevalence rates of certain diseases in monozygotic (identical) versus dizygotic (fraternal) twins, a very common finding is that there are higher concordance (meaning both twins have the trait) rates in monozygotic twins, providing evidence for the "nature" perspective since monozygotic twins are genetically identical. However, if monozygotic twins are identical, should it not be the case that if one monozygotic twin has a personality trait, the other one would, as well? As anyone who has met identical twins knows, their personalities, while often similar, are also often quite different in key ways—which supports the "nurture" side of personality development.

So it is that human behavior (and also intelligence—it is a fallacy to believe that one's intelligence can never change) is a combination of biological and environmental influences. However, even though there is wide consensus that both nature and nurture play a role in personality development, this does not mean that where one falls on the nature/nurture continuum is unimportant. Consider the case of something that virtually all of us have experienced at one point or another in life—depression. If you were a physician treating depression, how would you conceptualize this illness? If, on the one hand, you lean more toward the nature end of the nature/nurture continuum, you might view the depression as essentially biological in origin and perhaps would prescribe an antidepressant such as Prozac for treatment. On the other hand, if you subscribe to more of a nurture perspective, you might feel that therapy based on discussing real-life experiences that may have led to the onset of the depression would be the more effective route. In many cases, the best option might be a combination of these approaches.

Attitudes, Perceptions, and Attributions

Although their ideas provide useful frames to draw from, one does not need to be Sigmund Freud or B. F. Skinner to attempt to understand the personalities of others. We make these assessments every day when we come to conclusions about the personalities of those around us. These assessments are reflected in our attitudes, perceptions, and attributions.

Attitudes Successful leadership demands an understanding of attitudes and their manifestations in an organization. For our purposes, we'll define **attitude** as a series of beliefs and feelings held by people about specific situations, ideas, or other people. As shown in Table 4-2, three main aspects of attitudes include (1) affect, the emotional content of a situation; (2) behavior, specific actions taken in response to or in anticipation of a situation; and (3) cognitions, an individual's thoughts or perceptions of a situation.

In general, it is believed that people try to maintain a balance between these three components as they form attitudes. In some situations, the three components come into conflict and a skilled leader will consider feelings as well as behaviors in the attempt to promote positive attitudes.

Perception and Attribution We pay attention to people and objects in such a way that gives them meaning to us. That idiosyncratic aspect of perception can mean that two people can form two different impressions of the same evidence, as the classic illusion in Figure 4-1 shows.

Which did you see first, an old woman or a young woman? Can you see both now? Figure 4-1 shows how our perceptions of people are affected by a number of elements, including the characteristics of the person we perceive,

TABLE 4-2 The Components of Attitudes

Components	*Definition*	*Example*
Affective	Favorable or unfavorable feelings	The workers' feelings about the new regulations
Behabior	Human actions	The workers' performance
Cognitive	Beliefs, knowledge, understanding	The wrokers' beliefs about performance standards and supervision

FIGURE 4-1   **The Old Woman/Young Woman Illusion**

such as physical appearance, clothing, and verbal and nonverbal communication, as well as the ascribed attributes, including status, occupation, and personal characteristics.

Social perceptions have much to do with our impressions of people who are different from ourselves. Upon meeting a person with a disability, for instance, we may react by speaking too loudly, asking questions of others instead of speaking directly to the person, or not knowing what to say for fear of saying the wrong thing. Similarly, our first impressions of people whose accent is different from our own, or whose height, or clothing, or even vehicle is not like ours may be erroneous. (For example, would you expect a nun to drive a pickup?)

Our perceptions can be inaccurate for three main reasons: **stereotyping, selective perception,** and **perceptual defense.** We might negatively *stereotype* the person with an Italian accent by inferring connections to organized crime, or the person with a disability by assuming he or she is unable to respond to conversation. A stereotype can also be positive, as hearing a Scandinavian's accent and assuming the person must be a good skier. Frequent workplace stereotyping occurs with differences in age and gender.

Selective perception occurs when we see or hear only what we want to see or hear. Teenagers have marvelous powers of selective perception when they screen out parental requests. We select on the basis of our own experiences, needs, and orientations.

The third way to block perceptions is through *perceptual defense*. Typically, perceptual defense takes place when we distort or deny something that is too difficult to acknowledge.

Yet it is not only how we perceive people and events that affects our response to them; **attribution,** or the reasons we ascribe for our behavior, plays an important role. We interpret an event and then try to uncover its cause. Much depends on our view of ourselves and the world and seeing ourselves on a continuum as having a great deal of control over events or as being powerless.

✦ LEADERSHIP SKILLS ✦
Leader as Learner

Contrary to popular perception, leaders are not people who are always certain of themselves and their direction. Rather, leaders are people who are open-minded learners. What's more, they are not afraid to let others see them in this light. In fact, creating an environment in which learning and its natural byproduct, mistakes, are okay can be a potent tool to unite a group and inspire creativity, risk taking, and effort.

Today, those who practice leadership must be open to learning about their colleagues and followers. That includes their differences in personality and work styles, their lifestyle as it affects their effort, and the interplay of such factors as age, race, religion, sexual orientation, and gender. No one can be expected to grasp all the implications of such a wide range of differences, so leaders especially must show they are willing and able to learn. But interpersonal skills in understanding group members do not stop with the leader. The leader must promote such understanding among group members themselves, so they can empower each other and call forth and recognize each other's contributions.

JOHN BROADUS WATSON
"Father of Behaviorism," Advertising Pioneer

Born to a family of meager means in Greenville, South Carolina, John B. Watson rose to become the preeminent psychologist of the United States (and an influential figure in advertising) in the first half of the twentieth century. Along the way, he founded a movement— *behaviorism*—that continues to enjoy considerable influence in psychology today.

Working in the shadow of Freud—who placed great emphasis on introspection and events that take place and have meaning primarily within the realm of the mind—Watson was first and foremost interested in that which can be observed. Defining psychology as the "science of behavior," he pushed for the field to become more scientific in nature as he formed and chaired the first department of psychology in the country.

According to Watson, we are all born with three basic emotional reactions— fear, rage, and love. He felt that environmental events determine the time and the extent to which these emotions are expressed, and that science could be applied to condition certain responses in certain situations. He demonstrated his point in his most famous experiment—the Little Albert experiment—in which he conditioned a young boy to be fearful of rabbits after scaring the child each time a rabbit was presented. Through this and other experiments, he argued that human emotions, such as fear, are not due to biology or neurosis or unresolved feelings of wanting to sleep with one's parent or any other ideas put forth by Freud and his followers, but rather, to actual experience. In essence, Watson was saying that if he were given a young child, he could turn that child into anything one desired, given the right manipulation of the child's experiences.

It is not surprising that Watson, forced out of academia due to a sex scandal with one of his graduate students (whom he later married), found an easy application of his ideas in the world of advertising. Credited by some as the first to bring research into advertising, Watson pioneered the notion of understanding one's customers and their needs before attempting to sell any products to that customer. Prior to this time, most of advertising consisted of what we would now consider bland and entirely rational descriptions of products. Watson was in the vanguard of moving advertising from appealing to reason to a more emotion-based approach.

Watson also advocated capitalizing on children's emotions, but perhaps not as you might think. In fact, Watson used his research on children to advance an approach to childrearing that might appear extreme to some today, but was extremely influential in the early twentieth century. Watson summarized his beliefs on childrearing as follows: "Never hug and kiss them, never let them sit on your lap. If you must, kiss them once on the forehead when they say good night. Shake hands with them in the morning. Give them a pat on the head if they have made an extraordinarily good job of a difficult task. Try it out. In a week's time you will find how easy it is to be perfectly objective with your child and at the same time kindly. You will be utterly ashamed of the mawkish, sentimental way you have been handling it." To Watson, attending to crying children serves only to reinforce the crying. What children learn from this exchange when parents comfort them is, "If I want my parents' comfort, all I have to do is cry."

Fortunately, the days of scaring young children with rabbits are long gone, yet modified versions of Watson's behaviorism continue to have tremendous influence within current psychology. Today's behaviorism continues the legacy of focusing on the here and now and on that which is observable and measurable. It also maintains the belief that individuals can learn to control their emotions through a series of concrete steps, with particular emphasis on rewarding the positive versus punishing or ignoring the negative. Just as young children can be trained to fear rabbits, so also can individuals of all ages be trained to change their behaviors and conquer their fears.

(For more information visit http://www.brynmawr.edu/Acads/Psych/rwozniak/watson.html.)

◆ Chapter Summary

There are a number of ways that one can view intelligence. The world requires multiple talents, and to view a person as purely intelligent or unintelligent is likely to not be a particularly productive way of thinking. Rather, most of us likely grasp some things very quickly and others not as quickly. For example, a movie star may know how to light up the screen with inspired acting, but probably is not going to be as helpful to you as a more mechanically inclined person would be should your car break down in the middle of nowhere. Both the mechanic and the actor may possess approximately equal intelligence overall, but in different domains. As you move forward in your career or personal life, we urge you to think about the assumptions that you make about other people and their abilities and also to critically evaluate your own intellectual strengths and weaknesses. And remember, as the following box highlights, do not assume that a person who may have deficiencies in one area or at one point in time will not be able to thrive in other areas.

Our unique personalities affect our ability to lead. Whereas once it was believed that all leadership traits were inherited, modern psychological research supports a perspective that includes both biological and environmental contributors to personality development. We are born with certain dispositions toward leadership that can be aided, stunted, or otherwise altered by the experiences we have during the course of our lifetime. Every day, our personality affects our ability to lead through our perception and attitudes toward other people and situations.

✦ CREATE YOUR OWN THEORY ✦

Is intelligence a global or a contextual construct? Are leaders born, or are they made? Under what conditions does the development of one's true personality best thrive? If you were to try to motivate your classmates to achieve a certain end, which approach would best suit you? What do you think people are looking for in leaders, and what skills do you have that meet these needs? These are but a few of the questions we encourage you to consider in reflecting on this chapter.

Now let's reconsider the Leadership Moment at the beginning of the chapter. Based on your emerging theory of leadership, how would you analyze the changes that are taking place in Wally's work performance, and how can these be addressed? Do you feel that he is simply a lost cause, or are there interventions that could result in an improved performance? How would the issue of motivation play a factor in your analysis?

✦ Key Terms

attitude	IQ
attribution	intelligence
emotional intelligence	nature/nurture debate
g and s	perceptual defense
Gardner's eight forms of intelligence	personality

psychometric perspective

selective perception

stereotyping

tabula rasa

triarchic theory of intelligence

✦ Questions for Discussion and Review

1. What are some of the assumptions about intelligence characteristic of the psychometric model?
2. Name two people you know who possess each of the eight intelligences outlined by Gardner.
3. For each of Gardner's eight intelligences, describe a situation where possessing this intelligence would be a strength and where possessing a strength only in this intelligence would be a weakness.
4. What characterizes an *emotionally intelligent* leader?
5. What is the *nature/nurture* debate? What evidence supports each side? Where do most psychologists fall on the nature/nurture continuum?
6. Describe a situation in which your initial perception of a situation turned out to be inaccurate. What are the implications of personal attitudes and perceptions on leadership?
7. What is selective perception? How does it differ from stereotyping and perceptual defense?

✦ Online Self-Assessment Tool

The Keirsey Temperament Sorter is perhaps the most well-known and widely used self-assessment tool that examines individual personality traits. To learn more about this instrument and to take two short personality quizzes (one focuses on temperament, the other on character), we encourage you to visit http:///www.keirsey.com.

CHAPTER 5

Psychology II: Motivation

∎ ∎ ∎

Carol Roberts chaired the fundraising committee at her church. The committee ran the Annual Bazaar, which had raised $50,000 in previous years. The church was counting on this money being raised again. The event was only one month away, and she knew that her committee was way behind schedule in planning for each of the elements of the event. The committee members needed to be motivated to do their job.

Tom, Leroy, Gladys, and Renae were on the committee. Tom wanted to chair the committee but was not chosen for this task and since that time he had slowed down his output. Leroy loved to cook and host cookouts; however, he was not following this in his role as food coordinator. Gladys was a single mom of four talented children, and she explained that she simply had not found the time to organize the program. Renae loved teaching in the school where everyone enjoyed her skill and dedication. Unfortunately, she did not lead her committee as successfully.

Tomorrow, Carol is planning an important meeting for her committee. She knows they need to get in gear quickly.

1. What should she do?

2. Does each person need to be motivated differently? Can this be done in a small team? How about a large team?

3. How can Carol keep herself motivated?

4. What is the best way for a leader and/or follower to motivate you?

◆ MOTIVATION THEORIES

We all know or have seen people we consider to be great motivators. Successful leaders know how to motivate others, and they do this in large part by having an understanding of the needs of those they are trying to lead. Over the past 100 years, there has been an ever-growing body of research that has attempted to understand motivation and its core elements. What follows are brief descriptions of some of the most influential motivation theories and their application to leadership.

Hierarchy of Needs

You may have already learned about Maslow's **Hierarchy of Needs.** Psychologist Abraham Maslow claimed that humans possess certain levels of needs. He postulated that one's primary needs—for food, shelter, sex, and safety—have to be met before higher-order needs for esteem and self-actualization can be satisfied. By the same token, one cannot be motivated to achieve high-order tasks if lower-order needs have not been met.

As Figure 5-1 shows, this motivation can be accomplished in a variety of ways. For example, suppose you are in a volunteer group, attempting to coordinate efforts for a fundraiser. The other members of the group have rushed to the meeting without any chance for dinner. Maslow's theory suggests you won't be able to motivate them by appealing to their self-concepts if their stomachs are growling.

ERG Theory

The **ERG theory** refined parts of the Maslow model. Alderfer postulated that the main needs of humans are *existence, relatedness,* and *growth* (see Figure

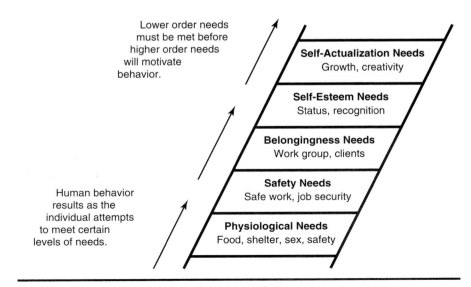

FIGURE 5-1 Maslow's Hierarchy of Needs

5-2), which are comparable to Maslow's five areas. Yet Alderfer also suggested that we can do things to satisfy more than one kind of need at a time, and he said our needs are not strictly hierarchical. For example, a person who has unmet relatedness needs (self-esteem needs in Maslow's model) may still look toward growth experiences (Maslow's self-actualization). In addition, the ERG theory notes that when an individual is frustrated in achieving a higher-level need, he or she might look to satisfying a lower-level one. This is termed a **frustration regression hypothesis.**

Although both Maslow's and Alderfer's theories are applicable to organizational settings, their work was primarily fueled by the desire to understand human needs across all settings. By contrast, a number of other theories have placed primary emphasis on examining work-related needs. The most notable are the works of Frederick Herzberg and Douglas McGregor.

Herzberg's Dual Factor Theory

Herzberg began his research by asking a simple question: What do people want from their jobs? After surveying accountants and engineers, he concluded that certain factors tended to be associated with job dissatisfaction, while a separate set of factors was linked with job satisfaction. He called this the **Dual Factor theory**.

Herzberg termed the factors whose absence can lead to dissatisfaction **hygiene factors.** They include job security, quality of supervision, interpersonal relationships, working conditions, and adequacy of pay and fringe benefits. If these factors are present in an organization, employees are not necessarily satisfied; however, Herzberg contended that their absence would be associated with high levels of dissatisfaction reported by many employees.

Those factors that portend satisfaction he called **motivational factors.** Among these are opportunity for achievement and advancement, responsibility, job challenge, and recognition. Although these factors in and of themselves do not predict job satisfaction, Herzberg noted that it was unusual to find highly satisfied employees where these factors were not present.

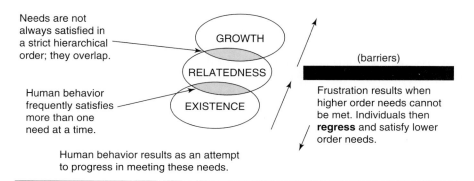

FIGURE 5-2 ERG Theory

Cognitive Factors and Personality

Leaders help people care, say Dean and Mary Tjosvold (1995), well-known authorities on leadership and team building. If followers are not motivated to accomplish a task, they suggest that leaders should be *psychologically savvy*. They must have the kinds of interpersonal skills that let them get others involved and working together in what they call the *cooperative bottom line.*

Effectively pulling in others to participate in a shared effort addresses individuals' needs to work toward self-actualization. But the Tjosvolds point out that it also is a good business strategy. "Life is aspiration. Learning, striving people are happy people and good workers. They have initiative and imagination, and the companies they work for are rarely caught napping."

McClelland's Trichotomy of Needs

According to McClelland, individuals differ in their need to control events and influence people. His **Trichotomy of Needs theory** identifies three main motives behind workplace behaviors—power, drive and achievement, and affiliation.

Power Motivation   Those with high drives for power are characterized by three traits: vigorous action and determination to use their power, thoughtfulness (some would call it scheming) about how to influence others' thinking and behavior, and concern about their standing with others (McClelland, 1975).

As we will see in the political science chapter (Chapter 8), both those who are leading and those who are following exert power at different times. Some theorists draw a further distinction between personalized power drives, in which people want power for their own reasons, and socialized power drives, in which people look to use their power for the good of others.

Drive and Achievement Motivation   Again, both followers and leaders can exhibit drive, or a strong pull toward getting things done. Some people demonstrate a high achievement motivation; that is, they love to be challenged and enjoy accomplishment for its own sake. People with strong achievement motivation have been described as consistently taking responsibility for success or failure, competitive, looking for feedback on their performance, taking moderate risks, and planning and setting goals for themselves.

By contrast, people—again, both leaders and followers—with weak achievement orientations are less motivated by solving problems, are not as satisfied by accomplishing the assigned tasks, and are looking for easier tasks.

Need for Affiliation   The third drive or need is for belonging, love, and connection with others. People with high affiliation needs work well with others and may be motivated by the interaction. According to McClelland, although people exhibit all three needs to varying degrees, only one usually motivates individuals at any given time.

McGregor's Theory X and Theory Y

Assumptions about what motivates collaborators can significantly affect the decisions that leaders make. Influenced by Maslow's work, Douglas McGregor proposed a continuum of beliefs held by managers about the motives of employees. At one end of the continuum, which he named **Theory X,** is the belief that people are motivated primarily by basic needs. Theory X leaders and managers hold the following assumptions:

- People inherently dislike work, and whenever possible will try to avoid it.
- Since people dislike work, they must be coerced, controlled, or threatened with punishment to achieve goals.
- People will avoid responsibilities and seek formal direction whenever possible.
- Most people place security above all other factors associated with work and will display little ambition.

A **Theory Y** leader, on the other end of the continuum, thinks that people are motivated by higher-order needs. Theory Y leaders base their behaviors on the following four assumptions:

- People can view work as an activity as natural as rest or play.
- People will exercise self-direction and self-control if they are committed to the objectives of the task.
- The average person can learn to accept and even seek responsibility.
- The ability to make innovative decisions is widely dispersed throughout the general population and is not necessarily the sole province of those in management positions.

Leaders should constantly evaluate their assumptions about the motives of others. Although no individual is likely to be a "true X" or a "true Y," the assumptions one makes can significantly affect the ability to practice leadership and inspire others.

Equity Theory

In this approach, people are thought to be influenced by their perceptions of the fairness of rewards for certain performances. Based on social comparison theory, **equity theory** suggests that people evaluate their own performance and their attitudes by comparing them to others. Developed by J. Stacy Adams at the University of North Carolina, equity theory posits that people consider two primary factors in evaluating equity:

1. The ratio of their outcomes to their inputs
2. The ratio of another's outcomes to inputs

Notice that these judgments are based on perceptions rather than objective data. A problem arises when a leader puts into place policies that are intended to be equal and fair, but that employees may see as preferential for some. This theory challenges leaders to consider the policies from the standpoint of the workers, both individually and collectively, in terms of fairness. Leaders will ask themselves whether some sectors are rewarded more than others, and in which situations resentments are likely to occur.

Equity theory further proposes that people will seek to equalize the ratios of outcomes (such as pay, recognition, job status) to inputs (such as effort, age, gender, experience, and level of productivity). Thus, if people feel they have been working very hard without receiving enough recognition for their efforts, at some point they will likely begin to produce less, moving the outcome/input ratio closer to 1. Conversely, when people feel they are being rewarded too much (a rare occurrence!), they will start to work harder so they can offset the inequity. Figure 5-3 outlines the basic tenets of this theory.

Expectancy Theory

Psychologist Victor Vroom first proposed the **expectancy theory** of motivation in 1964. Leaders benefit by having an accurate sense of the expectations employees bring to specific situations—they can use the information to help motivate performance.

As depicted in Figure 5-4, Vroom claimed that three principal components influence motivation:

1. *Expectancy*—an individual's perception of the likelihood that effort will improve performance
2. *Instrumentality*—an individual's perception of the likelihood that specific outcomes will be linked to their performance
3. *Valence*—an individual's perception of the worth of certain outcomes

Leaders can influence each of these components. For example, leaders can help collaborators improve their skills and abilities, thereby influencing expectancies. Leaders can also affect instrumentalities by offering support and advice. Finally, leaders can influence valences, or perceptions, by listening to others and helping them achieve the specified outcomes.

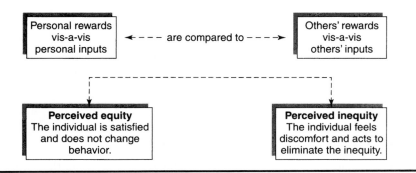

FIGURE 5-3 Equity Theory

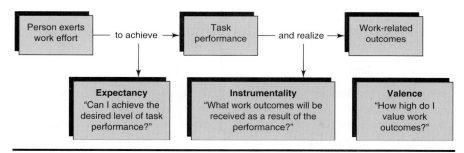

FIGURE 5-4 **Expectancy Theory**

Reinforcement Theory

Based on the notion that behavior results from consequences, **reinforcement theory** looks at the role of positive and negative reinforcers, not at people's needs or reasons for choices. There are three major divisions of reinforcement theory—classical conditioning, operant conditioning, and social learning theory. **Classical conditioning** was developed by Pavlov around the turn of the twentieth century through experiments in which he trained dogs to salivate when a bell was rung, thus associating two normally unrelated stimuli—the bell and salivation (see Figure 5-5). The dogs learned over time that whenever the bell would ring, food was sure to follow. The application to motivation is that humans will be motivated if they associate certain situations with desirable outcomes (e.g., playing soft music to set a romantic mood).

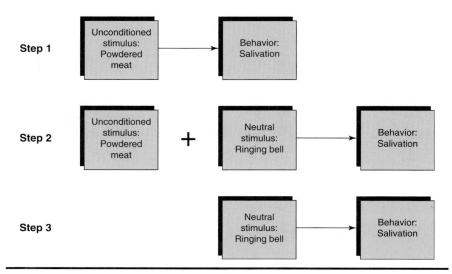

FIGURE 5-5 **Pavlov's Conditioning Experiments**

B. F. Skinner and other proponents of **operant conditioning** claimed that classical conditioning might be useful for dogs and primitive learning, but could not explain more complex learning. Skinner asserted that rewards are the major determinant of behavior; that is, reinforced behavior will tend to recur. Seen in this light, motivation can be thought of as finding the appropriate reward for the behavior that is desired. Obviously, this conditioning can go both ways. For instance, teachers have long known that praise or good grades or, in some cases, more concrete rewards such as stickers or candy or opportunities to engage in favorite activities, can shape a student's behavior. However, canny students have learned that looking incredibly interested and asking questions can help shape instructors' attitudes, and perhaps even their grading. The same operant conditioning dynamic exists between followers and leaders.

Modern behavioral learning theory has expanded on the classical and operant models to produce **social learning theory**. According to its proponents, such as Albert Bandura, learning is an active process, and the learner has more control than classical or operant conditioning would suggest. A person's cognitive processes affect his or her responses to the environment. In social learning theory, reinforcements or incentives are also seen to affect behavior. Most complex learning takes place via observing others and then imitating them. A common example is a young child taking cues from an older sibling and attempting new behavior that previously had been neither reinforced nor punished.

◆ THE EFFECTS OF HUMAN DIFFERENCES ON MOTIVATION

As if understanding the aforementioned intricacies of motivation isn't difficult enough, the range of human differences adds significantly to the mix. With our increasingly diverse population, including differences in race, gender, religion, physical ability, country of origin, age, personality style, and sexual orientation, the overwhelming interplay of factors becomes obvious. Although we cannot understand and predict all of the effects of these differences on motivation, we can at least recognize their presence and seek advice about the implications. Cultural preferences, for example, can turn what is intended as friendly eye contact into what is perceived as rude and offensive behavior. A reward that is clearly motivating for a young adult may be meaningless or denigrating to an older person. And expecting the same degree of physical effort from a person who may be weak from religious fasting but who prefers not to mention this is doomed to failure.

◆ THE LEADER'S ROLE IN MOTIVATION: DIFFERING VIEWPOINTS

In *Tough-Minded Leadership*, management consultant Joe D. Batten says,

> We must get rid of the old idea that a leader can give motivation. All motivation is self-motivation. We simply cannot and should not want to instill motivation externally. The excellent leader goes all out to provide

the climate, the stimuli, and the example, but all real motivation is self-generated. Only growing, actualized individuals can reach out beyond themselves in ways essential to true synergistic teams....We can know and lead others only when we are progressively learning how to know and lead ourselves.

The Dale Carnegie folks know all about this kind of motivation. In their book, *The Leader in You* (1993, pp. 51–52), Stuart R. Levine and Michael A. Crom discuss an employee going the extra mile to satisfy a customer:

> People will only want to perform like that if they feel like an important part of the organization. That's why employees need to be respected and included in a corporate vision they can embrace. That's why people need a stake in their work lives. That's why their successes need to be rewarded, praised, and celebrated. That's why their failures need to be handled gingerly. Do these things. Then stand back and watch the results roll in.

They go on to list three underlying principles that must be addressed for motivation to be effective:

1. Employees must be included in all parts of the process, every step of the way. Teamwork is the key here, not hierarchy.
2. People must be treated as individuals. Always acknowledge their importance and show them respect. They're people first, employees second.
3. Superior work must be encouraged, recognized, and rewarded. Everyone responds to expectations. If you treat people as if they are capable and smart—and get out of the way—that's exactly how they'll perform (p. 52).

In the highly competitive world of collegiate and professional sports, the difference between winning and losing often rests not on which individual or team has more talent (although this never hurts!), but on which team has the greater will to win. Essential to creating and sustaining winning teams is the presence of a head coach with the ability to motivate his or her players. What follows is a profile of one of college basketball's acknowledged master motivators, Pat Summitt, women's basketball coach at the University of Tennessee. The second profile, that of Rigoberta Menchu, tells the story of a woman of humble beginnings who motivated a subjugated people of Guatemala to stand up for their rights.

PAT SUMMITT
Rocky-Top Dynasty

For those readers who follow college basketball in the United States, a quick trivia question for you: Who is the active Division I coach with the most career wins? Mike Krzyzweski? Bobby Knight? Lute Olsen? Close, but not quite. If you answered Pat Summitt of the University of Tennessee, move to the head of the class.

First introduced as the women's basketball coach at the University of Tennessee at age 22, Summitt has since became the youngest coach to reach 300, 400, 500, 600, 700, and 800 career wins. Along the way, her teams have won six national championships and consistently are among the top two or three teams in the nation. In 2000, she became the Naismith Women's Collegiate Coach of the Century, and later that year she was inducted into the Basketball Hall of Fame in Springfield, Massachusetts. Future honors are likely—with 853 wins heading into the 2004–05 season and with retired Dean Smith's record 879 wins in her sight, Pat Summitt shows no sign of letting up on the competition anytime soon.

Although Summitt certainly has had her share of talented players, what makes Tennessee a powerhouse year after year is Summitt's ability to get the maximum effort and performance from these players. In a motivational book (which was the first motivational book written by a high-achieving female coach), entitled *Reach for the Summitt: The Definite Dozen System for Succeeding at Whatever You Do* (Broadway Books, 1998), Summitt outlines her twelve-step system for success. These *definite dozen* steps are:

1. Respect yourself and others.
2. Take full responsibility.
3. Develop and demonstrate loyalty.
4. Learn to be a great communicator.
5. Discipline yourself so no one else has to.
6. Make hard work your passion.
7. Don't just work hard, work smart.
8. Put the team before yourself.
9. Make winning an attitude.
10. Be a competitor.
11. Change is a must.
12. Handle success like you handle failure.

A quotation from Summitt in this book nicely captures her no-nonsense, hard-nosed, approach to motivating others. Writes Summitt, "I'm someone who will push you beyond all reasonable limits. Someone who will ask you not to just fulfill your potential but to exceed it. Someone who will expect more from you than you may believe you are capable of. So if you aren't ready to go to work, shut this book."

(For more information visit http://www.coachsummitt.com.)

RIGOBERTA MENCHU
The Guatemalen Peasant Who Won the Nobel Prize

A 37-year-old Mayan Indian woman leveraged the power of language to help rally the world behind the cause of the mistreated indigenous peoples of Guatemala. One of the first Indian activists to learn Spanish, the language of the wealthy landowners and military men running the government, Rigoberta Menchu clearly understood the importance of communicating with the "enemy."

In a similar way, she understood the importance of her fellow Indians keeping their own languages—upwards of twenty Indian dialects are spoken in Guatemala—to preserve their own culture. Once she mastered Spanish, Menchu began defending Indians' rights against a cruel government that all too often viewed Indians as easy prey. In addition, she also learned three of the principal Indian dialects.

Indians make up 60 to 80 percent of Guatemala's 10 million people, but they have repeatedly been subjugated by colonial powers and their descendants since the sixteenth century conquest of Central America by the Spaniards. Menchu believed that part of their vulnerability came from their cultural and linguistic isolation.

Descendants of the advanced Mayan civilization, today's Mayans reside on the mountaintops of Guatemala, living a simple life centered on respect for the land and close community ties. They frequently work on the coffee plantations of wealthy landowners.

Rigoberta Menchu learned to organize from her father, with whom she frequently traveled to villages across the country as a young child. She learned that the source of the government's terror against the Indians came from a concern over owning the land. She taught other villages to master the art of trapping government soldiers through a carefully rehearsed plan of hiding and surprising them, making the soldiers think they were armed.

After her father had been killed in an unsuccessful occupation of the Spanish embassy in Guatemala City and her brother and mother were tortured and killed, Menchu vowed to keep organizing the peasants. At a fraction over five feet tall, this powerful leader mobilized peasants, students, and workers in a series of strikes and demonstrations. As death threats escalated, she escaped to Mexico, where she still lives in exile.

Her insistence on nonviolence, despite the government's atrocities that included the deaths of her family members, attracted the attention of the world. Her efforts to bring peace and justice to Guatemala prompted two Nobel laureates, Argentina's Adolfo Perez Esquivel and South Africa's Bishop Desmond Tutu, to nominate her for the Nobel Peace Prize. The nomination itself was controversial, coming as it did amid the celebrations of the 500th anniversary of Columbus's "discovery" of the Americas. She was awarded the Nobel Peace Prize in 1992. She insists that the objective of the movement she heads is not to retaliate against the government's cruelty, but rather, to assure the basic human rights of the people of Guatemala who have no recourse.

She accepted the Nobel prize in 1992 in Oslo. As the chairman of the Norwegian Nobel Committee said, "By maintaining a disarming humanity in a brutal world, Rigoberta Menchu appeals to the best in us. She stands as a uniquely potent symbol of a just struggle."

One of her primary strategies as leader has been to teach other companeros to read and write Spanish so that Indians could learn to speak—and understand what the government was really saying—for themselves.

Her award was criticized by the Guatemalan government as well as by some U.S. conservatives in America, who saw her victory as a win for feminist, socialist, and violent causes.

With the $1.2 million award money from the prize, she has established a foundation for human rights of indigenous peoples in Guatemala and throughout the Americas.

(For more information visit http://www.nobel.se/peace/laureates/1992/tum-bio.html.)

◆ Chapter Summary

In this chapter we explored some of the major contributions made by the field of psychology to our understanding of leadership. This section highlighted a number of leading theories that attempt to understand what motivates individuals to behave in certain ways. There are no universal truths. Each theory takes a unique perspective on motivation and each needs to be understood within the context of a society made up of individuals from widely divergent backgrounds and beliefs. Skillful leaders do not subscribe strictly to any one of these theories, but rather seek to understand and adapt these approaches to their own home and work relationships.

How do psychological principles apply to leadership? We'll let the Tjosvolds (1995) have the last word here:

> Leadership is a "we" thing that requires both leader and employee. So too does using psychology. You will be more efficient if you involve your employees, colleagues and friends in helping you develop your psychology skills and strengthen your leadership competence. Learning unites leaders and followers in a common journey of self discovery and team development.... Leadership today is too complex and challenging to be left to one person; it's only successful when done together.

◆ CREATE YOUR OWN THEORY ◆

In this chapter, you have been exposed to a number of theories on how leaders can best motivate individuals and groups to achieve desired ends. Now it is your turn to consider to what extent you accept the premises put forth by these different theories.

As you engage in both leader and follower behavior, it's instructive to understand why you are making the effort to influence others. Those with personalized power drives are less likely to act as effective leaders, are less emotionally mature, and are more apt to try to manipulate others for their own goals. Those with socialized power drives, by contrast, tend to be more open to questioning and advice and less defensive. They also tend to see the bigger picture rather than the short-term snapshot.

Does Maslow's Hierarchy of Needs, Alderfer's ERG theory or Herzberg's Dual Factor theory influence your approach to leadership? If so, how? In the opening leadership moment, would Carol's response utilize any of these approaches? What can you use from these chapters on psychology in your own theory of leadership theory?

◆ Key Terms

classical conditioning

Dual Factor theory

equity theory

ERG theory

expectancy theory

frustration regression hypothesis

Hierarchy of Needs

hygiene factors

motivational factors

operant conditioning

reinforcement theory

social learning theory

Theory X

Theory Y

Trichotomy of Needs theory

◆ Questions for Discussion and Review

1. What distinguishes Alderfer's ERG theory from Maslow's Hierarchy of Needs?
2. What does Alderfer consider to be the primary human needs?
3. What are some of the distinctions between Theory X and Theory Y leaders? Do you know anyone who meets the criteria for either of these styles?
4. What is the primary difference between personalized and socialized power drives?
5. Is equity theory based on objective data or perceptions?
6. According to Vroom's expectancy theory, what three components influence motivation?
7. Compare and contrast Bandura's social learning theory with Skinner's operant conditioning theory and Pavlov's classical conditioning theory.

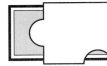

CHAPTER 6

Communication

■-■-■

George Ruth of Ruth's Consulting firm has a crisis brewing. For years, his consulting firm has made its reputation on its ability for rapid response. Now, as the company has grown and expanded to different cities across the country, communication breakdowns are happening nearly daily. As owner, he has emphasized team-based decisions and has worked very hard to empower firm employees not to come to him with every little decision. Yet, rather than enjoy their freedom, some employees still seek his approval for every move, slowing down the organization's response rate. Meanwhile, other employees are starting to take liberties and make decisions that affect the entire business without consulting anyone. In addition, he is having trouble finding ways of rapidly reaching all of his employees, who by now are spread out in offices in Boston, Chicago, Minneapolis, and Washington, D.C. All employees have e-mail accounts, but many check these accounts only sporadically. The companywide voicemail system is only a little better—often, individuals will leave a fellow employee a voicemail rather than walk down the hall and converse with that same person.

All of these factors are leading to the firm gradually losing its reputation for rapid response. If these communication breakdowns continue, Ruth worries, the whole business might collapse.

1. *What would you do?*
2. *What types of communication breakdowns are taking place? How would you label them?*
3. *Could some of these communication breakdowns have been avoided? How?*

Communication is, in many ways, at the heart of leadership. One can cr(
ingenious plan for reinvigorating a company, but if one is not able to con
cate this plan, it is not worth the paper it is written on. Successful leaders undei-
stand the nuances of communication and are able to alter their communication
style in order to meet the demands of specific situations. This chapter will introduce you to some of the main communication theories and will demonstrate that
there are many levels to communication. Throughout, we urge you to consider
which forms of communication are most comfortable to you and why and to think
about in which situations would certain types of communication channels (e.g.,
e-mail versus a phone call) be more effective than others.

Let's begin with some of the communication fundamentals.

◆ BASIC COMMUNICATION THEORY: THE TRANSACTIONAL MODEL OF ENCODING, CHANNELS, AND DECODING

Human communication is best viewed as a *transactional* process. That is, communication involves an exchange in which both sender and receiver determine
the meaning of the communication. Here is how the **transactional model of
communication** works. When a communication is made, it passes through several points between the sender and receiver (see Figure 6-1). When information
is communicated, the first step toward interpreting that information is called
encoding. The encoding process translates the communication into a set of
meaningful symbols (language) that express the communicator's purpose. The
resulting message is then transmitted through an available *channel*. Among the
many **communication channels** within organizations are face-to-face communication, memos, computer messages, and nonverbal cues, such as facial expres-
sions. The channels we use include devices such as telephones, fax machines,
computers, and, in face-to-face communication, our senses, especially hearing,
sight, and touch. Culture affects our choice of channels. For example, for messages with emotional content, some cultures ascribe more import to tone of voice
than to facial expression. Others, such as some African cultures, may place a
higher value on touching while conveying a message.

A story about a Turkish friend illustrates the disastrous effects possible when
cultural differences interfere with communication. Gungor was an extremely
outgoing, friendly person Art had met in the 1960s. He came to visit in New York
City, and was particularly excited about seeing the United Nations. Art showed
him how to use the bus and told him that he'd see him that evening. When Art
returned to his apartment that evening, his usually high-spirited pal was in the
dumps. He said that he had been bitterly disappointed. It was then that Art realized that he should have given him some pointers.

First, he should have been warned not to sit next to someone else on the bus
if other seats were empty. Nor to look at anyone else in the eyes, much less try to
engage them in conversation. He thought that people disliked him, while they
were actually protecting their space and their sense of safety—two elements vital
to anyone who has ever ridden public transportation in New York City.

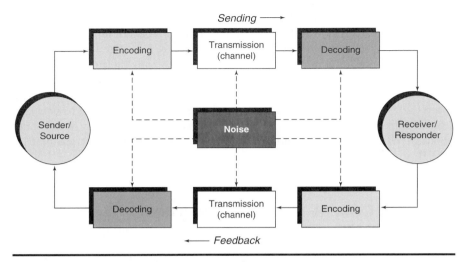

FIGURE 6-1 A Model of Interpersonal Communication Process
SOURCE: P. L. Hunsaker and C. W. Cook, *Managing Organizational Behavior*, Reading, Mass.: Addison-Wesley, 1986, p. 197. Copyright © 1986 by Philip L. Hunsaker. Reprinted by author's permission.

The final step in the transactional process is decoding. **Decoding** is a process of interpretation performed by the receiver of the message. Based on that interpretation, the receiver may structure a response, which then goes through the same process of encoding, transmitting (through one or more channels), and decoding. In our previous example, Gungor had tried to be friendly, but his message was lost in decoding.

Filters and Sets

We communicate to bring about a variety of outcomes, such as understanding, pleasure, and influence. But, as we all know, what we are attempting to say and what is actually heard by the receiver of a communication can be quite different! The original intent of a communication can be affected by a variety of factors, such as filters and sets. **Filters** are the physical and psychological factors that affect the message. From a physiological standpoint, a person may literally not be able to hear a message if he or she has ear damage, for example. Other major filters are factors such as exposure to the language being spoken, cultural differences in language usage, and the usage of slang. Thus, the original intention of a message may get lost in translation, leaving both sender and receiver confused or angry. Typically, though, filters are an aid to communication. Since we are not robots, we all use filters as a way of placing information in context or forming additional meanings to communications.

Sets, which are more elaborate forms of filters, describe a predisposition to respond in a certain way. For instance, people from the Middle East stand much closer to each other (6 to 12 inches) than people from the United States (18 to

36 inches). The distance cultural set had major implications during a series of negotiations about the Middle East. One Egyptian diplomat complained to the press that an American diplomat must not have been truly concerned about the negotiations. He explained that when the American talked to him, he stood far away, a clear sign to the Egyptian that he was withdrawing. The American, of course, was surprised by this accusation, asserting, rather, that he stood where he was comfortable. Neither the American nor the Egyptian diplomat had an adequate understanding of the cultural set of the other, and a miscommunication was the result.

Interference

Interference, or **noise,** refers to anything that distorts the message or distracts the receiver from accurately hearing the message. Beyond the usual kinds of noise we experience, such as loud music or the sound of jackhammers on the street, interference can include nonsound factors such as the room's stuffiness or lack of light, or other people's distracting behavior or strange dress. The more channels we use, the greater the chance for interference. For instance, speaking on the phone deprives us of seeing the other's facial cues. Communicating via e-mail involves its own set of established protocols, but alleviates tone of voice as well as facial cues and gestures.

Types of Communication

Throughout history, the methods through which communication is delivered have become increasingly sophisticated. A politician, for example, may devise a formal forty minute speech to deliver in Congress, a five-page press release for the media, a one page letter to send to supporters, and a thirty-minute sound bite to give in speeches in her home district—all on the same topic. Each form of communication has a different thrust and is intended for different audiences.

But one does not need to be a politician to devise different ways to communicate messages. We all utilize different forms of communication in order to meet our needs. What follows is a brief description of some of the major ways in which communication can be classified.

Verbal versus Nonverbal Communication   In some ways, this is the most basic communication distinction. **Verbal communication** describes communication put forth via speech. However, this is not the only way in which messages can be conveyed. It is said, in fact, that a message is conveyed more by **nonverbal communication** (e.g., facial gestures, body language) means than by actual words. When someone smiles while simultaneously saying he is angry, it is common to discount the anger. Yet nonverbal cues can also be ambiguous and open to disparate interpretations. A smiling angry person, for instance, could be squinting, trying to soften the anger by smiling, or expressing contempt. Or, the entire meaning of an extended verbal communication can be changed by one subtle wink or smile, indicating that the speaker was only kidding.

Intentional versus Unintentional Communication   Like the distinction between verbal and nonverbal communication, the difference between intentional and unintentional communication is quite intuitive. That is, **intentional communication** refers to communication that was consciously and purposefully delivered. Thus, when you receive a call from your partner and he or she asks you if you wouldn't mind picking up some milk on your way home from work, that is likely an intentional communication aimed at achieving a certain outcome—fresh milk. However, it is possible that this same communication could have **unintentional** components. That is to say, your partner might not have thought about this communication beyond thinking, "I would like to have some milk," but you, as the receiver, might give this message additional meaning. Perhaps you felt that your partner sounded somewhat annoyed on the phone. You might take this message to mean, "My partner is annoyed that he or she always ends up doing the grocery shopping, so is testing me to see if *I* will do the shopping." So you may come home with an armload of groceries, astonishing your partner who only wanted milk.

Every communication has an intended message, but it also, depending on the context and to whom the communication is offered, has the potential for unintended messages as well. The skilled leader is aware of this phenomenon and is always on the lookout to see if his or her communications are being received in the spirit they were intended.

Formal versus Informal Communication   **A formal communication** is built within the framework of an organization and follows a stated procedure. For example, circulating memos or posting information on the company Web site is, for many organizations, a formal mechanism for distributing information. On a smaller scale, staff meetings may be utilized for formal discussions on topics.

Informal communication channels are not formally sanctioned or created by the organization. Rather, they emerge within its everyday life. Similarly, informal groups in the workplace may emerge both across and within levels and departments and serve the interests of the members. Among the more common manifestations of informal communication is the **grapevine.** Rumors and beliefs—often given more credence than communication from higher management—are passed along the grapevine. This channel serves the social needs of group members but may be disliked by those managers or leaders whose communications are inadequate. These leaders may see the grapevine as creating much noise and distorting their messages. Table 6-1 describes some primary characteristics of the grapevine.

Upward versus Downward versus Lateral Communication   In the traditional workplace setting, there is often a status differential amongst those who are conversing. Thus, the same words may take on a different meaning if they are spoken by the CEO, as opposed to an entry-level employee. There are three different directions communication can take in a hierarchical structure. **Upward communication** consists of feedback given by employees to others higher in the corporate chain of command. This feedback can be given in a number of ways, such as via direct communication, surveys, memos, e-mail, and so on. Upward communication is to be encouraged. Managers who place rigid guidelines on

TABLE 6-1 Observations about Grapevine

1. The grapevine is a significant part of an organizational communication system with regard to (a) quantity of information communicated and (b) quality of information, such as its importance and its effects on people and performance.

2. The quality of management decisions depends on quality of information inputs that management has, and one useful input is information from the grapevine.

3. Successful communication with employees depends on (a) understanding their problems, (b) understanding their attitudes, and (c) determining gaps in employee information (the grapevine is a valuable source of these kinds of inputs).

4. The quality of management decisions is significantly affected by management's success in listening to and interpreting the grapevine.

5. The quality of management communication programs is significantly affected by management's capacity to understand and to relate to the grapevine.

6. The grapevine cannot be suppressed or directly controlled, although it may be influenced by the way management relates to it.

7. The grapevine has both negative and positive influences in an organization.

8. The grapevine can provide useful inputs even when information it carries is known to be incorrect.

9. In normal organizational situations, excluding situations such as strikes and disasters, the grapevine on the average carries more correct information than inaccurate information.

10. The grapevine carries an incomplete story.

11. Compared with most formal communications, the grapevine tends to speed faster through an organization, so it can affect people very quickly.

12. Grapevine communications are caused.

13. Men and women are approximately equally active on the grapevine.

14. Nonverbal communication is significant in interpreting verbal grapevine communication.

15. Informal leaders often serve as message centers for receiving, interpreting, and distributing grapevine information to others.

16. Typical grapevine activity usually is not a sign of organizational sickness or health; that is, grapevine activity is a normal response to group work.

SOURCE: From P. V. Lewis, *Organizational Communication: The Essence of Effective Management*, 3rd ed. (New York: Wiley, 1987), pp. 47–48. Reprinted by permission of the publisher.

upward communication and discourage feedback from lower-level employees stymie creativity and lose access to valuable ideas and suggestions.

Downward communication is feedback given by managers to their subordinates. Examples include performance evaluations, memos, policy statements, and so on. This information must be presented clearly and its relevance to the audience highlighted to ensure that it is not ignored.

Lateral communication is organized communication with peers. When done effectively, it serves to heighten the efficiency, clarity, and quality of information and further strengthen existing communication networks.

Figure 6-2 displays some of the core objectives for using upward, downward, and lateral communication.

✦ STRATEGIES FOR FACILITATING COMMUNICATION: THE ROLE OF LISTENING

Although much attention is given to the role of the sender in communication, only recently have we begun to focus on the critical importance of *listening* in effective communication. We all know that listening and hearing are quite different: hearing involves physiologically receiving the sound waves and neurologically processing the stimuli. Listening involves understanding, assigning meaning to what we hear, and remembering (short-term or long-term). Listening is a complex process that is only just beginning to be understood in the Western world. The Japanese language has seven words that describe levels of listening. Try to think of any synonyms in English!

Levine and Crom (1993) assert that listening is the "single most important of all the communication skills. More important than stirring oratory. More important than a powerful voice. More important than the ability to speak multiple languages. More important even than a flair for the written word" (p. 985).

Listening is an active process. It takes not only sustained concentration on what the other person is saying, but also attention to nonverbal cues such as gestures or other forms of body language. Nonverbal cues convey the message that you are listening and concentrating on what the other person is saying. Active listening can produce huge benefits. People everywhere love to be listened to, to find a receptive audience for their thoughts and concerns. Active listening does much to nourish a relationship and convey the sense that you respect that person. Table 6-2 provides key guidelines for active and effective listening.

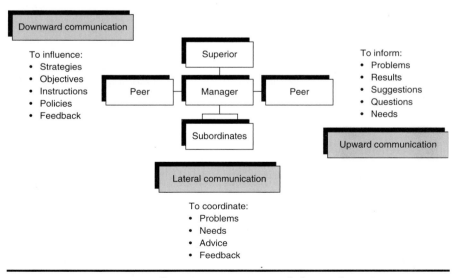

FIGURE 6-2 Directions of Communication and their Objectives

TABLE 6-2 Guidelines for Effective Listening

1. Stop talking. It is impossible to listen and talk at the same time.
2. Listen for main ideas.
3. Be sensitive to emotional deaf spots that make your mind wander.
4. Fight off distractions.
5. Take notes.
6. Be patient. Let others tell their stories first.
7. Empathize with other people's points of view.
8. Withhold judgment.
9. React to the message, not the person.
10. Appreciate the emotion behind the speaker's words.
11. Use feedback to check your understanding.
12. Relax and put the sender at ease.
13. Be attentive.
14. Create a positive listening environment.
15. Ask questions.

SOURCE: Philip L. Hunsacker and Anthony J. Alessandra. *The Art of Managing People.* New York: Simon and Schuster, 1986. Copyright © 1986 by Philip L. Hunsacker and Anthony J. Alessandra. Reprinted by author's permission.

Dean Rusk, former secretary of state under President Lyndon Johnson, understood the power of listening. His experiences in negotiating with political leaders across the globe convinced him that listening is "convincing people with your ears."

Factors Leading to Breakdowns in Communication

Within any organization, a number of factors can cause noise and thus contribute to the breakdown of communication. Sometimes these distortions are deliberate, and other times they are simply a component of human nature. Donnelly, Gibson, and Ivanecevich have identified the following factors as leading to communication breakdowns:

- Differing frames of reference
- Selective perception
- Semantic problems
- Filtering
- Constraints on time
- Communication overload

Differing frames of reference refers to the fact that senders and receivers bring to any communication diverse experiences and expectations, offering the potential for message distortion. What the sender intended to convey may not be interpreted in the desired manner because the receiver is approaching the message from a different perspective.

Selective perception occurs when the receiver attends to a certain portion of a message and ignores the rest. People particularly attend to statements that reconfirm their beliefs and often ignore or distort disconfirming statements. When people make these types of value judgments, they are selectively attending only to those portions of communication that are important to them. If people have poor source credibility, their message may be distorted or ignored by the receiver because the receiver does not find the senders to be a reliable source of information. Do we always believe what the boss tells us?

Sometimes poor communications can be attributed to **semantic problems,** which are misunderstood word meanings. This is a particularly salient problem when the sender and receiver hail from different cultures. Words with double meanings or culturally specific meanings run the risk of being misinterpreted by the receiver. Along the same lines, words can take on special meaning within a group and then be misunderstood by those outside the group because the sender has not clearly communicated its special meaning.

Earlier in chapter, **filtering** was described as a process in which information is broken down from larger to smaller bits by the receiver. In the context of factors leading to breakdown in communications, filtering takes on a different meaning. Instead of being a process utilized by the receiver of a communication, filtering in this context involves the manipulation of information on the part of the *sender* with the goal of restructuring it to be more pleasing to the receiver. Negative filtering can occur for a number of reasons, the most common being to cover up for a mistake or to try to impress another.

Time pressures can also contribute to distortion, because important words or steps in the communication may be omitted to obtain a desired outcome more quickly.

Finally, **communication overload** occurs when a person simply has too much information to decode in a reasonable time frame. The recent explosion of the electronic media often results in arriving at one's office to find dozens of messages waiting on the computer. A deluge of information limits our ability to absorb and respond effectively.

Improving Communications

Just as there are a number of potential impediments to communication, so, too, are there a number of ways to improve communication. The first step is to create a **supportive communicative climate.** According to Gibb (1965), this has six ingredients:

1. Using descriptive, as opposed to evaluative, speech
2. Taking a collaborative approach to problem solving
3. Communicating with spontaneity, rather than from hidden strategies or agenda
4. Demonstrating empathy—going beyond hearing what someone says and attempting to view the situation from the other's frame of reference
5. Promoting equality across and within levels of an organization
6. Trying to hear all sides of a debate rather than simply sticking to one's own agenda

Another important aid to communication beyond effective listening (discussed earlier in this section) is using feedback to increase understanding. Organizations with a highly hierarchical structure or limited opportunities for interaction across levels frequently have communication problems because no feedback is given. People in these cases are falsely assuming that their messages are being heard in the manner intended, when it is likely that just the opposite may be occurring. In other cases, people may not feel free to offer accurate information, so they filter their message to obtain a more positive response.

Leaders must understand the importance of both giving and receiving feedback. Table 6-3 offers guidelines for this process. Leaders also need to model giving effective feedback—that is, feedback that will help others to increase their performance. See Table 6-4 for a comparison of effective and ineffective feedback.

Expressing Feelings and Solving Conflicts

People express their feelings in a variety of nonverbal ways: by laughing, yawning, complaining, gritting their teeth. A goal of effective communication is to set a climate in which it is permissible, even expected, for people to express their feelings directly and openly. When people stop suppressing their feelings, others can understand more of what is going on and speculation shrinks. To do this, we must feel safe. We must trust that others will value what we say and try to understand our feelings and reactions from our perspective.

TABLE 6-3 Guides for Giving and Receiving Feedback

Criteria for Giving Feedback
1. Make sure your comments are intended to help the recipient.
2. Speak directly and with feeling, based on trust.
3. Describe what the person is doing and the effect the person is having.
4. Don't be threatening or judgmental.
5. Be specific, not general (use clear and recent examples).
6. Give feedback when the recipient is in a condition of readiness to accept it.
7. Check to ensure the validity of your statements.
8. Include only things the receiver can do something about.
9. Don't overwhelm; make sure your comments aren't more than the person can handle.

Criteria for Receiving Feedback
1. Don't be defensive.
2. Seek specific examples.
3. Be sure you understand (summarize).
4. Share your feelings about the comments.
5. Ask for definitions.
6. Check for underlying assumptions.
7. Be sensitive to sender's nonverbal messages.
8. Ask questions to clarify.

SOURCE: Philip L. Hunsacker and Anthony J. Alessandra. *The Art of Managing People.* New York: Simon and Schuster, 1986: pp. 202–213. Copyright © 1986 by Philip L. Hunsacker and Anthony J. Alessandra. Reprinted by author's permission.

TABLE 6-4 **Characteristics of Effective and Ineffective Feedback**

Effective Feedback Is...	*Ineffective Feedback Is...*
• Meant to help	• Meant to disparage
• Clear, specific	• Vague, ambiguous
• Immediate (if possible)	• Slow in coming, not tied to event
• Sensible and appropriate	• Inaccurate, inappropriate

Charismatic Leadership

Many call themselves leaders, but only a select few can truly be called *charismatic leaders*. In modern parlance, **charismatic leadership** involves a relationship between a leader and the persons being led in which the leader is believed to possess inspirational charismatic qualities. Currently a thriving area of research within leadership studies, the term *charismatic leader* brings to mind vivid images for many. For some, it may evoke images of influential religious or spiritual leaders, such as Martin Luther (see profile in Chapter 1) or Mother Theresa (see profile in Chapter 9). Others may think of great political leaders, such as Thomas Jefferson or Nelson Mandela (see profile in Chapter 1). Still others may think of less well-known men and women, such as a mother who, through the sheer force of her own personality, influences a school board to make a change, or a child who seems to make friends easily and is a natural leader. Charismatic leadership is at once a familiar and an elusive topic, one that does not easily fit into any particular definition, category, or discipline. We have chosen to discuss charismatic leadership in our chapter on communication because one common link between all charismatic leaders is that skilled use of communication is central to their leadership. Simply put, their perceived charisma is based on their ability to communicate.

The word *charisma* is derived from the Greek, meaning "divinely inspired gift." Once used only in reference to religious figures, Max Weber is credited with expanding this term to include secular leaders. Weber, a sociologist, argued that there are essentially three types authority structures for societies. In a **traditional authority system,** authority is granted based on traditions and unwritten laws separate from the individual personalities of the power wielders. A classic example is the passing of the crown to the eldest male upon the death of a king. A **legal-rational authority system** is characterized by the presence of a bureaucratic structure that governs the use and transition of power. An example is the transfer of power to the vice-president upon the death of the president of the United States.

A **charismatic authority system** is fueled by society's belief in the powers and abilities of the leader. Charismatic leaders are often seen as nearly superhuman, and power is given based on personal authority, not by laws or traditions. Examples run the gamut of heroes, villains, and those in between, such as the first Dalai Lama, Adolf Hitler, and H. Ross Perot.

◆ MODELS OF CHARISMATIC LEADERSHIP

Within the leadership literature, there are a number of theoretical models that attempt to define and describe charismatic leadership. Halpert (1990), in analyzing the nine characteristics of a charismatic leader put forth by House in 1976, determined that charismatic leadership is based on three dimensions: referent power, expert power, and job involvement. **Referent power** is based on the use of interpersonal skills to influence others. Referent power is not derived from formal authority, but rather is obtained through the formation of a relationship in which others come to trust and respect the individual with referent power. **Expert power** is similarly not necessarily based on a formal title or position, but, rather, is due to a person's specialized knowledge or skills. For example, one would not expect to find receptionists at the top of any company power chart, yet they are often the ones who know best how to get things done in the organization and, accordingly, individuals may bypass managers and turn to receptionists when they need help in specialized areas. The last component, **job involvement,** is reflective of the ability charismatic leaders possess to understand the organizational and social culture and to inspire others to be invested in their work.

According to Conger, charismatic leaders are effective communicators who utilize specific communication styles to communicate their vision. The two dominant styles are **management by inspiration** and **management by anecdote.** Management by inspiration occurs when leaders distinguish themselves in such a way that others feel inspired to follow them. Common rhetorical techniques that serve this purpose are the use of metaphors and analogies and adjusting one's message for different audiences. Management by anecdote, in which leaders use real or fictitious stories to communicate a point, is similarly a rhetorical technique commonly employed by charismatic leaders.

What happens when a charismatic leader is able to influence a large number of individuals and how does change come about? According to Conger (1988), charismatic leaders possess an ability to introduce quantum change in an organization. Conger suggests that these leaders progress through four stages, beginning with sensing opportunity and formulating a vision. Their strong sense for the needs of consumers and their equally powerful ability to dissect the flaws in the current organizational strategy help them develop a vision that is both exciting and realistic.

The second stage is articulating the vision. Charismatic leaders use their advanced communication skills to portray the vision's core aspects.

The third stage is building trust in the vision. As important as promoting the vision is, it is equally important that charismatic leaders sell themselves so that others see them as skilled and trustworthy. This trust-building is not accomplished by coercion, but rather, via methods such as personal risk taking, unconventional expertise, and self-sacrifice. Supporters of charismatic leaders not only subscribe to the vision, but they also respect the leaders and trust their ability to accomplish the vision.

The final stage is achieving the vision. Empowerment is instrumental in this stage, since it imbues followers with a sense of self-worth and belief in their competence to overcome obstacles. If followers believe in the vision and in their ability to overcome potential obstacles, they stand a far greater chance of achieving success.

From a different perspective, Hackman and Johnson (1996) believe that leaders must demonstrate communication skills in three primary areas—monitoring the environment and building relationships (linking), thinking and reasoning (envisioning), and influencing others (regulating). They conclude that charismatic leaders excel in all three areas, possessing superior skills in building personal alliances, creating an exciting vision, and inspiring others to help them to achieve this vision.

◆ IS CHARISMATIC LEADERSHIP ALWAYS BENEFICIAL?

At the extreme, a charismatic leader can inspire others to overthrow a corrupt leader or to turn around a failing business. Charismatic leaders are our heroes—they possess the skills, intellect, and courage to view things a different way and to inspire others to follow them in seeking change.

However, throughout history charismatic leaders have also played pivotal roles in mass killings, such as has been the case in mass suicides related to cults, during the Holocaust, and in the September 11 attack on the World Trade Center. Failures of charismatic leadership are typically less dramatic, though, and result from sources such as an underdeveloped or otherwise impractical vision or implementation of the vision and/or unchecked egoism leading to resentment among followers. When power is based largely on the leader's personal communication skills and skills of persuasion, there is the danger that those who follow charismatic leaders can become blinded to the equally valid ideas or opinions of others or will reject the charismatic leader after unfavorable events take place. Succession after the death or retirement of a charismatic leader is often problematic, particularly if the leader has not trained a replacement (which is often the case) and was not also a transformational leader (this term will be discussed in more depth in Chapter 9)—meaning that his or her efforts did not result in a system in which followers emerged more capable of leading themselves.

What follows are profiles of some well-known figures—all from different walks of life but having one thing in common: their charismatic leadership.

BARBARA JORDAN
Her Words Wore Boots*

My first thought upon hearing of Barbara Jordan's death was, "She was too young." She was only 59 when she died. Yet she long ago became one of our society's elders, a wise woman for our national village, a deeply rooted moral touchstone for an increasingly rootless nation.

She had always been wise beyond her years. She was only 29 when she became the first black woman elected to the Texas Senate, elevating the collective IQ of that chamber by several hundred points simply by showing up.

She was only 37 when, on the House Judiciary Committee, her eloquence lifted the squalid mess of Watergate out of the shadows of petty partisan politics and into the sunlight cast by our Constitution. As the measured tones of this stolid young black woman pealed across this nation, the oh-so-powerful white men of Watergate began to shrink into a foul-mouthed smallness totally unworthy of the offices they held. As she said then, Barbara Jordan was not willing to be an idle spectator of our

° Written by Katie Sherrod, 1996.

nation's government. She knew to her bones that she was the government—she and the rest of "We the People." She was that truly rare thing: a thinking patriot.

Why did she touch us so? I think it was because she always connected her prose to this passion, and thereby exalted both. Her words always wore boots, treading powerfully into our hearts and minds.

Blacks, and women especially, were enlarged and empowered by her words and example, but her wisdom and humor transcended race and gender. No one ever mistook Barbara Jordan for some mere token. She was wholly and completely herself. Moreover, she did not suffer fools gladly. I often saw her silence buffoons with a look—a skill that came in handy in the Texas Senate.

When her illness struck her in the late 1970s, we were bereft, mourning what might have been, perhaps even the first female and first African-American president.

But to mourn then was to underestimate Barbara Jordan. She had just come home, she hadn't given up. As she assumed the mantle of elder stateswoman and scholar, her influence continued to be felt in Texas and in Washington. Powerful men and women flew into Austin to sit at her feet, and she gave them all the same thing: unsparing honesty.

Her vast intellect was matched by her courage and integrity and, often, tempered by her wit. Even as her illness attacked her body, that magnificent voice went on. When he was about four years old, my nephew Nicholas heard her on the radio and asked me, "Is that God?"

I replied, "No, but it should be."

I think the idea of God as a black woman would have tickled Barbara Jordan. Now I find myself imagining all the great conversations going on up there on heaven's front porch—Barbara and God, voices rolling like thunder, laughter sparkling like rain.

We're gonna miss her for a long, long time.

(For more information visit http://www.beejae.com/bjordan.htm.)

RONALD REAGAN
The "Great Communicator"

"(I) won a nickname, 'The Great Communicator.' But I never thought it was my style or the words I used that made a difference: It was the content. I wasn't a great communicator, but I communicated great things..."

—Ronald Reagan, in his farewell address, 1989

In this era where public distrust—if not outright antagonism—toward U.S. leaders runs rampant, it is easy to forget that it was not that long ago when a U.S. president inspired confidence in many through phrases, stories, and unshakable optimism in the future. Reagan believed that God had given the United States a special place in history.

As discussed in this chapter, an integral component of charismatic leadership is having a vision. As former Reagan speechwriter Peggy Noonan wrote as part of *Time* magazine's "100 Most Influential Individuals of the 20th Century" series,

"Ronald Reagan knew, going in, the sentence he wanted, and he got it. He guided the American victory in the Cold War."

And boy, could he communicate that vision. Reagan's vision of America as a nation of destiny was tied to a speaking style that emphasized simplicity. Reagan was fond of saying that "there are simple answers—there are just not easy ones." Although many might not agree with him, when Reagan spoke, we understood what he meant. He fully believed that the United States was in the right and that it would emerge victorious in the Cold War and he inspired millions—including other key heads of state—to believe in him. Said former Canadian Prime Minister Brian Mulroney in a 1998 interview in *Vanity Fair*, "You know, when you've got a quarterback who can run, who can throw, and who can take a hit—and he's out there in the rain every Sunday—well, that idea got through to the allies. And when it did, everything jelled."

Born of humble origins in Tampico, Illinois, Reagan burst upon the national political scene late in the 1964 presidential campaign when he gave what is still referred to in some Republic circles as "The Speech"—in which he defended free enterprise and railed against communism so successfully that David Broder has called this speech, "the most successful national political debut since William Jennings Bryan electrified the 1896 Democratic convention with his 'Cross of Gold' speech."

Reagan possessed a legendary charisma such that even his political detractors were often drawn to him as a person and that carried him to high rates of popular support even in the midst of great scandals such as Iran-Contra during his second term. Wrote Greg Senf, "When those little red lights on the cameras lit up, he glowed like a man welcoming his best friend, and somehow he made you feel like you were his best friend."

Now THAT is a charismatic leader!

(For more information visit http://www.whitehouse.gov/history/presidents/rr40.html.)

Note: For more reading about Reagan and leadership, we recommend James M. Strock's *Reagan on Leadership: Executive Lessons from the Great Communicator* (1998).

HOWARD STERN AND OPRAH WINFREY
Media Moguls

Oprah and Howard—an unusual pair who are recognizable by their first names. One is the self-proclaimed "King of All Media" and the other's book recommendations become instant best-sellers. Both reach millions daily and inspired a series of imitators who have not neared their level of success. One show provides its listeners with a seemingly endless stream of naked women, unusual persons, and celebrity gossip (Stern has called himself "the man who has put the 'sin' back in syndication"), while the other has explicitly rejected "tabloid television" and is arguably the United States' most well-known and effective advocate for a host of causes.

Born less than three weeks apart in 1954, both Winfrey, an African-American female from rural Mississippi and Stern, a Jewish male from Queens, burst upon the national scene in 1986 with syndicated talk shows bearing their name. Both began as traditional professionals, but quickly made detours based on their charisma that turned them into superstars. As a sophomore at Tennessee State

University, Winfrey broke barriers when she became the first female and the first African-American news anchor in the Nashville market. After graduation, she continued as a news anchor in Baltimore, but the role of the detached news reporter was not for her. By age 22, she was hosting a TV talk show entitled "People Are Talking" and a career was launched.

Similarly, Stern graduated Magna Cum Laude from Boston University, having majored in broadcasting and film. Never the traditional disc-jockey, Stern stated in a 1984 *People* magazine article that it was at his first professional job post-graduation that "it dawned on me that I would never make it as a straight deejay. So I started to mess around."

At the time of Oprah's emergence on the national stage, Phil Donohue was the undisputed king of daytime television talk shows. Donohue's shows, which were the first to utilize the now ever-present format of the host moving across the audience with a microphone, were based largely on providing viewers with information. Invited guests were recognized experts, and discussions were rarely personalized. Oprah's style was different. Utilizing what Deborah Tannen terms *rapport talk*—the back-and-forth conversation that Tannen believes to be the basis of female friendship—Oprah also brought in experts, but also shared her own secrets. Said Winfrey in a 1986 interview, "The difference between Donahue and me is me. He's more intellectual in his approach. I appeal to the heart and relate personally to my audiences." Through the years, Oprah viewers have received updates on her love life and struggles with weight, and she has divulged information ranging from the mundane to the deeply personal, such as the revelation that she was raped as a child. By sharing herself with her audience, many people have formed a connection with Oprah that transcends television.

Similarly, listeners and viewers of the controversial Howard Stern show have come to learn much about its host, both through his radio and television shows and via his autobiographical book and movie *Private Parts*. Said Stern in a 1997 interview, "I always resented the label of 'shock jock' that the press came up with for me because I never intentionally set out to shock anybody. What I intentionally set out to do was to talk just as I talk off the air, to talk the way guys talk sitting around a bar." While, with its endless stream of scantily clad or naked females, it is on the surface the ultimate "guy" show, Stern's charisma and relentless honesty and openness have resulted in an extraordinarily loyal audience that often transcends gender. Stern has also managed to successfully turn seemingly difficult situations in his favor. When his show was pulled off six radio stations as a result of public outcry against on-air indecency in early 2004, Stern signed a multi-million dollar contract with Sirius Satellite radio.

Thus, while their personal interests and the content of their respective programs remain as divergent as ever, Winfrey and Stern have both built huge media empires based on charisma and openness. An unlikely pair, time seems to only solidify their hold on an audience that has followed their personal ups and downs raptly.

(For more information on Howard Stern visit http://www.howardstern.com; for information on Oprah Winfrey visit http://www.oprah.com.)

✦ Chapter Summary

Leadership in many ways begins with communication. Leaders who cannot communicate their ideas will rapidly find a diminishing audience for their efforts. Communication is something that we all know something about, yet is not easily defined. This chapter provides an introduction to basic communication theory and its application to leadership. At its core, communication involves a transactional process between sender and receiver, who both act on information based on their own perceptions of what is being communicated. Communication can be verbal or nonverbal, intentional or unintentional, formal or informal, and upward, downward, or lateral, depending on who the senders and receivers are and in what context the communication is being expressed.

Leaders know how to listen. In recent years, more attention has been given both to interpersonal barriers to communication and the role that active listening can play in facilitating communication. Communication will never be a wholly objective process, but skilled leaders are sensitive to the underlying dynamics behind communication and are adept at effectively utilizing the mediums through which communication can be offered.

✦ CREATE YOUR OWN THEORY ✦

Throughout this chapter, we have explored the many different ways in which communication can be put forth. As you reflect on these different approaches, which do you find to be your strengths? Are you, for example, an e-mail person, or do you prefer to talk face to face? In what context would either of these options be more preferable?

Also important to consider is the role that distortion can play in the receipt of a message. How well do you handle basic communication theory? What personal filters and sets do you bring into interpersonal interactions? What types of feedback are you primed to hear and accept, and what are your blind spots?

Are you a charismatic leader? If so, why, and if not, why not? Who are some of the charismatic leaders that you have known and what made them so? What are some of the perils of a leadership style based largely on the charisma of the leader?

Finally, what are the implications of all these considerations on your own theory of leadership? In our opening vignette, we presented the fictitious case of George Ruth, who is finding that as his firm expands in terms of staff size, communication mediums available, and geographic location of employees, it is getting harder and harder for him to communicate effectively. In this era when many of us already feel overloaded with access to communication (*Quick:* How many e-mail accounts, phone numbers, pagers, and mailing addresses do you have?), how should leaders work to reduce barriers to communication and ensure that others are able to receive information in a maximally effective way?

✦ Key Terms

charismatic leadership	job involvement
communication channel	lateral communication
communication overload	management by anecdote
decoding	management by inspiration
differing frames of reference	nonverbal communication
downward communication	referent power
encoding	selective perception
expert power	semantic problems
filters	sets
formal communication	supportive communicative climate
grapevine	transactional model of communication
informal communication	unintentional communication
intentional communication	upward communication
interference/noise	verbal communication

✦ Questions for Discussion and Review

1. Describe how communication is a transactional process. What are the steps within this process?
2. What are some examples of communication sets?
3. Describe three situations where interference has impeded communication.
4. Describe three situations where nonverbal signals can alter the meaning of a verbal communication.
5. What is the primary distinction between upward, downward, and lateral communication?
6. How is active listening different from hearing?
7. What are some of the main factors that can lead to a breakdown in communication?
8. What are some of the characteristics of a supportive communicative climate?
9. What is charismatic leadership? Is it always desirable?

CHAPTER 7

Philosophy and Leadership

LEADERSHIP MOMENT

Sanjay and Erica had a problem. They were asked to write a poem describing their philosophy of leadership. Sanjay told Erica that his dad had told him that leadership is doing "the right thing right." "It's that simple," he told Erica, "I have no idea how I can stretch it into 5,000 words."

Erica responded that she agreed that leadership had a lot to do with morality, but she realized that what was moral for some people might be immoral for others. She, for example, thought that hunting was immoral and that war between countries was immoral, yet she felt that after 9/11 we should protect ourselves and our leaders should lead this effort.

Sanjay responded that he agreed, but "hassling people who look different than the average American" at airports violated his philosophical beliefs and that our leaders should stop doing it. Erica replied that it is in our "self-interest to challenge people who could be more likely to be terrorists." Sanjay replied, "I guess it depends on your philosophy of leadership. I think I will get started on my paper."

1. *What is your view on searching people who fit the description of terrorists at airports?*
2. *Does your approach to leadership depend on your philosophy or approach to life?*
3. *Is a chapter on philosophy appropriate for a text titled* Practicing Leadership: Principles and Applications?

The conception of leadership, especially as defined by the current text, is intimately connected with the evolution of business organizations that developed in the past twenty years. Chandler (1977), in fact, sees the rise of professional class of business leaders as a nineteenth-century phenomenon.

The Greeks of the classical age had no shortage of great leaders, and they even made the matter of leadership an explicit issue for detailed inquiry, but they were specifically addressing military, moral, and political leadership. The profile of human excellence that emerges from these inquiries is useful for determining what the ideal leadership characteristics are in the abstract, whether they manifest on the battlefield, in daily life, or in the corporate boardroom.

Our proposal is to look at how leadership is treated in the moral and political sense, since that is a paradigm case of leadership that can be detected in philosophical works as old as the discipline itself. From these studies we will attempt to extract the abstract qualities that make a person an effective leader. Indeed, we shall title these sections to reflect the primary attributes that the thinker argued are central to effective leadership.

✦ THE GREEKS: THE LEADER AS HARMONIZER AND TEACHER

Leadership became an issue in Greece first and foremost in the military sense with the *Iliad* of Homer. That document, set against the epic struggle of the Trojan War, provides many personifications of how leadership was understood in a society presided over by a warrior nobility. The warrior was different from the farmer because he served a different function. What is more, one can perform this function well or poorly. To perform one's function well, one must cultivate the appropriate *arête*; that is, the appropriate virtue or excellence that enables the possessor to perform well. Homer's multiple characters provide a dimension of the warrior's excellence. As Werner Jaeger (1965) writes, "The ideal of decisive action and physical prowess belongs to Ajax, cunning and warrior's guile Odysseus, the unity of both of these qualities, as well as the possession of many other attributes belonging to the ideal warrior, are found in Achilles."

Yet, by the time of the Classical Age of Athens several centuries later, life had changed significantly from that of Homeric heroes. No longer a warrior society, the Athens of Pericles was an accomplished economic power with a bustling seaborne foreign trade. What's more, aristocracy had given way to democracy, empowering many more people from many different social classes. To these people, the heroes of the *Iliad* led lives very unlike their own. Thus, this ideal of leadership needed to be supplemented.

This was the Athens of Socrates (470–399 B.C.). As a philosopher, Socrates' pupil Plato made the problems of morality and politics central. In his treatment of the ideal city, the subject of the **ideal leader** becomes a dominant issue.

◆ PLATO'S *REPUBLIC*: IDEAL LEADER IN THE IDEAL CITY

In the multilayered dialogue of the *Republic*, **Plato** engaged a wide range of issues central to the moral and political life of human beings. His treatment in the *Republic* of justice, politics, morality, and education, as well as the more speculative issues of the nature of knowledge and reality, provide an excellent summary statement of Plato's thoughts at that point in his life.

Before presenting the ideal city presided over by ideal rulers, Plato articulated a portrait of the political status quo. What emerges is a vision of a cynical society that has turned its back on traditional religious values and replaced them with a thorough-going relativism based on the primacy of power and self-interest.

The fundamental premise is that it is human nature to be self-interested. People are motivated by their desire to expand their power over other people and over desirable objects—wealth, influence, position, and so on. The population can be divided into those who are weak and those who are strong. The strong take their opportunities as they arise, while the weak are reluctant to do so. Laws are fabricated restraints placed on human desire and are created in an attempt to introduce some degree of order into the chaotic situation. Since laws run contrary to human desire, in that laws serve as obstacles to human will, they are selectively obeyed: the strong will obey the law only when they must—when the fear of being caught and punished is real. When such a threat is not present, the strong will break the law and thus satisfy their desires.

Assuming a self-interested human nature, coupled with the conviction that there are no absolute meanings to core value conceptions, the leader is that individual who is cunning enough to dupe others into entrusting him or her with power. As the shepherd, the leader appears to have the best interests—the comfort and security—of the flock at heart. In reality, and unbeknownst to the flock, the leader's real concerns are to advance his or her own interests at the people's expense.

Thus, the qualities of the ideal leader in this view are strength, cunning, and the ability to cultivate a believable façade. Such leaders manipulate the public for their own advantage. The people believe that their leaders love them and genuinely want their safety, security, and happiness. Yet, in the end, this ruler desires nothing different than the shepherd, and the public is like so many unknowing sheep.

This is the position that **Socrates** must refuse. In the course of his construction of the ideal city, we find that the exceptional few who will be its leaders are distinguished by certain talents that are then refined by a specially tailored education, with the result being a cultivation of wisdom.

It is clear that in Plato's opinion, not everybody is suited for this leadership role. Potential rulers are chosen from the population because they possess certain inborn traits and because of the lessons they have learned from experience. Consequently, Plato selected those who love unchanging truth, hate untruth, are moderate with money, are neither petty nor mean, do not fear death, and have a good memory. This is philosophical nature that serves as the basis for the true leader's character. On their own, these characteristics do not guarantee a good leader; rather, they are the starting points for cultivating the quality of leadership.

The proper education can refine these qualities to the point where excellence of wisdom emerges. Such truth is found only in the realm of abstract thought, which requires the development and exercise of the highest intellectual capacities found in the human mind. The educational curriculum relies on mathematics and philosophy, which orient the mind toward the abstract, the universal, the unchanging; in short, the Truth. These abstract ideas, called **Forms,** are the carriers of universal and immutable truth.

The ultimate Form for Plato, however, was the Form of the Good. Knowledge of the Good is the most abstract and difficult knowledge to master. It is so complex that in a dialogue, Socrates admitted to his friends that he himself was incapable of providing a ready definition of this Form.

Yet, so much hangs in the balance. Without knowledge of the Good, the rest of our knowledge will come to little. Our deliberate actions will be foiled.

Thus, the ideal city constructed by Plato is an intellectual aristocracy, governed by the elite who, in contemplating the Good, have acquired the virtue of wisdom. Wisdom is viewed as the ability to make sound judgments, not about particular matters, but rather "about the city as a whole and the betterment of its relations with itself and other states." The men and women who possess this wisdom will translate their abstract knowledge of the Good into concrete practices: good laws, good public policy, a coherent and excellent program of education, all to the benefit of those who live in the city.

Socrates meant to illustrate that the truly wise ruler leads in order that those who are led can develop their potential as human beings and thereby prosper. In one metaphor, the ruler is compared to the physician, who alone among all people is permitted to administer harsh medicine to sick patients to effect a cure. The physician is permitted to do this because it is only the physician who possesses the special knowledge required to administer such drugs. The leader must, likewise, attend to the benefit of the led. This daunting task may require that the ruler do things that, like medicine, result in short-term pain. The ultimate goal, however, is same as that of the physician: the well being of those to whom the leader attends.

Plato depicted the leader as harmonizer of people, as the improver of those whom he leads, and as an individual of rare intellectual qualities.

✦ THE LEADER AS PROVIDER OF RESOURCES AND GUIDE TO OTHERS

Conspicuous on the intellectual scene of the thirteenth century was **Thomas Aquinas** (1225–1274, A.D.). Christianity had become the official religion of the late Roman Empire, and thus was also an intellectual focal point for the world that had succeeded the Roman era. Early Christian authors, such as St. Augustine (354–430, A.D.), had developed philosophies incorporating Platonic ideas within the framework of the Christian religion. The result was a rich lineage of Christian Platonism that numbered among its company such figures as Augustine, Anselm, and Bonaventure. Theirs was a hierarchical universe with God standing at the summit. In many ways, the human world was a microcosmic version of the universe, and the traveler in that universe, the human soul, must by its own choices proceed to union with God.

Aquinas drew from this tradition, as well. However, unlike his predecessors, he had to reconcile the Christian and Platonic threads of his thoughts with the newly recovered works of Aristotle, which had been lost to the Christian West since the emperor Justinian closed the Greek philosophical schools in the sixth century. During this period, the great Arab thinkers of the Middle Ages had studied the works of Aristotle closely. Much of Aristotle was not as compatible with Christian ideas as was Plato. Thomas Aquinas came of age in this period of cultural turmoil, and his great achievement was creating a Christian philosophy that accommodated the obvious genius of Aristotle.

#3   His writing on politics offers an insight into the qualities to be found in the ideal leader. His ideal monarch has the qualities derived from the divine model. A determinate feature of reality is that there is always a distinction between the part that rules and that which is ruled. Aquinas wrote:

> In all things that are ordained towards one end, one thing is found to rule the rest. So, too, in the individual man, the soul rules the body. Likewise, among the members of a body, one, such as the heart or the head, is the principle and moves all the others. Therefore, in every multitude there must be some governing power.

Thus, he wrote, "Let the king recognize that such is the office which he undertakes, namely, that he is to be in the kingdom what the soul is in the body, and what God is in the world." In discovering what God does in the universe, one discovers what "it is incumbent upon a king to do."

The king emerges as the teacher of virtue as well as the caretaker of human needs. The effective leader "should have as his principal concern the means by which the multitude subject to him may live well." Cultivation is crucial to living well, and the monarch must undertake this as a primary task. Beyond providing the goods needed for a comfortable life, the king must do what is necessary to cultivate virtue in the subjects. The ideal leader gives his subjects what they need to be as fully human as they can be. The result is the happiness of this world and the divine bliss of the next.

#3   The ideal leader, given Thomas Aquinas's political ideas, assumes the role of a teacher, improver, and moral paradigm for the people who are led. By embodying the highest standards of behavior in terms of goodness and nobility, the leaders contribute to the improvement of those who look to them for leadership. The overall result is a community that approximates the idea of self-sufficient and thriving union of individuals, each of whom enjoys the resources needed to function in an optimally human manner.

✦ THE LEADER AS MEDIATOR OF INDIVIDUAL SELF-INTEREST

The seventeenth century was a period of turmoil in England. Along with the international conflicts with the Dutch, the domestic scene saw the scourge of civil war, the execution of the king, the turbulence of Oliver Cromwell, and, ultimately, the victory of Parliament over the monarch in the Glorious Revolution of 1688–1689. During this period of upheaval, England nurtured two of her greatest political theorists, Thomas Hobbes and John Locke.

Thomas Hobbes

Despite England's insularity, **Thomas Hobbes** followed the Continent's intellectual developments closely, specially regarding the new science being fashioned by Galileo and Descartes. Hobbes's insight was that human beings likewise emerge as material bodies in motion, with a native desire for power. Human life becomes, then, a ceaseless quest for power, and the pursuit of those things that accrue greater power. He concluded that such a nature would, in the absence of strong law and governmental authority, convert social life into a war of each against all.

In his most celebrated chapter of *Leviathan*, Hobbes described the natural human condition as one of universal war, a world of perpetual violence and fear in which the life of human beings is "solitary, poor, nasty, brutish, and short." Just as the moving material bodies in nature, he saw human beings in motion in the political world, inevitably colliding over the pursuit of objects that promise to expand power. Without a powerful leader, political society, he said, cannot avoid the cataclysm of civil war.

However, Hobbes offered a solution: the **Laws of Nature,** which reason is able to discover, lay down the precepts that rescue humans from the civil war of their natural condition and pave the way to the peace of civil society. These laws instruct humans to seek peace, to fight with every advantage of war should peace not be possible, and to be content with that amount of liberty that one will allow all others to possess as well. His solution was to create sovereign power by a contractual agreement made by all those who live in society.

Yet, the peace that these laws establish is fragile. Human desire for power, and their willingness to dominate others in its pursuit, is simply too strong.

The primary attributes that the effective leader must possess, according to Hobbes, are strength and the ability to instill sufficient fear to keep the subjects obeying their agreements. Recall that human nature is self-interested, and that in the absence of a strong sovereign there is nothing but chaos.

John Locke

John Locke proceeded from a statement of human nature in which humans are capable of reason yet also susceptible to passions. Reason, he said, indicates to all who consider it that all human beings have a right to life, liberty, health, and possessions.

The Laws of Nature goes on to counsel respect for each other human being as a locus of reason and these rights. However, humans are not unfailingly rational. Passion encourages some to desire what others possess, and in the absence of organized society and political authority, humans will soon slide into a state of war. Passion will incline some to violate others' rights to life, liberty, and possessions. The legislative power is the primary function of government leadership, which he defined as the power "which has the right to direct how the force of the commonwealth shall be employed for preserving the community and the members of it." The executive power that carries out the laws must reside somewhere else and is "visibly subordinate and accountable" to the law-making function of the government.

For Locke, fundamental decisions about policy should be made at a broadly based level with much participation. The executive leader acts on the decisions thus made and carries them out in the interest of the community. Failure to do this effectively leads to the recall of the executive power.

#5   Both Hobbes and Locke envisioned leadership in terms of keeping peace among the members of society, although the difficulty of doing this varies. Hobbes paints a more cynical picture in which the desire for power is so fundamental and overpowering that the leader must resort to fear as the primary mechanism for leadership. Locke, by contrast, sees humans in more rational control of their lives, capable of rectifying the disruptions that are sparked by passion. The leader, according to Locke, guarantees that each respects the rights of others and refrains from their violation. Beyond that, leadership remains outside of people's lives, allowing them to pursue their own interests without undue interference.

The two profiles that follow represent thinkers who have profoundly affected modern society. Machiavelli was the philosopher who took a more realistic position than many of his predecessors, accounting for the frailties of human nature. Mahatma Gandhi, by contrast, was a leader who was deeply influenced by pre-modern philosophical thinkers and who formulated his own philosophy of truth and nonviolence in his quest for the freedom of his countrymen.

MACHIAVELLI
The Pragmatic Leader

In sharp contrast to the God-centered, Christian worldview of Thomas Aquinas are the very worldly and unflinching views of Niccolo Machiavelli (1469–1527), a career diplomat immersed in the political intrigues of the Florence of his days. He wrote *The Prince* during his enforced leisure following the expulsion of the Medici as a summary of what he learned during his years of practical experience. Machiavelli addressed the work to Lorenzo de Medici, who ruled Florence from 1469 until his death in 1492, to exhort him to unify Italy.

With Machiavelli we pass into a world more familiar to the modern reader. Like ours, his society was commercial, with the primary form of wealth no longer land but money. The powerful were those who engaged in commerce in some manner as merchants, traders, or bankers. Indeed, what he says about the political life of the prince is readily applicable to the uncertain and risky world of commercial affairs.

Machiavelli's name has become synonymous with one who delights in manipulation, without any scruples in doing what it takes to achieve an apparent good. Suggestive of calculation, manipulation, and the desire for power, *The Prince* does not disappoint on a cursory first reading. He describes the prince as one who would establish a new principality not by inheritance, but rather, through force. The leadership qualities Machiavelli set down figure against this backdrop.

First, Machiavelli was loath to construct any ideal city or ruler that lived solely in the imagination. His gaze was directed purely and without apology at this world. He spoke not about human failings, nor did he lament that humans are not better than they are. Rather than creating utopia, Machiavelli sought to give the future ruler the best possible advice about dealing with friends, enemies, conflict, flatterers, and the ever-changing tides of fortune.

Human beings reveal themselves as less than the image of God. Governed by desire and greed, they take offense at minor injuries, break faith without regret, and switch loyalties with startling speed. The prince, he said, who would be successful in such a world must be a student of military affairs and must comb history for the appropriate role models to emulate:

> [I]mitate the fox and the lion, for the lion cannot protect itself from traps, and the fox cannot defend himself from wolves. One must therefore be a fox to recognize traps, and a lion to frighten wolves.... Therefore, a prudent ruler ought not to keep faith when by so doing it would be against his interest, and when the reasons that made him bind himself no longer exist. If men were all good, this percept would not be a good one; but as they are bad and would not observe faith with you, so you are not bound to keep faith with them.

Gone is the inclination to view the successful leader as a microcosm god, as Aquinas had, or as the optimally human philosopher-ruler, as Plato had. Machiavelli asserted that there are times when others must be pampered and times when they must be crushed, times when one must be kind and times when one must be cruel. The prince who learns this will be successful; the prince who insists on being virtuous rather than merely appearing so will come to ruin.

In terms of the personal qualities of the prince, Machiavelli was no less cynical in his approach. While Plato spent much time defining the virtues necessary for the proper functioning of human beings and Aquinas stressed the cultivation of virtue among the vital projects the monarch must undertake to lead the people, Machiavelli offered a startling alternative view. In the turbulent world of political power and intrigue, the actual possession of virtue may be less advantageous than vice. Addressing the qualities of mercy, faithfulness, humanity, sincerity, and piety, Machiavelli wrote that it is not necessary for the prince to actually possess these qualities:

> but it is very necessary to seem to have them. I would even be bold to say that to possess them and always observe them is dangerous, but to appear to have them is useful. Thus it is well to seem merciful, faithful, humane, sincere, religious and to be so; but you must have the mind so disposed that when it is needful to be otherwise you may be able to change to the opposite qualities.

Neither Plato nor Aquinas could have put another end above the pursuit of Good. In stating that the end justified the means, Machiavelli subordinated the Good to some other, more attractive end. This end includes power, order, and stability.

Fortune, what Machiavelli called "the ruler of all our actions," also assumes significance for the leader. He called fortune the chance elements in events, and in colorful, sometimes notorious metaphors, likened it to a river raging out of control and a woman who can only be brought under control by the bold and impetuous young man who will conquer her by force. Above all else, he asserted, the effective prince must be able to foresee future contingencies so that he can bring them under control. The successful prince will be able to do this most of the time; nevertheless, even the most successful can't completely control fortune.

With Machiavelli, we experience the beginnings of the passage to modernity. The transcendent values of the ancient world, the religious values of the medieval world and the artistic values of the Renaissance world are not prized here. Leadership, instead, lives within a complicated matrix of greed, faithlessness, power, and chance. The task of the leader is to secure some degree of stability, order, and control in this swirling maelstrom of experience. Even the most effective leaders live precarious existences that are only as secure as their control over the unforeseeable.

MAHATMA GANDHI
The Father of a Nation

Mohandas Karamchand Gandhi was born in 1869 in the western state of Gujarat in India. His early days were not remarkable—members of his trader-class family were not politically active although some of them had served in minor government positions when India was under the British rule. Gandhi went to London to study law and then tried unsuccessfully for a couple of years to establish a law practice in Bombay (now known as Mumbai). His practice finally became a success when he moved to South Africa in 1893, where he lived for the next two decades.

His life in South Africa turned out to be much different than life in India. While there, he experienced racial discrimination first hand when he was thrown out of the first-class compartment of a train reserved for white people. The incident was a turning point in his life and inspired him to fight for human rights and racial equality in South Africa. Drawing inspiration from various sources such as the Hindu sacred texts, Western religious philosophies, and the writings of Tolstoy, Ralph Waldo Emerson, and Henry David Thoreau, Gandhi developed his own personal philosophy of truth and nonviolence that served as a basis for his struggle for political and human rights for Indians in South Africa. As a result of his persistent efforts that included his first civil disobedience campaign, the South African government, in 1914, signed an agreement promising to alleviate the problems of the Indian community there.

When he returned to India in 1915, he found that word of his success in South Africa had earned him a great deal of respect in his home country. Soon after his return, he joined the Indian National Congress, India's major political party leading the struggle against the British. While Gandhi was in favor of opposing the British rule, he was against the militant ideology of Lokmanya Tilak, the leader of the Indian National Congress. For the first few years upon his return to India, Gandhi's political activities were limited only to a few instances where he was convinced that nonviolence would prove successful. Soon, he started becoming more active, and in 1920 took on the role of the leader of the Indian National Congress after Lokmanya Tilak's death.

Gandhi's transformational leadership led to dramatic changes in the society in which he lived. Practicing a minimalist lifestyle and promoting the ideology of "simple living, high thinking," he insisted that *ahimsa* (nonviolence) and *Satyagrah* (truth-force) were the tools to overcome the British. He called for Indians to refrain from violence even when they faced physical brutality at the hands of the British. He encouraged boycotts of anything British and led hunger strikes and peace marches to stand up for his belief. One of his most famous marches was the Salt March of 1930, which protested the British law that made it illegal for Indians to produce salt. Indians were only allowed to buy salt from licensed producers, which were all British owned. Gandhi was joined by thousands of people on the march, which lasted twenty-four days and ended with people making salt from seawater.

It is important to note that Gandhi's nonviolence did not imply a passive or evasive strategy. He believed in confrontation, but without physical violence. Even so, it was hard for many to believe that a battle of this magnitude, a whole country's freedom, could be won without weapons and bloodshed, particularly since hundreds of Indians had been killed at the hands of the British in the struggle for independence. He faced plenty of opposition, even within his own party. Gandhi, however, was able to not only convince the nation of the wisdom of his beliefs but was also able to demonstrate their validity—as a result of his efforts and the "Quit India" Movement he launched in 1942, India eventually won her independence from the British in 1947.

Gandhi transformed more than India's political situation. He believed in power at the grass roots and set up several organizations to bring development and autonomy at the village level. He was determined to get rid of the social evils that plagued the predominantly Hindu Indian society. Gandhi, a Hindu, fought the age-old Hindu caste system that branded certain castes as untouchables. He referred to the untouchables as *Harijans* (children of God) and spread the message of equality of all human beings. His efforts to promote communal harmony between Hindus and Muslims earned him several enemies among the Hindu nationalist groups. His pro-Muslim stance led to his assassination in 1948 by a Hindu nationalist who blamed him for India's partition into India and Pakistan.

Gandhi was, and still is, respected as one of the greatest leaders of his time. His ideas have influenced several other leaders, including Martin Luther King Jr. The people of India called him *Mahatma* (great soul) and *Bapu* (father). He was willing to stand by his beliefs in withstanding severe criticism, jail time, even physical illness, and was ready to face death rather than give up his ideals. He was truly the father of Indian independence.

✦ Chapter Summary

In this chapter, we trace the evolution of Western philosophical views of leadership. Beginning with the Greeks, Plato's notions of leaders as harmonizers and teachers are discussed. St. Thomas Aquinas's view that leaders must embody the highest standards of behavior is then presented. In marked contrast are Machiavelli's writings, steeped in the political intrigue of his day. Gandhi represents the modern-day applications of some of the ideologies of philosophical thinkers.

✦ CREATE YOUR OWN THEORY ✦

Of the various philosophers and philosophies discussed in this chapter, which do you most identify with? Do you have a philosophy upon which you base your leadership style? If we asked your family, friends, business associates, and your competitors to describe your philosophy of leadership, what would they say? Is it consistent with your statement? What issues, challenges, and opportunities evolve when you are leading and following people whose philosophy is very different from yours?

✦ Key Terms

Forms

ideal leader

John Locke

Laws of Nature

Plato

Socrates

Thomas Aquinas

Thomas Hobbes

✦ Questions for Discussion and Review

1. What are some of Plato's views on the nature of human beings and the characteristics of the ideal leader?
2. How did Socrates' conceptualization of a leader differ from that of Plato?
3. How did Thomas Aquinas's work contribute to our understanding of leadership? What characteristics did he attribute to the ideal leader?
4. What are the Laws of Nature, and how are they beneficial, according to Hobbes?
5. How do Hobbes and Locke differ in terms of their views on the amount of control people have over their lives?
6. How are the views of each of the individuals presented in this chapter reflective of the culture and historical time period in which they lived?

CHAPTER 8

Political Science: Power and Leadership from the Top

∎ ∎ ∎

LEADERSHIP MOMENT

You're dean of the graduate school and the administration's representative on a committee designed to address the concerns of graduate students. A small but growing group of graduate students has been pressing the university to provide larger stipends, to pay some or all of their health insurance costs, and to demonstrate more respect for the role of graduate students in the university. One of the graduate student representatives on the committee has sparked the ire of the committee's one faculty representative—an individual chosen without graduate student input. This student reported in a meeting summary sent out to a graduate student organization e-mail list that the faculty member "seemed unsympathetic to graduate student concerns." At the next meeting, without any advance warning, the professor lashed out in a disrespectful and confrontational manner at the graduate student. Although you do think the graduate student could have exhibited better judgment by choosing her words more carefully, she certainly didn't deserve to be treated like this.

1. *What would you do?*
2. *What power issues are at play in this scenario?*
3. *How might your perspective change if you were the president of the university? What if you were a member of the graduate student government?*

It is impossible to understand fully the notion of leadership without an understanding of certain fundamental principles of political science. Many would argue that leadership is about the exercise of power and political science is, at its core, a study of what constitutes power, who has it, and how it is exercised. As many have explained, politics, much like leadership, is about who gets what, when, and how. Understanding our own answers to these questions sheds lights on how we evaluate leadership, regardless of whether we are referring to the competency of a president, the effectiveness of a dean, or the skills of a company's chief executive officer (as well as all the intermediate levels of leadership necessary in both a democracy and most good companies).

Just as good managers must consider the needs of their employees along with the needs of the company, a truly great president must be attentive to the needs of the people—as the position is elective—and to the larger needs of the nation and the public good. When discussing presidential leadership (which we will do in further detail), the question arises as to whether great leaders are born, are formed, or both. Are the presidents consistently ranked as great by academics and the public—Washington, Jefferson, Lincoln, and FDR—great because of their innate personality traits or because of the extraordinary times in which they served? Just as a so-called ordinary person like Miep Gies (profiled in Chapter 1) points to the times in which she lived as the trigger for her extraordinary actions, the great presidents seem to have been born with the necessary ingredients to respond to the clarion calls of history effectively.

◆ POWER

Political theorists and scientists debate issues about power and its exercise. Theorists have articulated competing and complementary theories of the state, which have evolved in conjunction with the development of the modern state in the post-Machiavellian period. Power, in this sense, has to do with how to order society, whether we are referring to the power of Hobbes's *Leviathan* (discussed in Chapter 7) or the power exercised by elective representatives. **Power,** as it relates to leadership, is more about regulating the relations of individuals to each other. Power, for our purposes, can be defined as the potential influence over the attitudes and behaviors of one or more target individuals.

Influence is the degree of actual change in the target person's attitudes or behaviors. **Influence tactics** are, therefore, behaviors that one person uses to affect another's attitudes or behaviors. Examples of influence tactics include appeals to reason, emotion, and inspiration, as well as consultation, ingratiation, exchange of favors, the formation of coalitions to influence a particular target individual or group, pressure tactics, and more coercive tactics based on one's position of authority.

The power of individuals shapes the types of tactics they can use to influence others. Those with more power have a larger array of tactics from which to choose. In many ways, a democracy is an exercise in influence tactics as those in power seek to influence others in positions of power and the broader public seeks

to influence those with power to better represent their interests. I
those with more money and education are often more effective
those in power, just as managers and upper-level employees are mc
influencing a company's operations.

According to a workplace survey of 165 managers cited by Robbins (1993), the
following seven strategies are the most common tactics used to obtain influence:

1. *Reason* (most often cited)—using facts and data to make a logical or
   rational presentation of ideas
2. *Friendliness*—using flattery, creating goodwill, acting humble, and
   being friendly prior to making a request
3. *Sanctions*—using organizationally derived rewards and punishments
   such as preventing or promising a salary increase, threatening to give
   an unsatisfactory performance evaluation, or withholding a promotion
4. *Bargaining*—using negotiation through the exchange of benefits or
   favors
5. *Higher authority:* gaining the support of higher levels in the organization to back up requests
6. *Assertiveness*—using a direct and forceful approach such as demand-
   ing compliance with requests, repeating reminders, ordering individuals to do what is asked, and pointing out that rules require compliance
7. *Coalition building*—getting the support of other people in the organization to back up the request

The survey also found that managers chose influence tactics depending on
four factors: their relative power, their objectives, their expectation that the other
person would comply, and the culture of the organization. Effective leaders must
understand the types of influence tactics being used in their organizations as they
seek to develop a shared vision. In addition, those lower on the organizational
totem pole should be aware of their managers' tactics so that they understand
what is expected of them.

Figure 8–1 portrays a way of viewing the distinctions between power
and influence.

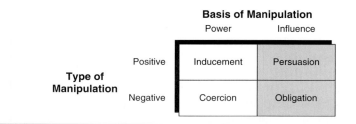

FIGURE 8-1   Different Forms of Manipulation
SOURCE: Reprinted from *Business Horizons*, March–April 1987. Copyright 1987 by the foundation
for the School of Business at Indiana University. Used with permission.

Sources of Power

Before we talk about where power comes from, we should define power as it relates to our discussion of the intersection of leadership and political science. According to DuBrin (1995), organizational politics is defined as the informal approaches to gaining power through means other than luck or merit. French and Raven (1975) found that managers derive power, as such, from five sources. This model is worth discussing in greater detail because of its wide acceptance. We know that leaders have power, but almost all individuals have power in some form or other, which means that leaders and followers both exercise power from different sources simultaneously.

1. **Expert power**—based on knowledge or competence. The expertise could range from understanding how to make a strong presentation or how to get an invoice processed in an organization to demonstrating how to harness nuclear energy. Clearly, followers also can be experts, as when a mechanically adept student rescues the professor's class by fixing the video recorder.

2. **Referent power**—based on relationship and personal drawing power. Leaders who attract others by their style or charisma demonstrate referent power. For instance, a student dressed in a novel or unusual way may inspire others to dress similarly.

3. **Legitimate power**—bestowed by formal organization. Also known as *position power,* this type comes with the sign on the door and the title on the letterhead. However, the real power may lie elsewhere in the organization. Sometimes the most powerful person in an organization is the administrative assistant who controls the schedule and access of the titular head.

4. **Reward power**—the ability to offer and withhold types of incentives such as status, promotions, salary increases, or interesting assignments. Followers can reward leaders' behavior through their praise, enthusiasm, or obvious support.

5. **Coercive power**—the ability to force someone to comply through threat of physical, psychological, or emotional consequences. Parents generally possess this power, as do children, which is why they often get favorable results from throwing a tantrum in a crowded store.

In addition to understanding the different sources of power, it is equally important to assess the effectiveness of different types of power. According to Nelson and Quick (1996), reward and coercive power both might produce the desired results, as long as the manager/leader is present. Coercive power, however, has the potential unintentional consequence of placing the manager in the role of a "Big Brother" who must constantly monitor the actions of employees. Reward power also requires managers to watch over the shoulders of employees to determine who deserves a reward. Both types of power, therefore, foster growing dependence on managers. Those who expect to receive rewards or to be coerced into action take their cues from their managers.

Legitimate power—as embodied in the T-shirt slogan, "Because I'm the mommy, that's why!"—has its place, but ultimately is less effective in helping organizations achieve their goals and in fostering employee satisfaction. Referent power and expert power are the most effective, especially from an organizational perspective. However, charismatic leaders must be careful not to lose sight of common goals. Expert power is most closely associated with task performance and employee satisfaction, which is not surprising because it can empower followers as much as leaders.

Position or Personal Power

Yukl (1994) and others describe power in different terms, asserting the existence of two types of power—position and personal power. **Position** (or *legitimate*) **power** is derived from one's place in the organization (see Figure 8–2). The amount of an individual's position power varies depending on organizational policies and union contracts. Position power gives individuals various kinds of power, including:

- Authority (the right to influence others in specific ways)
- Control over information
- Control over who does the work and where they do it
- Control over rewards and punishments

Personal power, by contrast, is derived from an individual's personal attributes (see Figure 8–3). Leaders who have expertise, are likeable, and are attractive often possess this power, which they can use in interactions with subordinates as well as superiors. Personal power comes from a variety of sources, including referent and expert power. Control over information and its distribution can give an individual personal power. Association power, which occurs when an individual has influence over somebody else with power, also can provide an individual with personal power. Personal power cannot be gleaned by knowing somebody's title.

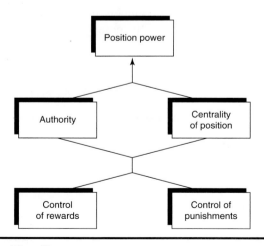

FIGURE 8-2 Position Power

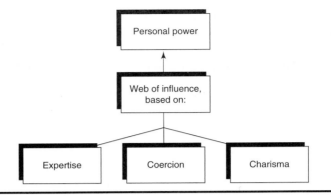

FIGURE 8-3 **Personal Power**

Rosenbach and Taylor (1993) suggest another lens through which to view power. They break power down into three components:

1. *Power over*—the traditional view of power as domination
2. *Power to*—enhance other people's power or power as empowerment
3. *Power from*—being able to resist the power of others' unwanted demands

Finally, Etzioni (1993) describes three types of organizational power—coercive, utilitarian, and normative (see Figure 8–4).

Coercive power, as we have noted, compels certain behavior with threats or fear. **Utilitarian power** is exercised through providing rewards. Those with **normative power** can influence members of an organization to act in certain ways by arguing that something is the "right" thing to do. According to Etzioni, organizations fall within three types:

1. **Alienative**—those whose members are primarily unhappy, negative, and don't want to be part of the organization

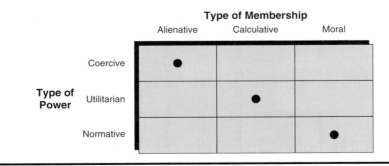

FIGURE 8-4 **Etzioni's Power Analysis**

2. **Calculative**—those whose members are constantly assessing the tradeoffs of belonging and ceasing to belong
3. **Moral**—those whose members make sacrifices to further the larger cause

◆ EVALUATING INFLUENCE TACTICS

The Ethical Perspective

Managers and leaders of all sorts must make constant decisions about the influence tactics they choose to use. Blanchard and Pearl (1980) suggest several questions we should ask ourselves before seeking to influence others:

- Is it legal?
- Is it balanced?
- How will it make me feel about myself?

Mohandas Gandhi, one of the twentieth century's most influential leaders (profiled in Chapter 7), proposed an equally humane form of evaluation:

> Whenever you are in doubt, or when the self becomes too much with you, recall the case of the poorest and weakest man who you may have seen, and ask yourself if the step you contemplate is going to be any use to him. Will he gain anything by it? Will it restore him control over his own life and destiny? Will it lead to swaraj, that is, self- government for the hungry and spiritually starving millions? Then, you will find your doubts and self melting away. (Nair, 1994)

Although most tactics can be used in a manipulative manner, DuBrin (1995) offers a framework for the ethical exercise of influence:

- Leading by example
- Using rational persuasion
- Developing a reputation as a subject-matter expert
- Exchanging favors and bargaining
- Legitimizing a request
- Making an inspirational appeal and showing emotion
- Consulting with others before making a decision
- Forming coalitions
- Being a good team player

Do the Means Justify the Ends?

DuBrin also devised a list of dishonest and unethical influence tactics:

- Deliberate Machiavellianism by advocating the ruthless manipulation of others for one's own ends

- "Gentle" manipulation by falsifying statements or arguing that everybody else has already followed the request
- Coercion via threats, criticism, excessive demands
- Debasing or demeaning oneself to control others
- Upward appeal, going over a person's head to influence his or her actions
- Passive control by sulking, ignoring, or otherwise giving someone the silent treatment
- Ingratiation and charm
- Joking and kidding (which can be either ethical or manipulative, depending on tone, tact, and situation)

Most of us have witnessed first hand the negative and positive uses of power. McClelland (1975) describes a different type of positive use of power, which he calls **social power** and defines as the positive expression of power unleashed by achieving group goals. According to McClelland, managers are most successful when they combine a high need for social power with a relatively low affiliation need. These leaders, he says, exhibit four characteristics regarding power:

1. They believe in the validity of the authority system from which they draw their power. They are comfortable with influencing others and being influenced. They believe in the organization.
2. They enjoy their work and bring to it a sense of order. They value work beyond its income-producing ability.
3. They are altruistic, believing that their well-being is linked with the corporation. They put the company first.
4. They believe in seeking justice above all else and that justice should extend to the workplace.

✦ HOW DO INDIVIDUALS ACQUIRE AND LOSE POWER?

The balance of power between individuals and among individuals in organizations rarely remains static. Several leading theories help us understand how people obtain, maintain, and lose power in organizations. These are the vertical dyad linkage and the social exchange theory.

Vertical Dyad Linkage

The phrase 'vertical dyad linkage' refers to the relationship between a pair of supervisor and subordinate. According to this model, the leader's style differs from one dyad to another (i.e., with from one subordinate to another). In certain instances, a leader and a small group of followers share a high degree of mutual attraction and influence. These select few people, the *in-group,* are typically quite loyal, committed, and highly trusting of the leader. These leaders most often exercise reward, legitimate, and coercive power to influence their followers.

What are the implications for leadership in such situations? Effective leaders are those who avoid creating groups of insiders and outsiders because such a cleavage is divisive and reduces overall group performance. Some leaders find that the best way to improve group performance is to make everybody feel a part of the in-group. In fact, charismatic leaders (those with referent power) have a striking ability to do so.

Social Exchange Theory

According to the **social exchange theory,** leadership is a transaction between leaders and followers, both of whom benefit in the process. The benefits may include status, praise, identity, money, or other types of rewards. When the benefits each receives are close to equivalent, the relationship between leader and followers is most effective. According to this line of reasoning, members of a group can stockpile "points" by demonstrating loyalty, problem solving, and so forth. Leaders may emerge from a leaderless group based on how many of these types of points they have earned.

Once leaders have power, why would they give it away? Ironically, you will acquire more power by sharing the power you have with others. When followers increase their power, they perform better, thus raising the overall productivity of the group. This practice of sharing power is also known as *empowerment.* For examples of how managers view empowerment differently than leaders, see Table 8–1.

TABLE 8-1 Differences in the Empowering Process as a Function of Role: Leaders Compared with Managers

Empowering Process	*Leader Activities*	*Manager Activities*
Providing direction for followers/subordinates	Via ideals, vision, a higher purpose, superordinate goals	Via involvement of subordinates in determining the paths toward goal accomplishment
Stimulating followers/ subordinates	With ideas	With actions; things to accomplish
Rewarding followers/ subordinates	Informal; personal recognition	Formal; incentive systems
Developing followers/ subordinates	By inspiring them to do more than they thought they could do	By involving them in important decision-making activities and providing feedback for potential learning by giving them training
Appealing to follower/ subordinate needs	Appeal to needs of followership and dependency	Appeal to needs for autonomy and independence

SOURCE: Burke, W. Warner. "Leadership as Empowering Others," Table 4, p. 73, adapted as submitted. In S. Strivasta and Associates, *Executive Power.* Copyright 1986 by Jossey-Bass, Inc. Publishers.

Leaders can empower followers/subordinates through a variety of methods, including:

- Rewarding and encouraging followers in visible ways. Certificates, worker-of-the-month recognition, membership in certain clubs, and so on can serve as incentives.
- Creating a positive work environment. Confident and comfortable workers are willing to take on more challenges.
- Showing confidence. Empowering leaders tell their followers verbally and nonverbally that they have confidence in their abilities.
- Promoting initiative and increasing responsibility with appropriate rewards. The followers' motivation to take on greater responsibility increases if the rewards are perceived to be appropriate.
- Starting small. Take on larger changes one step at a time.
- Praising initiative, even when results fall short. This encourages innovation and reinforces a positive work environment.

✦ PRESIDENTIAL LEADERSHIP IN THE UNITED STATES

When political scientists in the United States study leadership (please note that in this section, for purposes of brevity, we are focusing our examination only on presidential leadership in the United States—other countries have different presidential histories and traditions), they often focus on presidential leadership and its implications for democracy. Naturally, the modern presidency differs greatly from the presidency as conceived of by the founders and described in the Constitution. Even though much has changed during the course of our history, the past is prologue. Presidents remain constrained by constitutional limits on their authority, even as **extraconstitutional powers** have come to play a larger role in the exercise of presidential power. Having thrown off the shackles of monarchy and the trappings of aristocracy, the founders were concerned most with the potential abuses of concentrated power as they set out to forge our national government.

From 1781–1788, the Articles of Confederation governed the new United States. Remember that the Articles lacked an executive office and reserved many rights to coequal state governments. The weaknesses of the national government under the Articles propelled our founders toward an uneasy compromise between the excessive power of monarchy and the national power void of the Articles. Indeed, concerns about tyrannical power resulted in the divided and representative system of government that we still have today. States share power with the national government, and the national government itself is divided into three branches with separate but overlapping powers (checks and balances). The U.S. president operates under a Constitution ratified more than 200 years ago yet leads a country in a world vastly different from that of the men who wrote the document.

Sources of Presidential Power

Delegates to the Constitutional Convention grappled with many difficult and complex matters, such as how much power to give to the national government, how much should remain with the states, and how best to balance power between the executive, judicial, and legislative branches of government. Debates about the executive prompted some of the greatest controversy. At the beginning, everything about the form and function of an executive officer was open for discussion. Many at the convention opposed the idea of an executive officer because they feared the president would be nothing but a king in plain clothes. Others, Alexander Hamilton chief among them, argued that a strong executive officer would be necessary to safeguard the republican system. After all, only a unitary figure with certain powers can act quickly during crises to protect the nation, and a president with republican virtues would be able to rise above the more parochial concerns of Congress—especially those of the House of Representatives, whose members each represent small fragments of the total population—to represent the national interest. In particular, delegates "wanted an executive that was strong enough to check a runaway legislature, but not so strong as to become despotic" (Milkis and Nelson, 1999).

Under the Constitution, the president received several specific powers, including the power to:

- Act as commander in chief of the military
- Serve as head of state
- Veto acts of Congress
- Convene Congress
- Appoint executive branch officials
- Make treaties
- Grant pardons

From the start, however, our nation has debated what constitutes the proper exercise of presidential power. Hamilton, for instance, believed that the president had the authority to act where the Constitution was silent. In other words, he believed the president wasn't limited to the specific powers outlined in the Constitution but had the latitude to expand **presidential authority** where necessary to better serve the nation.

Gradually, the powers of the presidency have expanded to include many powers not specifically listed in the Constitution. Presidents George Washington and Thomas Jefferson—despite Jefferson's belief in a more limited executive—began augmenting the powers of the presidency from the beginning, and today presidents regularly exercise powers neither envisioned by the founders nor spelled out by the Constitution. These extraconstitutional powers include but are not limited to:

- Congressional grants of power
- Executive orders

- Prestige and material resources of the office
- Going public
- Use of information, especially in the areas of military and foreign policy

Although early presidents began expanding presidential power in new ways, presidents throughout the nineteenth and into the early twentieth centuries typically played a more traditional, limited role in the American political system. Indeed, during much of the nineteenth century, for instance, Congress took the lead in determining public policy for the nation. As a result, members of Congress—Daniel Webster and John Calhoun, for instance—remain better known than certain nineteenth-century presidents (think of Millard Filmore, for example). However, the gradual expansion of presidential powers, coupled with the trauma of the Great Depression and World War II, reshaped the American presidency.

During the presidency of Franklin Delano Roosevelt (see profile at the end of the chapter) the traditional model of the presidency gave way and the modern presidency emerged. To meet the challenges of the Depression, FDR enhanced the powers of the presidency exponentially. The breadth and scope of the federal government grew during this period as well, as the *alphabet soup* of New Deal programs—the WPA, TVA, SEC, and many more—emerged to help the country recover. In addition, FDR changed the executive office of the president through the Executive Reorganization Act of 1939, which institutionalized the presidency by increasing the number of staff and offices that directly report to the president and by expanding presidential control over existing government departments and agencies.

Today, as Theodore White has written, the moment a new president takes over constitutes "the most awesome transfer of power in the world—the power to marshal and mobilize, the power to send men to kill or be killed, the power to tax and destroy, the power to create and the responsibility to do so, the power to guide and the responsibility to heal—all committed in the hands of one man."

Exercising Presidential Leadership

An examination of the presidency begs many of the same questions as an examination of leadership in general. For instance, are great men born or made? Of course, some modern presidents have been stronger than others—Jimmy Carter ranks as a particularly ineffectual president while Ronald Reagan (profiled in Chapter 6) used his skills as the Great Communicator to remold American governance. What explains the difference? Do men make history or does history make men? The *great-man theory* of history fuels the idea that Americans expect greatness from presidents, as history is moved forward and shaped by great men. As we evaluate the American presidency, we must also consider whether the office itself limits or facilitates presidential leadership.

In his book, *Presidential Power and the Modern Presidents,* Richard E. Neustadt (1990) develops an understanding of presidential leadership modeled after FDR, whom he upholds as the ideal U.S. president. Neustadt, and others, were struck by the incongruity between what we expect of our presidents and the constitutional powers of the president, which he considers to be limited in nature. What explains the exception of Roosevelt and what does that suggest about the nature of presidential leadership? Neustadt argues that the power of the presidency is the power to persuade and to influence, particularly through bargaining. His book endorsed the extraconstitutional powers that FDR used so effectively and that Neustadt considers so important given the weakness of the president's actual legal powers. Neustadt explains that the Constitution does not give presidents the powers they need to be strong leaders, but the Constitution's system of separation of powers requires a strong executive to unify the government.

The essence of presidential power, he says, is the power to persuade, which depends on both a president's professional reputation and his public approval ratings. In other words, "The power to persuade is the power to bargain. Status and authority yield bargaining advantages" (Neustadt, 1990). The president's responsibility is to maintain his potential to exert influence through the decisions he makes because his power is a function of those decisions. Because FDR used his power so effectively, Neustadt holds him up as a model of an ideal president.

While Neustadt specifically addresses the power of presidents, many of his lessons apply to broader questions of leadership. As he explained, "The purpose here is to explore the power problem of the man inside the White House. This is the classic problem of the man on top in any political system: how to be on top in fact as well as in name. It is a problem common to prime ministers and premiers, and to dictators, however styled, and to those kings who rule as well as reign. It is a problem also for the heads of private "governments"—for corporation presidents, trade union leaders, and churchmen."

If Neustadt's ideas are correct, then much of a president's effectiveness as a leader depends on his abilities, such as what type of public and private communicator he (or, someday, she) is. What other factors might affect presidential leadership?

Whether liberal, conservative, or independent, the public in general expects a president to have a vision and to adhere to that agenda diligently. It makes sense, therefore, that presidents with forceful and charismatic personalities tend to be popular. Such individuals are most likely to harness the persuasive forces of the presidency and lead the country down the road of progress. Are the paths presidents take predetermined by their personalities, the historical moment in which they serve, or something else? Do presidents, as some suggest, remain true to their personality types and so act in predictable ways, or is presidential leadership more a function of a president's ability to break free of such constraints? What else might influence presidential leadership? What if Roosevelt had served during another historical time? Would he still be considered one of the few irrefutably great U.S. presidents or would another time have proved limiting? Without a Depression to confront or a war to wage, how would Roosevelt have accomplished what he did?

While most of us don't want to cede control of our destiny to historical forces, it is difficult to imagine FDR president during another era. In *The Politics Presidents Make,* Stephen Skowronek (1993) argues that the historical times in which a president serves are paramount. He examines the institution of the presidency in terms of historical times, asking several questions, including what presidents past and present have in common, what conditions of leadership they share, and what they do to succeed or fail. Skowronek looks for historical patterns to enhance our understanding of the presidency. Power for him centers on the idea of repudiation, by which he means a president's ability to carve out his own path by repudiating that of his predecessor: "The power to recreate order hinges on the authority to repudiate it." Presidential authority, according to Skowronek, is the legitimacy of a president to do what he wants.

Types of Presidential Authority in the United States

There are four types of presidential authority: the reconstructionist, the disjunction, the articulation, and the preemptive. Presidents, in Skowronek's view, are most effective when they can negate what has come before and so offer a new vision of their own. The personality of presidents, understandably, turns out to "reflect characteristics of the office under different circumstances" rather than characteristics of the individual. Skowronek says that an examination of the institution from a historical perspective reveals certain patterns that are much more than coincidental. He concludes that various times call for various responses from the president. What becomes known as a president's personality and/or character thus derives from the period in which he serves. Presidents are likely to heed the clarion call of history and march to its beat. Presidential power is, hence, delineated by forces largely out of the hands of individual presidents, and what they can achieve is, to an extent, predetermined. So, while Neustadt says modern presidents should model themselves after FDR, Skowronek disagrees. "Roosevelt succeeded magnificently, but it does not follow that if we could just get more people like Roosevelt into the office, the problems and dangers the presidency poses would recede."

In this view, individuals are captives of history to a certain extent. Do you agree? Can you reconcile this idea with the notion that great men and women shape great events and are, therefore, the forces that move history forward? Is leadership derivative of individuals in positions of power, or does the process of leadership transcend the character of individual leaders? How much should leaders, presidents or not, heed the times in which they serve? Can you think of leaders who have defied the limits of their historical times, thereby, perhaps, remaking history? Can effective leaders create moments ripe for leadership? Or, is it the right combination of personality and historical opportunity that provides for presidential greatness?

Evaluating Presidential Leadership

In a *Presidential Studies Quarterly* (2000) article, presidential scholar Fred Greenstein describes qualities associated with presidential success. He sets forth six types of skills that particularly influence presidential effectiveness:

1. Skills as a public communicator
2. Organizational capacity, which is defined as the "ability to rally colleagues and structure their activities effectively"

3. Political skill

4. Vision, meaning a president's ability to organize the administration around a clear set of public-policy goals

5. Cognitive style, which is the way in which presidents process all the information they receive

6. Emotional intelligence, meaning "the extent to which the president is able to manage his emotions and turn them to constructive purposes rather than be dominated by them to undermine his public performance" (Greenstein, p. 180)

In the wake of former President Clinton's impeachment and his rather scandal-laden presidency, it is not surprising to consider how significant a president's emotional intelligence may be. Nixon stands out as perhaps the most emotionally compromised U.S. president, but as Greenstein points out, Lyndon B. Johnson, Carter, and Clinton all lacked a certain amount of emotional stability. "The vesuvian LBJ was subject to mood swings of clinical proportions. Jimmy Carter evinced a rigidity that impeded his White House performance. The lack of self-discipline of Bill Clinton led him into actions that resulted in his impeachment."

Should we do a better job screening presidential candidates with some degree of emotional instability, or are there benefits to having had such individuals as president? Clearly communication skills were key to the success of Ronald Reagan. Is it good or bad that a president can compensate for less than exceptional skills in other areas by being an effective speaker? Of course, George H. W. Bush's problem with the "vision thing," as he called it, proved problematic in his 1992 campaign against Bill Clinton. Keeping in mind that leaders of all sorts wield power, how do these traits that Greenstein identifies translate into other arenas? Can the head of a company or a manager be effective without emotional intelligence? Vision is important for obvious reasons for presidents, but what about for managers and leaders of smaller groups? Will people be motivated to follow somebody who lacks a cohesive vision for the future?

Which type of power—personal or position—do you think is more effective? As you read the three profiles that follow, think about whether leadership inherent in one's character or is acquired. FDR and other modern presidents shifted power back to the president and away from Congress (especially compared to the balance of power typical of the nineteenth century), giving presidents center stage in our political system. According to Yukl, those who lead through personal power have more influence over us. Do you agree? Of course, many leaders, such as Margaret Thatcher of Great Britain and Lee Kuan Yew of Singapore, have successfully utilized both.

FRANKLIN DELANO ROOSEVELT
The Man behind the New Deal

Born into a wealthy Hudson Valley, New York, family in January 1882, Franklin Roosevelt enjoyed all the privileges money could offer, along with the love of his two devoted parents. He attended high school at Groton and moved from there to Harvard University, where he became editor of the *Crimson*. How did a man from such a background become a champion of downtrodden Americans and the most progressive U.S. President? How did FDR come to sympathize with Americans from all walks of life, and especially the third of a nation left "ill-housed, ill-clothed, and ill-fed" in the wake of the Depression?

It took more than the sense of noblesse oblige he inherited to transform FDR into the leader he became. In his twenties, Roosevelt spent a few years in the business world before quickly moving into the political career that would fill the rest of his life and, ultimately, would change the nation and even the world. As a young man not long out of Harvard, Franklin married his distant cousin, Eleanor Roosevelt, whose uncle, Theodore Roosevelt, gave her away at her wedding. FDR in many ways modeled his political career on TR's, though FDR was a Democrat and TR a Republican. Like Teddy Roosevelt, FDR first served in the New York state legislature (1910–1913), then as assistant secretary of the navy under Woodrow Wilson (1913–1920), and governor of New York (1928–1932) before finally being elected president in 1932. But TR and FDR shared more than just a career trajectory. They both stand out as two of the leading progressive presidents in U.S. history. Franklin Roosevelt, however, carved out his own path, leaving a legacy that has outdistanced that of TR.

His family and educational emphasis on social responsibility help explain why he embarked on a career in public service and why he exhibited reformist leanings as a young man. However, many point to his battle with polio as a turning point in his life. He contracted polio in 1921 at his boyhood summer home on Campobello Island located off the coast of Maine. Before polio, he was known as a capable man but not as an intellectual and certainly not as a man destined to transform the nation. The famous quote of Justice Oliver Wendell Holmes seems to reflect what many thought about FDR, that he had a "second-class intellect. But a first-class temperament." Although the country never knew the extent of his paralysis, FDR in fact became a paraplegic, never regaining the use of his legs despite years of effort. He spent much of the 1920s adapting to his condition by building his upper body strength so that he could appear to walk. While he focused on recovery, Eleanor became his eyes and legs, giving speeches and keeping Roosevelt's name current in Democratic circles. Elected four times to the presidency and in office for twelve years before his death on April 12, 1945, FDR was able to keep the extent of his disability from most Americans.

Many biographers have noted that his experiences with polio left an indelible mark on FDR, perhaps explaining in part how a man of wealth developed empathy for those in need and how a nation in need found a kindred spirit in a man who never had to work to earn his way. As the noted scholar Robert Dallek has written, "Afflicted by a crippling Depression, Americans took psychological hope from a president who, after losing the use of his legs, had surmounted his handicap to become governor of New York and president of the United States."

In addition, Roosevelt's quest for a cure brought him to Warm Springs, Georgia, where he spent many months recuperating and where he vacationed during his years as president. His time there brought him into contact with a rural poverty he might otherwise never have witnessed, and that may have prompted some of his antipoverty programs.

Despite his inability to walk, FDR never considered retiring to his family's country estate, as his mother assumed he would. Instead, he rose to the challenge, revealing many of the personality traits that make him one of our nation's greatest presidents. During weeks of pain following his initial bout and through years of stubborn and grueling exercise, FDR revealed a raw courage that impressed those around him. Just as he refused to believe he would be unable to reenter politics, he never doubted that the country would recover from the Depression's devastation and that the Allies would prevail in World War II. As he told the American people, "The only thing we have to fear is fear itself." More than anything else, FDR gave Americans hope.

Indicative of the leadership flare and forceful personality he demonstrated throughout his presidency, Roosevelt broke precedent by flying to Chicago in 1932 to accept the Democratic Party's nomination in person. After assuming the presidency in March 1933, Roosevelt acted swiftly to deliver his New Deal to the American people. He continued to break new ground as president, creating the modern presidency and remaking the federal government.

During our nation's darkest hour, FDR showed Americans only confidence and optimism. His famous Fireside Chats carried his resonant voice into living rooms across the country, signaling to the American people that recovery was on the way. FDR ushered in numerous programs to confront the Depression head-on during his first hundred days—the single most active period of American government—and throughout his twelve years in office.

(For more information visit http://www.whitehouse.gov/history/presidents/fr32.html.)

MARGARET THATCHER
Britain's "Iron Lady"

Margaret Thatcher was not only Britain's first woman prime minister, she was the first female prime minister of any European country. She surprised most political commentators when she led her Tory party to victory in the country's general election in 1979.

Growing up as the younger daughter of a lay Methodist minister, Ms. Thatcher learned early on to stand behind her own decisions regardless of other people's opinions. Unbounded determination helped her win a scholarship to Oxford, where she held leadership positions in the Conservative Association.

She continued working for the conservative position, and became the youngest woman candidate in the country when she stood for local election.

Despite losing twice in a row, she managed to increase the conservative vote by nearly 50 percent and proved herself a capable, hard-working politician.

She married, had twins, went to law school, and practiced as a barrister specializing in taxation law, but she kept her eye on the goal of being elected to Parliament. After several disappointments, she reached her goal in 1959.

Ms. Thatcher rose to prominence in the conservative Tory party, and in 1961 was appointed secretary to the ministry of pensions and national insurance. From 1964 to 1970, she emerged as an opposition spokesperson to the Labour party, then in power. As the minister of education (after the Conservatives won the 1970 general election), she was dubbed the "most unpopular woman in Britain" for her controversial views on education, including discontinuing free milk for students over seven and increasing school milk charges.

After Conservative Edward Heath lost in the 1974 general election, Ms. Thatcher announced that she would seek the party's leadership. Although no one took her seriously at first, she emerged the victor after two ballots.

Then, in 1979, she won a narrow victory in a no-confidence vote over James Callaghan, who became the first prime minister to be voted out of office since 1924.

Having campaigned on the promise to "turn the tide against socialism," she introduced legislation to reduce government spending in health care, housing, social security, and education while increasing support for the military and reducing taxation, particularly for the wealthiest people.

She was roundly criticized in Parliament and in the media for what her opposition called "the savage attack on the welfare state." Undaunted, she declared that the country was "sick and needed a dose of strong medicine."

Despite a major victory in quelling the civil war in Rhodesia and helping to hold free elections that resulted in black nationalist leader Robert Mugabe winning, she faced increasingly difficult times at home: massive unemployment, rising numbers of businesses closing, and widespread public uproar over her economic policies. Nevertheless, Ms. Thatcher won three consecutive general elections and held office continuously longer than any British prime minister since Gladstone.

She has been lauded and sneered at for her persistence and her willingness to challenge conventional wisdom. Indeed, even her rise to the top was a great challenge. She was the epitome of an outsider, coming not from the aristocracy of the party, but rather from a provincial town and middle-class parents. Most significantly, she was an outsider in terms of gender.

Writing in the *Atlantic Monthly* (Dec. 1991), Geoffrey Wheatcraft explains:

> She was cut off by the "homosocial" traditions of her party, which thirty years ago were very strong and are scarcely weak even now. It was a chaps' party—chaps who had known each other at school, at university, in the army; chaps who met to talk and drink in the House of Commons smoking room or the clubs of St. James Street. This was a camaraderie from which the lowborn were mostly excluded, and a woman was by definition

entirely excluded. And so Margaret Thatcher had to plow her own furrow, make her own friends, and attack the citadel of power from outside.

(For more information visit http://www.margaretthatcher.org/.)

LEE KUAN YEW
Nation Builder

The world's longest-serving prime minister, Lee Kuan Yew ruled Singapore from its inception as an independent country in 1959 until stepping down in 1990. Born in Singapore in 1923, he attended Raffles College there before going to England to study law at Cambridge.

After returning to Singapore in 1950, he threw himself into politics and rose to the top spot in the government in 1959. His accomplishments in Singapore are legendary: turning the economy from manufacturing to high-tech, transforming the infrastructure of the country to a modern-day exemplar, nearly eliminating crime and unemployment, and creating one of Asia's foremost health care and educational systems. Today, per-capita income in Singapore is higher than in England. Singapore boasts the world's busiest port and the third-largest oil refinery in addition to its role as a global center of manufacturing and service industries—all this in a tiny country almost totally lacking in natural resources.

His forthright, confrontational personality seems decidedly un-Asian. *Time International* describes Lee as "living by the conflict theory of management: you either dominate or are dominated." He experienced being dominated, first by British colonial rule and later by the often-brutal Japanese occupation in World War II.

When he came to power, he didn't hesitate to become the dominator. His style of governing was often described as "soft authoritarian," although his opponents might not agree with the "soft" designation. Lee promoted a culture that stressed discipline, avoiding drugs, and encouraging tolerance among the races.

In 1994, an American teenager convicted of a crime in Singapore was sentenced to caning. Despite torrents of opposition, including a personal plea from President Clinton, Mr. Lee defended his government's corporal punishment approach as an effective way to stem crime.

Lee characterizes American society as an overly permissive society that has lost its ethical and moral underpinnings. He asserts that the United States should not try to impose its model of government elsewhere, especially on Eastern nations whose cultures do not lend themselves to a democratic approach.

Since retiring as prime minister in 1990, Lee continues to serve the country in the newly created position of "senior minister." Former President Nixon was one of his many admirers, writing that if he had lived in a different time and place, Lee might have "attained the world stature of a Churchill, a Disraeli or a Gladstone."

✦ Chapter Summary

In this chapter, we've explored the link between political science and leadership. As we know, leadership requires the exercise of power, and political science studies the distribution and use of power. We've reviewed the influence tactics individuals in power use and the sources and types of power exercised by those in positions of authority. Finally, we've examined presidential leadership as a means of analyzing how leaders exercise power once they have it and the dilemmas associated with the exercise of power in a democracy.

✦ CREATE YOUR OWN THEORY ✦

This chapter has focused on the importance of understanding power and its many forms and dimensions. Which types of power do you exhibit, and which do you respect and/or fear? Have there been times where you have seen power used unethically? What forms of unethical power usage disturb you the most, and how can you best use your talents to challenge this unethical behavior?

Also heavily emphasized in this chapter was presidential leadership. Which skills do you think are most important for a president to have? Can a president in today's world get by with poor skills in any of the above areas? What, in your view, is the most serious deficiency a president could have? How important is vision to leadership? What does the experience of George H. W. Bush reveal about vision and the public's understanding of the presidency? What does his son seem to have learned from George the elder?

Do great brains make great presidents? How important is exceptional cognitive ability to presidential leadership? How did high intelligence shape Carter's presidency? Has Clinton's high I.Q. been an advantage or a hindrance? How does the media affect our perception of presidents?

What characteristics would your ideal president exhibit? Think back to our opening Leadership Moment. If you were president of the university, how would you handle a tenured professor who was misusing his positional power? If you were a student at this school, how might you challenge this abuse of power, or would you?

✦ Key Terms

alienative organizations

calculative organizations

coercive power

expert power

extraconstitutional powers

influence

influence tactics

legitimate power

moral organizations

normative power

personal power

position power

power

presidential authority

referent power

reward power

social exchange theory

social power

utilitarian power

vertical dyad linkage

✦ Questions for Discussion and Review

1. What types of leaders are most effective? Why?
2. What are some of the ways leaders seek to influence followers?
3. What are different sources of power, and which types are more associated with effective leadership?
4. How do you define personal power?
5. How important is it for leaders to be ethical?
6. Define empowerment and its place in leadership.
7. What is the difference between constitutional and extraconstitutional powers?
8. What is the cornerstone of presidential leadership, according to Neustadt?

✦ Online Self-Assessment Tool

To learn more about how your points of view on leadership match up with the strengths and weaknesses of a host of modern leaders, visit http://www.humanmetrics.com/rot/politicalsuccess/HPSSQ.asp.

CHAPTER 9

Management and Leadership

■ ■ ■

LEADERSHIP MOMENT

Gail and Howie were leaving their management class when Gail said, "Hi, Howie, I just heard that you were chosen captain of the cheerleading team. I guess you will now need to implement some of the management and leadership stuff we have been discussing in class."

"Thanks," Howie replied. "I guess so. I am a bit confused. I am not the coach or administrator of the squad. Paid people have those responsibilities. I am also not the manager. We don't have one, but the basketball and baseball teams do. I do have several administrative responsibilities, but it doesn't sound right to say I manage cheerleaders and I'm not sure I can lead cheerleaders. I believe captain is a middle rank of military officers, but we don't function like they do, and no one on the team outranks me. I have no idea why I am called captain, but I also don't know what else to call it!"

1. *Why do they often call the leader of a team—even a team of cheerleaders—captain?*
2. *What is the difference between a captain, coach, administrator, manager, or leaders?*
3. *Which of those titles are you most comfortable being called?*

Much of where we are in our understanding of leadership is a function of where we once were. This chapter provides some anchoring points as you progress on your leadership journey, providing information on the key concepts of management. Management and leadership are often confused, but we will attempt to describe both and how they interact.

Peter Drucker (1974) wrote:

> The emergence of management in this century may have been a pivotal event in history. It signaled a major transformation of society into a pluralistic society of institutions, of which managements are the effective organs. Management, after more than a century of development as a practice and as a discipline, burst into public consciousness in the management boom that began after World War II and lasted through the 1960s. (p. 2)

> Every developed society has become a society of institutions...every major task, whether economic performance or health care, education or the protection of the environment, the pursuit of new knowledge or defense is today being entrusted to big organizations designed for perpetuity and managed by their own management. On the performance of those institutions, the performance of modern society—if not the survival of each individual—increasingly depends.

Although the effects of management have been felt throughout history, it was first described more than 100 years ago during the Industrial Revolution as factories developed and we began to systematically study its impact. **Management** has been defined as the coordination of human, material, technological, and financial resources needed for an organization to reach its goals (Hess and Siciliano, 1996, p. 7). Or, to return to Drucker (1974, p. 17), management is "a multipurpose organ that manages a business and manages managers and manages workers and work."

With such far-reaching definitions, just what is it that managers do? It is commonly agreed that five functions make up a manager's job: planning, controlling, organizing, staffing, and leading (see Figure 9–1). The addition of continuous improvement as a sixth function of management is a relatively new phenomenon.

Although these charts seem fairly straightforward, defining management becomes much more difficult because none of the functions is really discrete; they are all interconnected. Further, not every manager is involved in each of the functions. One way to distinguish between management functions is to designate different levels of managers. Top-level managers, for instance—the chief executive officers, presidents, and senior vice presidents—spend most of their time in the two functions of planning and organizing. They oversee the big picture.

First-line, or front-line, managers are typically involved in the nitty-gritty of daily operations. These are the foremen, crew chiefs, and supervisors. Thus, first-line managers tend to spend much of their time in leading and controlling.

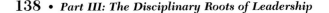

Management

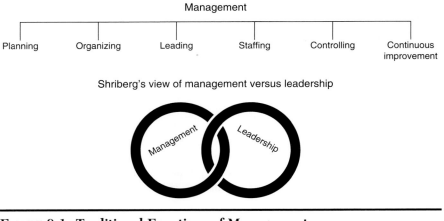

| Planning | Organizing | Leading | Staffing | Controlling | Continuous improvement |

Shriberg's view of management versus leadership

FIGURE 9-1 **Traditional Functions of Management (including Leadership)**

◆ LEADERSHIP VERSUS MANAGEMENT

Perusing the bottom half of Figure 9–1 prompts a basic question for this text—indeed, for any participant of a class in leadership. Is leadership merely a subset of management? Some management proponents argue that, yes, leadership is one facet of management. The military, for example, asserts that leadership is a totally definable skill, a science that can be learned. Their training manuals outline the behaviors that typify leadership, so that to lead one must simply acquire those skills and behaviors (see Chapter 13 for a detailed discussion on military leadership).

We disagree. Along with other leadership theorists, we maintain that leadership is a piece of the pie, a part of management, but that there is a good bit of leadership that cannot be considered a subset of management. Leadership and management share some characteristics, but each is also separate and distinct. For a useful depiction of the distinctions between leadership and management, see Tables 9–1 and 9–2.

These tables do not define leadership and management, as neither is synonymous with nor a subject of the other. They describe leadership as both a process and a property (Jago, 1992). The process of practicing leadership is integral to this text, because it envisions leadership as a noncoercive influence that shapes an organization's culture and people and motivates participants toward a common goal. The property is the characteristic attributed to the people who are perceived as leaders (Yukl, 1995).

A person, then, may be skilled as a leader or manager or both—or neither. The skilled leader definitely needs to understand the principles of management. This brings us to the question: What is doing management all about? How does it vary from doing leadership?

Yukl (see Table 9-3) describes eleven managerial practices. At all levels of management, most of these tasks take up the time of managers. How they approach these tasks describes whether they are managers or leaders—or both

TABLE 9-1   **Distinctions between Management and Leadership**

Activity	Management	Leadership
Creating an agenda	Planning and budgeting. Establishing detailed steps and timetables for achieving needed results: allocating the resources necessary to make those needed results happen.	Establishing direction. Developing a vision of the future, often the distant future, and strategies for producing the changes needed to achieve that vision.
Developing a human network for achieving the agenda	Organizing and staffing. Establishing some structure for accomplishing plan requirements, staffing that structure with individuals, delegating responsibility and authority for carrying out the plan, providing policies and procedures to help guide people, and creating methods or systems to monitor implementation.	Aligning people. Communicating the direction by words and deeds to all those whose cooperation may be needed to influence the creation of teams and coalitions that understand the vision and strategies and accept their validity.
Executing plans	Controlling and problem solving. Monitoring results versus plan in some detail, identifying deviations, and then planning and organizing to solve these problems.	Motivating and inspiring. Energizing people to overcome major political, bureaucratic, and resource barriers to change by satisfying very basic, but often unfulfilled, human needs.
Outcomes	Produce a degree of predictability and order and has the potential to consistently produce key results expected by various stakeholders (e.g., for customers, always being on time for stockholders, being on budget).	Produces change, often to a dramatic degree and has the potential to produce extremely useful change (e.g., new products that customers want, new approaches to labor relations that help make a firm more competitive).

SOURCE: Reprinted with permission, by The Free Press, a Division of Simon & Schuster Inc. from *A Force for Change: How Leadership Differs from Management* by John P. Kotter. Copyright © 1996 by John P. Kotter, Inc.

TABLE 9-2   **Distinctions between Managers and Leaders**

Personality Dimension	Manager	Leader
Attitudes toward goals	Has an impersonal, passive, functional attitude; believes goals arise out of necessity and reality	Has a personal and active attitude; believes goals arise from desire and imagination
Conceptions of work	Views work as an enabling process that combines people, ideas, and things; seeks moderate risk through coordination and balance	Looks for fresh approaches to old problems; seeks high-risk positions, especially with high payoffs
Relationships with others	Avoids solitary work activity, preferring to work with others; avoids close, intense relationships; avoids conflict	Is comfortable in solitary work activity; encourages close, intense working relationships; is not conflict averse
Sense of self	Is once born; makes a straight-forward life adjustment; accepts life as it is	Is twice born; engages in a struggle for a sense of order in life; questions life

or neither, as shown in Tables 9-1 and 9-2. For example, a skilled manager approaches the challenges of organizing and staffing by establishing structure for accomplishing the task requirements, staffing the structure with people who have the required skills, delegating responsibility, providing policy and procedure guidelines, and creating methods to monitor the results. A skilled leader approaches the challenge of developing a network to achieve an agenda by aligning the people. The leader communicates direction by words and deeds to everyone whose cooperation may be needed to create an effective team. The leader ensures that the team understands and accepts the visions. Then the team is free to create the necessary strategies and activities to accomplish the task. Some individuals use a combination of both approaches, and some use neither. Although some tasks (such as customizing a software control system) may be seen as more management and some tasks (creating a synergistic team) as more leadership, both are needed, and an effective management team has both.

"Managers do things right and leaders do the right thing," is a statement attributed to many sources. In the right things needed to be done right, managers often are expected to balance efficiency—the use of the minimum possible resources to produce an expected outcome, and effectiveness—the ability to accomplish a goal.

The "what" both managers and leaders do is described by Yukl's eleven management practices (Table 9-3). Most managers spend some time each day doing these activities. They may do them from either a manager's or leader's perspective.

Are these activities also done by students? Do some students do them from a leader's perspective and some from a manager's? Table 9-4 lists Mintzberg's (1979) ten primary roles of a manager. Do you agree with this list? What would you change, add, or remove?

Much of the current debate on leadership has evolved from competing theories on management, as the next section describes. John Pepper, the former chairman of the board and CEO (twice) at Procter & Gamble describes his view of leadership and management in an essay prepared for this text.

✦ LEADERSHIP SKILLS ✦
John E. Pepper

Leadership is an intriguing subject for me, and I'm happy to offer my observations about its development. First, a definition. Leadership to me is the particular process of guiding, directing, and motivating an organization to outstanding achievement in the organization's fundamental purposes.

Leading, then, involves articulating the appropriate vision, helping to develop what I call stretching objectives, making the right strategic choices to achieve the objectives; and implementing effective deployment plans to ensure that the resources and other necessary means are available to reach those objectives.

Leaders must also set the standards that guide the growth of the organization's culture and its results. Further, leaders must communicate with people so as to inspire them to exceed their previous achievements.

Clearly, the kind of leadership I'm describing pertains to all manner of activities, including a football team, an industry, a city, a nation, a household.

TABLE 9-3 Definition of the Eleven Managerial Practices

1. INFORMING: Disseminating relevant information about decisions, plans, and activities to people who need it to do their work, answering requests for technical information, and telling people about the organizational unit to promote its reputation.

2. CONSULTING AND DELEGATING: Checking with people before making changes that affect them, encouraging suggestions for improvement, inviting participation in decision making, incorporating the ideas and suggestions of others in decisions, and allowing others to have substantial responsibility and discretion in carrying out work activities and making decisions.

3. PLANNING AND ORGANIZING: Determining long-term objectives and strategies for adapting to environmental change, determining how to use personnel and allocate resources to accomplish objectives, determining how to improve the efficiency of operations, and determining how to achieve coordination with other parts of the organization.

4. PROBLEM SOLVING AND CRISIS MANAGEMENT: Identifying work-related problems, analyzing problems in a timely but systematic manner to identify causes and find solutions, and acting decisively to implement solutions and resolve important problems or crises.

5. CLARIFYING ROLES AND OBJECTIVES: Assigning tasks, providing direction in how to do the work, and communicating a clear understanding or job responsibilities, task objectives, deadlines, and performance expectations.

6. MONITORING OPERATIONS AND ENVIRONMENT: Gathering information about work activities, checking on the progress and quality of the work, evaluating the performance of individuals and the organizational unit, and scanning the environment to detect threats and opportunities.

7. MOTIVATING: Using influence techniques that appeal to emotion, values, or logic to generate enthusiasm for the work, commitment to task objectives, and compliance with request for cooperation, assistance, support, or resources; also, setting an example of proper behavior.

8. RECOGNIZING AND REWARDING: Providing praise, recognition, and rewards for effective performance, significant achievements, and special contributions.

9. SUPPORTING AND MENTORING: Acting friendly and considerate, being patient and helpful, showing sympathy and support, and doing things to facilitate someone's skill development and career advancement.

10. MANAGING CONFLICT AND TEAM BUILDING: Encouraging and facilitating the constructive resolution of conflict, and encouraging cooperation, teamwork, and identification with the organizational unit.

11. NETWORKING: Socializing informally, developing contacts with people who are a source of information and support, and maintaining contacts through periodic interaction, including visits, telephone calls, correspondence, and attendance to meetings and social events.

In my experience, I've found that certain qualities characterize the most effective leaders. I've identified four major benchmarks.

A Compelling Vision Every effective leader I've known has possessed a personally felt vision and goals. Deep commitments that they are not only willing, but anxious to share with others.

There's almost a spiritual dimension to the conviction these leaders have about the purpose of the organization for which they are responsible. Think about the great football coaches—Lou Holtz, George Allen. They both had unwavering commitments to their teams' excellence.

Simply put, if you don't believe in something passionately, you cannot be an effective leader. Yet it goes well beyond the passionate belief, to a concern for

TABLE 9-4 Mintzberg's Roles

Role	Description
Figurehead	The manager, acting as a symbol or representative of the organization, performs diverse ceremonial duties. By attending Chamber of Commerce meetings, heading the local United Way drive, or representing the president of the firm at an awards banquet, a manager performs the figurehead role.
Leader	The manager, interacting with subordinates, motivates and develops them. The supervisor who conducts quarterly performance interviews or selects training opportunities for his or her subordinates performs the role of leader. This role emphasizes the social-emotional and people-oriented side of leadership and deemphasizes task activities, which are more often incorporated into the decisional roles.
Liaison	The manager establishes a network of contacts to gather information for the organization. Belonging to professional associations or meeting over lunch with peers in other organizations helps the manager perform the liaison role.
Monitor	The manager gathers information from the environment inside and outside the organization. He or she may attend meetings with subordinates, scan company publications, or participate in companywide committees as a way of performing this role.
Disseminator	The manager transmits both factual and value information to subordinates. Managers may conduct staff meetings, send memorandums to their staff, or meet informally with them on a one-to-one basis to discuss current and future projects.
Spokesperson	The manager gives information to people outside the organization about its performance and policies. He or she oversees preparation of the annual report, prepares advertising copy, or speaks at community and professional meetings.
Entrepreneur	The manager designs and initiates change in the organization. The supervisor who redesigns the jobs of subordinates, introduces flexible working hours, or brings new technology to the job performs this role.
Disturbance handler	The manager deals with problems that arise when organizational operations break down. A person who finds a new supplier on short notice for an out-of-stock part, who replaces unexpectedly absent employees, or who deals with machine breakdowns performs this role.
Resource allocator	The manager controls the allocation of people, money, materials, and time by scheduling his or her own time, programming subordinates' work effort, and authorizing all significant decisions. Preparation of the budget is a major aspect of this role.
Negotiator	The manager participates in negotiation activities. A manager who hires a new employee may negotiate work assignments or compensation with that person.

SOURCE: These roles are drawn from H. Mintzberg, *The Nature of Managerial Work* (Englewood Cliffs, N.J.: Prentice-Hall, 1979).

achieving the organization's basic purpose—its highest values—at the highest possible level. And then constantly improving that performance.

At P&G [Procter & Gamble], this means serving the consumer, winning in the marketplace, and achieving both financial and share leadership. It also means building a place of employment that attracts the best people around and helps them fulfill their ambitions. This aspect of leadership focuses on one's belief in innovation, growth, continuing improvement, and contribution to the company.

The most effective leaders at P&G, then, are those who believe deeply in the aforementioned values and who continually define what they mean, as well as how best to achieve them. Of course, these central values are shared by others at the company.

The question becomes, how does one develop this compelling vision? Let me address that on a personal level. I've worked at defining my personal goals, as well as those of my department/subsidiary, and as the years have gone by, the company.

I have found a personal mission and priority statement very helpful in defining my goals long before they became so trendy. More than twenty-five years ago, I started what has become a personal tradition. I write down on a piece of paper what I want to do and what I want to contribute; where I need to improve; and what lessons I've learned. For these twenty-five years I've pulled out that piece of paper every six months or so.

It has been more than just a reminder to me. It has helped me build a deeper commitment to certain purposes and values and priorities, including superior products for the consumer, innovation, taking the offensive, and respect for the individual.

Personal commitment to a mission is vital, and it simply can't be manufactured. No matter what area you pursue, the capacity to be completely dedicated to a career or mission or strategy or tactic is all-important to its success. For the capacity to be totally dedicated is the foundation of a compelling vision, one that can be shared by others.

The kind of true leadership that involves taking risks and putting oneself forward as an example requires that the individual have deep convictions about a set of principles or a project that needs to be done.

The Ability to Inspire Once the vision is in place, a leader must then have the capacity to inspire others in its pursuit—not blindly or unquestioningly, but with enough fervor to achieve the goals.

In my experiences, I've found leaders with different characteristics who persuade others to pursue the vision. Part of this infectious nature of leadership is due to the importance of the mission itself. Yet part also comes from a burning desire within the most effective leaders for action—to win—to contribute—to serve.

This brings us to the question of appetite. The appetite for pushing oneself to be the best we can be and to help others be the best they can be. This drive springs from different sources within us, and from a mixture of sources. Many people's drive is sparked by a deep commitment to serving others.

All of us, I believe, are pushed by the drive to win, to be our best selves. To keep improving.

For me, the three greatest drivers in my work and life have been to serve, to be the best I can be, and to win.

Winning is something we all understand. In our highly competitive business, people won't succeed if they aren't winning against the competition. Competition provides a great benchmark, and, frankly, it spurs the adrenaline. Winning is fun.

Service is another great motivator—service to consumers, shareholders, our communities, and employees. Better service than before, better service than our competitors, better service in the absolute. That points to the quality of our products, and in having major preferences in consumer acceptance versus competition. It comes down to the value of our products.

Going into a country in Eastern Europe where we've never sold before, providing products of a quality consumers have never seen before—that's service. That's rewarding.

And it's service to employees, employees who stake their lives with the company, to offer them the training and the environment where they can grow to their fullest. In Eastern Europe, China, and Russia, young men and women can contribute in ways they've never before imagined.

It's service, too, to the communities where we work. We're involved in education and in other fields where the leadership of P&G can help. In addition, we serve the environment directly through our products and our processes.

That drive to be all you can be keeps you learning and growing. Each of the strongest leaders I've known would describe these drivers—the ones that enable them to inspire others in their vision—somewhat differently. Yet in all cases the drives are honestly felt and experienced, and ones we must nourish.

Initiative, Focus on Results, Courage, and Tenacity The most effective leaders I've known take the initiative to make the biggest personal difference, the most significant personal contribution they can. Whatever action they're focused on, they're fully engaged in trying to make things better than they are at present. Real leaders don't wait for permission. And their willingness to jump into the situation makes work fun for them, and for those around them. Their initiative also produces results that are recognized and rewarded.

These men and women have a laser-like focus on results. Their inner drive propels them to make things happen and get things done, producing a better tomorrow than today. They display an enormous amount of energy and capacity.

True leaders have the kind of personal courage that fuels their pursuit of their convictions, even when this means persisting against significant opposition. They're unafraid to say and do what may be unpopular. To do what they're convinced is right. These leaders are transparent.

They are forceful advocates for what they believe in, even—indeed, especially—when that goes against the grain.

Most of the biggest decisions I've been involved in have been controversial. The decisions have come about because someone had the courage to persist with a point of view.

Many of P&G's largest brands today were subjects of controversy when they began. Take Bounce Dryer-Added Fabric Softener. There were many who wondered whether putting a sheet in a dryer would appeal to consumers. In fact, the patent was turned down by other companies and almost by P&G until someone with a strong conviction that this could be made into a high-performing, high-value product persuaded the company to proceed. And now Bounce is one of our most successful brands, highly accepted by consumers and providing excellent returns to Procter & Gamble.

In the same way, these leaders have the courage to take command, to be decisive, to ask for action. After they've reviewed all the options and the discussions and debates have run their course, these leaders reach the point where they must step out and exercise their own responsibility.

One example we encountered in the 1980s was the need to bring a regional focus to our operations in Europe. Through much of our history, we had operated almost as separate fiefdoms—each country on its own. That was fine in some respects, but it became clear that it was necessary to focus our research and development efforts against a narrower group of projects if we were to achieve true performance and value breakthroughs for the consumer. We also had to rationalize our production sourcing in Europe so that we could achieve greater reliability and lower costs for consumers. That required a major change in mindset in the way we operated. It was very controversial. Ultimately, as the head of European operations, I needed to make the decision that this was the right way to go in the future.

In order to carry out this responsibility for decision making, it is essential to deal with problems head-on and not avoid them. Overcome difficult obstacles rather than put them off. With that conviction, I've always aimed to tackle the toughest problems first.

Persistence   Finally, my great leaders don't give up. They push on and on. It reminds me of my favorite story about Winston Churchill. After he retired from public office, he was asked to address the students and faculty at his grammar school. As you can imagine, the headmaster was very excited and told the students to prepare to hear one of the greatest talks they'd ever hear in their lifetimes.

The day arrived and Winston Churchill walked out on the stage with a small piece of paper, on which was written a few notes. He peered down at the audience, over his glasses, and said:

"Never, never, never, never give up."

And with that, he turned around and went back to his seat. Initially, the audience was surprised and let down. They'd expected so much more. But in time, they came to view it as the most important talk they could have heard. It summarized a lifetime of experience in just six words.

I've never forgotten this. I never will.

(John Pepper is the former CEO and chairman of the board of Procter & Gamble. Currently, he is a cofounder and trustee for the Freedom Center and senior vice president for finance at Yale University.)

✦ THE EVOLUTION OF LEADERSHIP FROM SCIENTIFIC MANAGEMENT

Most management historians see leadership theory evolving from classical management work—most prominently, the work of Taylor, Fayol, and Weber—in the late nineteenth and early twentieth centuries.

In the 1890s, **Frederick Taylor,** the father of **scientific management,** felt that workers performed below their true abilities and that what they needed was proper direction and support. He drew on his engineering background to find the most efficient way to perform specific tasks. Applying his scientific management principles to the task of loading slab steel onto railroad cars, he meticulously analyzed each component of the job, then trained a handpicked man to follow his directions precisely for each part of the task. Further, Taylor agreed to pay this man on a per-piece basis, a significant departure from standard practices at the time and one he predicted would encourage greater productivity. As a final step, Taylor arranged for the worker to focus only on the specific task of loading the steel, and Taylor, as the manager, oversaw related aspects, such as when and how the railroad car would be moved. The productivity gains were remarkable: productivity for this worker increased nearly fourfold. Taylor's experiment won over many who had been skeptical about such scientific approaches to work.

Specifically, Taylor called for four things:

1. A "science" for every job, including standardized work flow and work conditions
2. Carefully selected workers with the right ability to do each job
3. Careful training with proper incentives
4. Clear planning by managers

In 1916, **Henri Fayol** helped to further delineate the principles of management by setting forth five major management elements: planning, organizing, commanding, coordinating, and controlling. In the 1920s, sociologist **Max Weber** brought to the study of management the concept of bureaucracy, including a clear division of labor, a hierarchy of authority, formal rules and procedures, impersonality, and merit-based evaluations. Weber's notions of bureaucracy had none of the negative connotations that bureaucracies have today.

After World War I, when there was a tremendous increase in the demand for consumer goods, the **Hawthorne effect** was conceptualized. Simply put, as Ellen Mayo (1953) explained, if management increased its attention to workers, productivity also increased. From these findings the human relations movement evolved, drawing on Maslow's hierarchy of human needs and McGregor's Theory X and Theory Y (discussed in Chapter 5). Leadership theory continued to develop from these early works.

Beginning in the 1940s, the **quantitative management** perspectives (management science) emerged. This approach centers on applying mathematical models and processes to decision-making situations. **Operations management** focuses directly on applying management science to organizations. All leaders depend on information and management science as the basis for much of the information used by decision makers. One of the century's leading theorists on management, W. Edwards Deming, began his career as a physics instructor and then moved on to statistics. From this base, he molded the highly influential principles of quality. (Deming and the quality movement are discussed later in this chapter.)

Management information science, commonly referred to within organizations as MIS, is the process of collecting, processing, and transmitting information used to support all managerial functions. As the twentieth century progressed and computers and cyberspace became the norm, increasingly managers have begun to utilize the MIS system.

Since the 1960s, we have seen other developments in management that have directly affected leadership. For instance, leadership scholars have examined management skills at different levels with an understanding of the impact of technical, conceptual, interpersonal, and diagnostic skills on top managers, middle managers, and first-line managers, as shown in Figure 9–2. The discussion has yielded useful information for both leaders and managers.

Similarly, the debate over whether management (and leadership) is a science or an art has also influenced the dialogue. Those who argue that leadership is a science believe that the issue can be approached in a logical, rational, objective manner. They stress the use of management science and hard data. Others, however, who feel that intuition, experience, and instinct are crucial, rely heavily on interpersonal and conceptual skills.

✦ CONTEMPORARY MANAGEMENT ISSUES

Among the more contemporary management issues, the systems approach to organizations has had significant effects on leadership theory. This approach depicts a system as a set of interrelated parts that work together as a whole to achieve goals. In this view, organizations were originally considered **closed systems;** that is, they were not affected by outside events or situations. In reality, all organizations are **open systems.** They must deal with the environment to survive.

Clearly, then, individuals can't lead unless they have a thorough understanding of the organization as an open system, along with an appreciation of the makeup of the external and internal forces impinging on it. From the systems theorists came the word **synergy,** which describes the product of separate parts working together, making something more than merely the total of the separate parts by themselves.

The systems approach also suggests that managers consider the organization's internal forces, such as the subgroups and the effects of these subgroups on the entire organization. (For example, see Chapter 6 for a discussion of the grapevine and its potential impact on organizational communication.)

	Management skills—different skills are needed at different levels			
	Conceptual	Technical	Diagnostic	Interpersonal
Top management	XXXXXXXXX	XXX	XXXXXXXXX	XXX
Middle management	XXXXXX	XXXXXX	XXXXXX	XXXXXX
Front-line management	XXX	XXXXXXXXX	XXX	XXXXXXXXX

FIGURE 9-2 **Management Skills—Different Skills Are Needed at Different Levels**

Although classical management theory states that there is only one best way to resolve an issue, today there is widespread agreement with the **contingency theory,** which suggests that appropriate behavior in a given situation depends on a wide variety of variables, and that each situation is different. What might work in one company with one set of issues, employees, and customers might not work in a different company with different issues, employees, and customers. See Figure 9–3.

Although it is impossible to address the impact of globalization on management and leadership theory in a few short paragraphs, it's indisputable that the impact of markets across the world on U.S. business has meant a significant change in perspectives. Organizations are being affected by the increasingly broad sweep of day-to-day life. How can it be considered anything but a sea change when we can electronically access the latest figures on the Hong Kong stock market and in the next minute communicate via the Internet with a consultant in Eastern Europe? Never again can business ignore global implications for organizations, as the U.S. auto makers learned to their peril in the 1980s.

Management has formed a key basis for leadership theory. Both classical and contemporary issues have provided vital data and insights for leaders and followers.

Today we discuss the modern workplace as a learning organization—one that is constantly engaged in solving problems and understanding future challenges and opportunities. Learning organizations continuously experiment and learn from their endeavors. They use teams as their primary means of organizing. They understand that workers must be empowered and information widely shared. They understand the power of e-business, the Internet, and e-commerce, but they value the individual and the creativity of groups of individuals.

◆ THE QUALITY MOVEMENT

In recent years several proponents of a more comprehensive approach to ensuring quality in products and services have emerged. The teachings of these quality gurus often contrast starkly with the prevailing beliefs of managers. In the 1950s, as Japanese business tried to rebuild after World War II, these quality teachers were well received, but they were shunned in the United States until the 1980s, when Japanese companies exerted tremendous pressure on U.S. business. Apparently, necessity is also the mother of radically new approaches to leadership, as industrial leaders in both countries only adopted the new approaches when they were desperate.

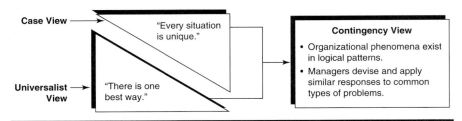

FIGURE 9-3 The Contingency View of Management
SOURCE: Figures from *Management,* 3rd ed., by Richard L. Daft; Copyright © 1994 by the Dryden Press. Reprinted with permission.

W. Edwards Deming

The best-known quality pioneer worldwide was Dr. W. Edwards Deming of the United States. Deming (1900–1993) was raised on a homestead in Wyoming with a strong ethic not to waste anything. He was quite a scholar, studying engineering and math before completing a Ph.D. in physics. During summers between school sessions, the young Deming worked in sweatshop-style factories, where he developed a deep sympathy for the working person. Although Deming started by teaching statistical quality control, he gradually developed a system of fourteen points. Fittingly, he tinkered with the wording and explanation of some of these points up to his death at age 93. Deming believed that while minor improvements might be possible by choosing to perform some of the points, skipping any of them would greatly diminish the total success. **Deming's fourteen points** form a manifesto of what is wrong with traditional Western-style management (Deming would not call traditional practices leadership; he would call them management). Because many leaders initially found Deming's points counter to their normal way of thinking, they rejected them. Others willingly accepted some points, but disagreed with others. The fourteen points are shown here in Deming's own words, although many other writers have adapted them. Numerous books, articles, study groups, and seminars have been devoted to understanding Deming's ideas. For a man who had minor influence in his own country until age 80, Deming will long have a profound influence on the United States and the world.

Deming's Fourteen Points

1. Create constancy of purpose toward improvement of product and service, with the aim to become competitive and stay in business, and to provide jobs.
2. Adopt the new philosophy. We are in a new economic age. Western management must awaken to the challenge, must learn their responsibilities, and take on leadership for change.
3. Cease dependence on inspection to achieve quality. Eliminate the need for inspection on a mass basis by building quality into the product in the first place.
4. End the practice of awarding business on the basis of the price tag. Instead, minimize total cost. Move toward a single supplier for any one item, on a long-term basis of trust.
5. Improve constantly and forever the system of production and service, to improve quality and productivity, and thus constantly decrease cost.
6. Institute training on the job.
7. Institute leadership. The aim of supervision should be to help people and machines and gadgets to do a better job. Supervision of management is in need of overhaul, as well as supervision of production workers.
8. Drive out fear so that everyone may work effectively for the company.
9. Break down barriers between departments. People in research, design, sales, and production must work as a team, to foresee problems of production and use that may be encountered with the product or service.

10. Eliminate slogans, exhortations, and targets for the work force asking for zero defects and new levels of productivity. Such exhortations only create adversarial relationships, as the bulk of the causes of low quality and productivity belong to the system and thus lie beyond the power of the work force.

11. Eliminate work standards (quotas) on the factory floor. Substitute leadership. Eliminate management by objective. Eliminate management by numbers, numerical goals. Substitute leadership.

12. Remove barriers that rob the hourly worker of his right to pride of workmanship. The responsibility of supervisors must be changed from sheer numbers to quality. Remove barriers that rob people in management and engineering of their right to pride of workmanship. This means *inter alia,* abolishment of the annual or merit rating and of management by objective.

13. Institute a vigorous program of education and improvement.

14. Put everybody in the company to work to accomplish the transformation. The transformation is everybody's job.

Source: W. Edwards Deming, *Out of the Crisis* (Cambridge, Mass.: MIT Center for Advanced Engineering Study, 1986), pp. 23–24.

Joseph Juran

Dr. Joseph Juran was born in Romania, came to the United States as a boy just before World War I, and spent his youth performing odd jobs to earn money for his family. Trained as an engineer, he worked for Western Electric Company in a variety of engineering and quality-related assignments. Juran and Deming were influenced by some of the same people and ideas early in their careers. Juran received a law degree working at night, then worked for the U.S. government during World War II and taught engineering for several years. In 1951, Juran published his acclaimed *Quality Control Handbook,* which many people still consider to be the quality "bible." On numerous occasions Juran traveled to Japan, where he taught middle and upper managers the importance of direct managerial involvement in improving quality. Management, he told them, was as important to quality as the statistical approaches they had already started to use. In fact, the combination of statistical and management approaches has proven exceedingly effective in Japan and elsewhere.

In contrast to Deming's demands for an overthrow of Western-style management systems, Juran focused on improving current management systems, thereby showing concern for practical quality improvement issues.

Juran's quality improvement model, sometimes referred to as a breakthrough sequence, consists of the following ten tasks:

1. Convince important decision makers that the improvement is needed.

2. Set logical improvement goals based on a reasonable plan.

3. Organize a project team to reach the goals with specific guidance on what to do.

4. Provide the team adequate training.

5. Identify the causes of the problem.
6. Develop a set of possible approaches to solve the problem, select one approach, and implement it on a small scale.
7. Evaluate the results.
8. Improve the approach, if needed, and implement it.
9. Overcome the resistance that some people are bound to have concerning the new methods.
10. Standardize the approach to maintain the improvement through training, control charts, and so on.

Juran has proven to be very accurate in predicting the direction of quality. As far back as the middle 1960s, he warned the Western world that Japan would overtake them in quality and productivity because of their quality improvement efforts. Now Juran calls the twentieth century the Century of Productivity. By the end of the century there was greater worldwide supply than demand of most products and services. The result, he says, is that customers can increasingly demand excellent quality, and companies that do not produce it will go out of business. Juran believes this trend will be so strong that he has already named the twenty-first century the Century of Quality!

Now that we have scratched the surface of the ideas of two leading quality experts, what lessons for leaders can we draw from them? We envision the lessons grouped under four primary paradigms.

Leadership Paradigms

1. **Quality must be a systematic approach.**
   Minor improvements may result from using some of the quality concepts and tools, but major improvement requires that they be used as an integrated whole. The Malcolm Baldrige National Quality Award in the United States has become the most common framework for describing the various parts of Total Quality Management. The Baldrige framework states that leadership is what fuels a quality effort. Without active, direct leadership, improvement will not happen.
2. **Customers are the reason we do everything we do.**
   Every time we answer the phone, fill out a piece of paper, cut metal, or answer a question it is because someone needs the output of that action. That someone is a customer, either external or internal to our organization. We need to identify that customer and his or her needs and treat satisfying those needs as our reason for existing.
3. **Leaders must understand long-term thinking.**
   Because our goal must be the long-term viability of our organization, we must frequently make decisions that help in the long run, but may cost us money or inconvenience now.
4. **Quality improvement requires a series of different thinking patterns.**
   Instead of always thinking in linear logic, we must frequently think

first in a divergent manner such as brainstorming possibilities, then in a convergent manner such as prioritizing or selecting.

Teams develop in a predictable progression that leaders must understand and plan for. Leaders generally need to develop more influencing skills for dealing with teams rather than just directing them. For example, teams often make decisions using consensus for which all team members must truly agree. Teams also need to be empowered to make some decisions that previously may have been made at levels higher in the organization. If leaders suggest teams will get to make decisions, but then do not actually let them because the decision does not conform to what the leader wants, all efforts are likely to backfire. Finally, measuring team process and results and establishing appropriate reward and recognition systems place demands on leaders (see Figure 9-4).

Another challenge to management is having to organize the efforts. Traditionally organization charts are neat and clean where all employees have one boss and the organization is created around various functions (tasks) or divisions (business units). Today, many people report to two or three or more "bosses" in matrix organizations or organizations that are team or network based.

Developing profiles for this chapter created an interesting challenge. CEOs, presidents, and others in senior positions expect to be called leaders, not managers. However, from our perspective they need to have both skills. They also need to understand the value of teams, diversity, ethics, and many other skills discussed throughout the text. We decided to profile two skilled people from the business world. Herb Kelleher, whose name has become synonymous with Southwest Airlines because of his emphasis on teamwork and quality, and Maureen Kempston Darkes, who effectively managed and leveraged diversity in an international company. A

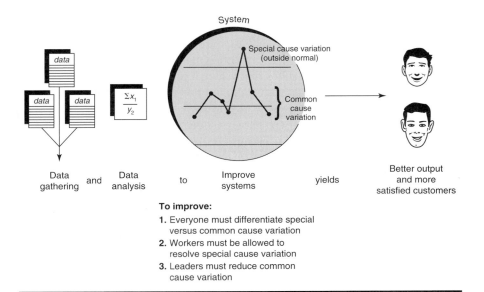

To improve:

1. Everyone must differentiate special versus common cause variation
2. Workers must be allowed to resolve special cause variation
3. Leaders must reduce common cause variation

FIGURE 9-4 Using Facts

third profile, that of Robert C. Macaulay, exemplifies some of the same principles, but in the context of a not-for-profit organization.

HERB KELLEHER
The Man that Made Southwest Airlines Fun—and Profitable

Southwest Airlines has a track record that would be remarkable in any industry—it was America's best performing stock from 1972 to 2002 and has been in *Fortune*'s top-ten companies for each of the last six years. But the fact that it has been able to sustain its growth through a turbulent industry, change of leadership, and the threat of new entrants is nothing short of amazing. In the months following the terrorist attacks on September 11, 2001, the U.S airline industry was one of the hardest hit, as flights were grounded and panic set in among consumers. While major carriers like United Airlines, Delta, and U.S. Airways struggled to stay afloat, Southwest Airlines flourished, continuing to post profits quarter after quarter. How did Southwest do it? To understand the foundations behind the success of the only airline in the United States that has made money every year since 1973, it is necessary to understand Herb Kelleher, the man whose inimitable management style has made the airline what it is today.

Kelleher, known in the industry as Herb, has been with Southwest since its first planes took to the air. Armed with a business plan that originated on a cocktail napkin, Kelleher co-founded Southwest Airlines in 1971 with just four planes and less than seventy employees, positioning it as a low-cost, no-frills provider of air transportation. To avoid having to follow the pricing regulations of the Civil Aeronautics Board, its flights operated only within the state of Texas, and soon became immensely popular because of its surprisingly low fares. The airline flies point-to-point, deviating from the more popular hub-and-spoke model followed by other airlines, serves no meals, has no assigned seating, and charges no fees to change same-fare tickets. Instead of electronic entertainment, it has "fun" flight attendants that amuse the passengers with their activities.

Kelleher is the man behind creating the culture that makes this organization unique. His down-to-earth demeanor and maverick nature have endeared him to the employees and are reflected in the airline's offbeat culture. The eccentricities of this airline and its employees have, in turn, captivated the hearts of customers. The walls at the company's headquarters are covered with pictures of everything from employees' pets, to Kelleher dressed as Elvis, to stewardesses in mini skirts. But frivolity is not all the airline is about—it is very serious, even conservative, when it comes to managing its finances. The company keeps a tight rein on its costs and maintains an investment-grade rating on its debt. Finding the perfect balance of methods and madness, of passion and quirkiness, Kelleher has created a distinctive atmosphere that is impossible for competitors to replicate.

Although he stepped down from his position as CEO in 2001, he continues to be involved with the organization as a member of its board of directors. Kelleher's formula for success is straightforward: "Ask your employees what's important to them. Ask your customers what is important to them. Then do it. It should be that simple."

MAUREEN KEMPSTON DARKES
Managing Diversity at GM Canada

Maureen Kempston Darkes assumed the presidency of GM Canada on July 1, 1994. As the first woman to head Canada's largest industrial company, she has attracted intense media scrutiny. Her young administration boasts several ground-breaking changes in GM Canada's corporate culture.

The former vice president of corporate affairs and general counsel for GM Canada notes that she always enjoyed setting direction and trying to create something of value. From her early days with GM, she has been very interested in ensuring that people could have a voice in the company.

"I was a founding member of the Women's Advisory Council," she says, explaining that the group works to ensure that employees can genuinely participate in the business. "It's a very strong group that provides me with feedback and insight about a number of issues." Kempston Darkes credits the Council with helping her develop new policy, such as the flexible working hours and alternative work schedules recently adopted by the company.

"What's interesting about the flexible working arrangement," she says, "is that we originally looked at it for women. It turns out, however, that it's really been used more by people moving toward retirement age. It helps them transition. Every time we become more flexible we serve more people, and we develop a better product."

Valuing Differences A leader, says Kempston Darkes, must provide clear vision, motivation, and guidance. "But leadership is also about counseling and mentoring. The end result is creating an environment where people can fully participate."

"People, after all, are our most important resource. Unless we can focus on their unique abilities, we're not fully utilizing our resources," she asserts.

Dealing with diversity is a key component of leadership to her. "To me, the challenge is creating a culture where people can contribute to the company regardless of sex, cultural difference, age, any other kind of difference. When we can create this climate, we can better understand our workforce, the marketplace—the whole environment."

She stresses the connection between diversity in the workforce and the increasingly diverse marketplace. "If I have a very diverse sales force, I can better relate to that market. Or take a look at the college graduates. I want to attract and retain talent. That means recruiting them, but also once they're here, making sure they're respected and considered. So this is not just about managing diversity. It's about valuing diversity. And there's a quantum leap between the two."

She has directed her senior management staff to examine every aspect of GM Canada's corporate culture in an attempt to value diversity. "We're very much in the beginning stages here. Our goal is to have a fully empowered workforce."

Listening "For me," she says, "real listening begins with understanding the customer base. So any leader should be prepared to be out in the field. I spend a considerable part of my time in the field."

Listening makes good business sense. "Sloan said it best: 'The quickest way to profit is to serve the customer in ways the customer wants to be served.' We do that and then ask ourselves, 'How can we exceed that?'"

"If we're pushing up market share, it's because we listen to the customer better and translate what he/she wants into products or services."

One example is 24-hour roadside assistance offered on any new car or truck purchased from GM Canada. "Why do we know that's important to the customers? Because they told us," she says.

Leaders must also listen to the workforce, Kempston Darkes says, and they must be willing to appreciate constructive feedback. "Our business is so competitive, you can't have a huge ego. You have to continually get better, and you can't do that sitting still."

To promote accessibility, she shuns the traditional grand executive office in favor of a smaller, less imposing one with a glass conference room next door. "It's symbolic that I and my senior managers are quite open."

GM Canada has also instituted a less formal dress code, which the employees monitor themselves. Depending on outside contact, the employees don't have to wear ties. Further, there is no executive dining room, no preferred parking. "It's symbolic, of course," she says, "but we're trying to promote the idea of openness and teamwork."

Insisting that she wants to hear what employees have to say, she adopts what she calls "a no fuss routine." On her frequent stops at dealerships and plants across Canada, she talks to people, asking them questions and giving them the chance to offer their own ideas and suggestions.

"I come back and work on those ideas. Empowered people have so much to contribute. Most people want to be able to contribute. The most frustrating thing in the world is to have an idea but no one willing to listen to it."

Finally, Kempston Darkes asserts that leaders must have a sense of balance. "Home and family are very important. Workaholics get a lot accomplished, true, but they can be too hard on others. You're more able to understand your employees when you search for the balance yourself." She and her husband have recently built a log home an hour north of Toronto, where they try—not always successfully, she admits—to escape for quiet time together.

(Maureen Kempston Darkes is currently GM group vice president and president, Latin America, Africa, and Middle East [LAAM], effective January 1, 2002. For more information visit http://www.roadandtravel.com/celebrities/pw_kempstondarkes.html.)

ROBERT C. MACAULEY

The Pebble Beginning the Ripple Effect

On April 4, 1975, the world was shocked to learn that a U.S. jet carrying 243 Vietnamese orphaned toddlers and infants crashed into the dense jungles near Tan Son Nhut. Nearly a third of the children were burned to death, while the remaining were critically injured. The Pentagon announced that it would not have the resources necessary to help the remaining maimed children for another ten days.

Dissatisfied with the excuse of bureaucracy as a reason to delay aid to dying children, Robert C. Macauley, a paper broker from New Canaan, Connecticut, decided that if the U.S. government wouldn't take action, *he* would. Within twenty-four hours of hearing about the crash, Macauley wrote a check for $251,000 to charter a Boeing 747 to rescue the children. To cover the expense, he and his wife, Alma, mortgaged their house. Within forty-eight hours, the children were rescued: "...by the time my $251,000 check to Pan Am bounced, the children were in the United States," says Macauley. His wife believes it was an even trade, "the bank got the house and Bob got the kids."

Pope John Paul II took notice of Macauley's extraordinary action. In 1981, Poland was under martial law and the country's medical supplies were virtually gone. The Pontiff invited him to Rome to discuss Poland's crisis. "I'm not even Catholic, but when the Pope asks a favor, you comply," says Macauley. Far exceeding their $50,000 goal, Macauley organized efforts that ultimately airlifted more than $3.2 million worth of aid to Poland.

With two successful missions under his belt, Macauley became the founder of AmeriCares in 1982. In its mission statement, AmeriCares defines itself as a "non-profit disaster relief and humanitarian aid organization, which provides immediate response to emergency medical needs and supports long-term humanitarian assistance programs for all people around the world, irrespective of race, creed or political persuasion."

Today, Macauley is CEO of this non-profit organization, and he receives no salary from AmeriCares. A graduate of Yale University and a former lieutenant in the U.S. Army, Air Transport Command, African Middle East Wing in WWII, Macauley is also the founder of a multimillion dollar paper products company, the Virginia Fibre Corporation (now Greif Bros. Corporation). Additionally, he is advisor to the National Executive Service Corps and New York Medical College.

Robert C. Macauley's story exemplifies how one man's belief that he can make a difference can literally change the world for the better. His efforts have snowballed, influencing both world and religious leaders alike. AmeriCares is associated with numerous long-standing ministries, including the Order of Malta, Mother Theresa's Sisters of Charity, and Help the Afghan Children. Known for consistently being one of the first relief organizations to arrive at the scene of a disaster, since its establishment AmeriCares has provided more than $3.4 billion in aid to more than 137 countries. And all this began with one man's refusal to sit idle while children suffered. In response to a disaster, rare is the individual who is confident enough to use his or her own sense of helplessness and compassion toward others as a catalyst to take action: "When human lives are at stake, you act now and worry about the red tape later," says Macauley.

(Written by Laura Schwarber.)

◆ Chapter Summary

This chapter touches on three areas of study that have shaped the growing field of leadership. Management, like leadership, can be characterized by a variety of definitions. The ambiguity, in fact, has spawned some controversy over whether leadership is a subset of management, or vice versa. The authors review this issue and assert that, although the two fields share many features, each has its own separate elements. The beginnings of scientific management are traced and contemporary systems approaches are described.

Following John Pepper's remarks about leadership, the chapter continues with a discussion of the quality movement and two of its early quality leaders, W. Edwards Deming and Joseph Juran. A final section discusses implications of the quality movement for leadership and the various ways of organizing leadership teams. The chapter ends with profiles of Maureen Kempston Darkes of GM Canada and the unique management practices at Southwest Airlines.

✦ CREATE YOUR OWN THEORY ✦

Are you a manager or a leader? Or perhaps a combination of the two? In what situations do you find it easier to lead? What is your perspective on the attributes of quality circles?

Now let's revisit our opening Leadership Moment. After reading the various aspects of management and leadership, do you feel that Howie's primary responsibility at this time is managing? Or is it leading?

✦ Key Terms

closed systems	management
contingency theory	Max Weber
Deming's fourteen points	open systems
Frederick Taylor	operations management
Hawthorne effect	quantitative management perspectives
Henri Fayol	scientific management
Juran's quality improvement model	synergy

✦ Questions for Discussion and Review

1. What does Fayol identify as the five key functions of management?
2. What is the primary distinction between early management theories (i.e., Taylor, Fayol, Weber) and contemporary theories?
3. Do you see management as being more an art or a science? Why?
4. According to Deming, what were the key historical factors behind Japan's embracing of modern quality principles before U.S. managers did?
5. What are some common themes linking Deming's fourteen points? Which points seem particularly important to you, and why?

6. What are some of the paradigms that Total Quality Management demands of leaders?

7. To what extent do you feel that TQM principles will be a factor in leadership development and practices in the twenty-first century?

✦ Exercises

Exercise 9.1   Leading versus Managing

You are the Regional Director of the American Heart Association. As such you are responsible for the eighteen local offices in your territory. Listed on the next page are a number of typical activities. Please identify them as management or leadership by placing a check mark in the appropriate columns. Some activities could fall in either category. In that case, classify them based on the way you would actually perform the activity.

Exercise 9.2   Leading versus Managing: Follow-up

1. Which activities/functions in the previous exercise could be classified as either management or leadership, in your opinion?

2. In two or three sentences, explain why each of those activities/functions could be an example of both management and/or leadership.

3. Briefly explain why you classified those particular activities/functions the way that you did.

4. Were there any activities/functions for which you disagreed with the answer key's classification?

5. If so, why?

Activity/Function	Management	Leadership
1. Supervising the development of the budget at each of the local offices.		
2. Hiring, firing, and evaluating the eighteen local directors.		
3. Conducting an annual retreat with the local directors to set specific objectives for the coming year.		
4. Preparing and submitting quarterly reports to the national executive director about the work of each chapter.		
5. Mediating conflicts at the local level and between the eighteen directors.		
6. Visiting each chapter monthly in order to motivate and inspire each staff.		
7. Speaking at endless Rotary, Kiwanis, Lions' Clubs and other civic groups in the region		

in order to articulate the mission and need for the American Heart Association.

8. Solving problems that local directors are unable to.

9. Monitoring the budgets of the local chapters closely since there are few contingency dollars if budgets aren't met.

10. Spending quality time on substantive, long-range plans for the association.

11. Attempting to influence policy at the national level because of the changes observed locally.

12. Forming ad hoc teams from various local offices to deal with unexpected/unusual or regional issues and opportunities.

13. Reviewing and adjusting the fund raising time-line for each office.

14. Participating in the selection of key leaders in each local fund campaign.

15. Keeping local directors and staff members energized and excited as the long months of fund-raising continue.

16. Keeping the local directors and staff focused on final details after the fund campaign ends.

17. Continually searching for new and innovative ideas about solving the age-old problems in not-for-profit organizations.

18. Developing and implementing the high-risk strategies if they have the potential for big payoffs.

19. Scheduling personal "thinking time" each week to try and remain focused on the big picture and removed from the food of daily minutia.

20. Reading and promptly responding to the numerous reports, correspondence, and requisite forms from local offices, national headquarters, and constituent groups in your five-state region.

Key

1.	M	6.	L	11.	L	16.	M
2.	M	7.	L	12.	L	17.	L
3.	M	8.	M	13.	M	18.	L
4.	M	9.	M	14.	M	19.	K
5.	M	10.	L	15.	L	20.	M

Teaming and Leadership[1]

■ ■ ■

LEADERSHIP MOMENT

You are the coach of your ten-year-old daughter's youth soccer team. After winning its first game, the team hit a rough patch, losing six games in a row. Several of your assistant coaches, as well as several parents, are bothered increasingly by this trend and lobby you to "instill more discipline" in practice and to start playing weaker team members less. Your players, at first indifferent to whether they won or lost, are now catching on to their parents' unrest—at your last practice there were two different times when players screamed at each other for perceived mistakes, with one saying, "You're the reason we keep losing." You thought that coaching was going to be relaxing, but you're starting to realize that, if this team does not start pulling together—and winning—soon, the season may be a real unpleasant one.

1. What would you do?

2. Which would you emphasize more, winning or team building? How are they interrelated?

3. How would you address the multiple coaching philosophies of the parents of your team members?

4. How would you address the increased fighting among team members?

---

1. This chapter is based in part on Chapter 3, "Management, Quality, and Team Building," written by Arthur Shriberg and Tim Kloppenborg for *Practicing Leadership: Principles and Applications* (2002), John Wiley Inc.

Leadership and management theorists have long struggled with meeting the needs, concerns, and expectations of organizations and each of its stakeholders as they balance individual needs. Organizations, like individuals, have their own life cycles and personalities.

In recent years, increasing emphasis has been placed on teams, teamwork, and *teaming.* Teams may be single or multipurpose. They may be single focus or multifunctional. They may exist for brief periods of time or may continue indefinitely. The leadership challenge involved differs depending upon the type of team involved and its life cycle, mission, and purpose. In this chapter, we look at three types of teams:

1. **Traditional teams:** Teams that remain relatively stable over time and physical space
2. **Virtual teams:** Teams composed of members spread over geographically remote areas
3. **Project teams:** Teams created for short periods of time to accomplish a specific task

To understand leadership roles, a team can be viewed as static or dynamic. Static teams are often examined at various points to ensure that the group is functioning well over time whereas dynamic teams are analyzed typically at different stages in their development.

All organisms go through various stages of development on their journey to maturity. Team organizations are no different. There is an emerging belief that teams go through five stages of development on their journey to maturity. These stages are forming, storming, norming, performing, and adjourning.

Forming, the initial stage of team development, is marked by a period of acclimation. This is when individual team members begin to form impressions about their colleagues' personalities, work habits, social habits, and thinking styles. Group members are often quite uncertain about their roles during this period and are likely to defer to a group leader for guidance. During the second stage of group development, **storming,** group members begin to feel more comfortable around each other and individual personalities begin to emerge. Team members may start voicing their expectations and opinions about the group as a whole and about their roles within it. As a result, the storming phase often is characterized by conflict, disagreement, and disorganization. It is often a challenging stage both for the group and its leader because the group's effectiveness depends on adequately managing the many issues that bubble up during this stage of development. To move through this stage successfully, team leaders should promote the open sharing of ideas and viewpoints, while allowing for a productive level of conflict. The remaining conflict carries the team into the next phase, **norming,** which occurs when team members begin to accept and understand each other. Conflict is resolved. Team identity emerges, and the team's goals are clarified. During this stage, team leaders must promote unity.

In the **performing** stage, emphasis in placed on completing team tasks and accomplishing team goals. Team members have established their roles, and procedures have been agreed upon. This phase is marked by conflict resolution and open communication. During the performing stage, team members typically demonstrate a high commitment to the team and to its goals. Leaders should focus on directing actions toward task accomplishment. Not all teams go through the final stage, **adjourning.** Permanent teams, for instance, never prepare for termination as teams working together for shorter periods do. Teams that reach this stage, however, focus on wrapping up final details and achieving all the team's goals. Team performance is less of a priority, and team unity is often quite high. Team members are often proud of their accomplishments but may also feel forlorn about the team's dissolution. Team leaders should assist team members with their transition into new roles and provide closure to their team experience along with thanks for completing the task.

◆ TRADITIONAL TEAMS

A team can be defined as two or more people who have developed processes to accomplish one or more specific goals. Traditionally, work teams are made up of individuals that work in physical proximity to each other but bring complementary skills to the task at hand. Teams, often called by other names such as task forces, quality circles, or steering committees, may be found at all levels of the organization and are created because there are specific advantages that they bring to the organization.

Advantages to Working in Teams

Teams often provide many benefits. One of the most significant is the enhanced performance provided by the team approach. Teams often perform better and more quickly than do individuals working alone. There are many reasons for this. For instance, teams have access to a more diverse set of knowledge and skills than individuals do on their own. Moreover, the team approach allows members to deal immediately with problems as they arise, rather than dealing with the delays that departmentalization can cause. And because multiple people will be working on the same project, mistakes can be caught more readily. Teams also are more innovative than individuals, and teams often provide the additional benefit of increasing employee satisfaction and motivation—much to the surprise of management. This is so because individuals see the fruit of their efforts pay off in teams in a way that they haven't when working outside of teams—and this motivates team members to work even harder. Not surprisingly, this tends to reduce turnover and absenteeism.

Barriers to Effective Teamwork

Although well-run teams enhance organizations, poorly functioning teams can lower morale and reduce organizational effectiveness. One of the most common hazards of teamwork is **groupthink,** which is the impairment in decision making and sound judgment that can occur in highly cohesive groups. It occurs when group members dismiss information that undermines their position, shun dissidents, and unify around a decision that might be unsound. **Social loafing** also can cause problems. Although teams often motivate individuals, some team members may reduce their effort if they believe nobody will notice.

Leading Teams

Zaccaro, Rittman, and Marks (2001) report that successful team performance is a product of team members successfully integrating their individual actions, the team's ability to perform in complex and dynamic environments, and the team leader's ability to define directions and organize the team. All teams, regardless of their forms and functions, are typically headed by a team leader. In generic terms a leader manages by whatever means, to ensure that all functions critical to both task accomplishment and group maintenance are managed effectively (Zaccaro et al., 2001). Manning and Curtis have compiled a set of behaviors from the works of Glenn Varney, Jon Katzenbach, and Douglas Smith who state that successful leaders develop successful teams through eleven time-tested practices:

1. Showing enthusiasm for the work of the group
2. Making timely decisions based on agreed upon goals
3. Promoting open-mindedness, innovation, and creativity by personal example and a conducive work climate
4. Admitting mistakes and uncertainties and modeling honesty as a virtue
5. Being flexible in using a variety of tactics and strategies to achieve success
6. Being persistent
7. Giving credit to others for the team's accomplishments and meeting people's needs for appreciation and recognition
8. Keeping people informed about progress and problems, celebrating victories and fine-tuning efforts
9. Keeping promises and following though on commitments, earning the trust and confidence of others
10. Training for success: master fundamentals and practice for perfection
11. Putting others first and self last—embodying the spirit of the caring leader

Although Manning and Curtis's eleven best practices provide a solid foundation for understanding and evaluating team leadership, teams are so diverse that no one set of leadership practices truly meets the needs of all teams at all times. However, successful team leaders do seem to share at least one characteristic that makes them effective—they integrate the skills and activities of team members in a way that best suits the team's needs. Group leaders need to utilize the expertise of group members at all stages of a team's life cycle. It is the leader's responsibility to identify who holds the appropriate knowledge, skills, and abilities needed to complete a task and to exploit, by whatever means possible, each team member to the fullest extent.

✦ VIRTUAL TEAMS

Thus far, we have focused on traditional teams, those that are located in the same geographic location and are stable over a period of time. Although there has been much talk about virtual workplaces in recent years, we have yet to become a society where individuals work predominantly in virtual settings, interacting with colleagues and team members through computers, phones, faxes, and other tools. The majority of work settings today remain largely traditional in that workers tend to work fixed hours in a fairly fixed location or locations. However, with the realities of a global market place and the ease of global communication, increasing numbers of workers spend part of their time in virtual settings—communicating via the Internet with colleagues and/or customers across the globe, for instance.

Virtual teams are composed of people working together across time and distance, toward a common goal, through the use of **information and communication technologies** (ICTs). Virtual teams, if properly managed, have tremendous potential for both the individuals and for organizations as a whole. Managing virtual teams involves maintaining close relationships with team members in different locations without the many face-to-face meetings typical of traditional teams. Organizations can offer virtual employment to attract and retain the best talent from across the globe. The key to success for virtual teams is for team leaders to recognize and address promptly the many social issues that may otherwise undermine the team's effectiveness.

Barriers to Effective Virtual Teamwork

Lack of trust is one of the biggest hurdles faced by members of a virtual team. Trusting a person one has never met or seen goes contrary to most people's instincts. Although studies have reported that many global virtual teams may experience a form of "swift" trust when faced with a common collaborative task, this trust often does not last very long (Jarvenpaa & Leidner, 1999). For this reason, virtual teams need to pay special attention to trust.

Another factor that contributes to the under-performance of virtual teams is the team members' fear of losing their personal identity and ownership of ideas (Wagner, 2004). In a virtual team, individuals are more likely to have to blend their unique ideas with those of the group. Contributions of virtual team members are stored in databases, which are the property of the organization. This creates a certain level of discomfort among those who do not want to give up ownership of their ideas and may actually cause such people to hold back their ideas for fear of losing the rights to them.

Another issue faced by virtual teams, particularly those that are only partly virtual and contain some traditional members, is that of parity. Those that are in traditional work settings may feel less privileged than their virtual counterparts, or vice versa. For instance, if an office has an emergency closure due to local weather conditions, should the virtual employees at another location be allowed to work? Perception of differential treatment can lead to interpersonal problems within the team, as well as problems at an organizational level in the form of lawsuits.

Additional social issues arise when virtual teams incorporate members from different countries and cultures. E-mail, for instance, is one of the most commonly used means of communication for teams that are spread over different locations, particularly in the United States, in spite of its obvious weaknesses of not being able to provide multiple cues that telephone and face-to-face meetings can provide (Markus, 1994). However, many Asian countries do not favor e-mail as much as the West does. There are several possible explanations for why this is true. Some authors attribute the Japanese preference for faxes to the fact that Japanese characters are harder to replicate in e-mail but can be drawn easily in a fax (Straub, 1994). Aversion to using e-mail or misreading e-mail content could also result from more deep-rooted cultural value systems. For instance, in Korea, the social order based on the teachings of Confucius dictates that subordinates should show respect to seniors in every form of communication. There is a widespread apprehension among Korean workers that e-mail does not adequately communicate respect and may eventually cost them a promotion (Lee, 2002). Although the media richness of e-mail is sufficient for most American or European team members even with its limited cues, it may be sorely lacking in appropriate cultural protocol from the perspective of their Asian counterparts.

Leading Virtual Teams

As attested by the steady outpouring of books on the subject, leading a regular team is a challenging task. Even when team members are all present under one roof, motivating them and resolving conflict are aspects that, if not dealt with effectively, can adversely impact the team's effectiveness. With virtual teams, the team leader can no longer stroll down the hall to assess the mood of her team or discuss challenges, opportunities, and concerns over lunch. The complexity of virtual teams makes the task of team building even more challenging. Some team leaders feel a sense of loss of control when they cannot see their team. Others feel that their ability to monitor performance and give feedback can be severely limited as a result of not sharing the same physical space with their team members. Although there is little empirical evidence to support these apprehensions, problems do arise in leading a team that is scattered over different geographic locations and time zones.

A visionary leader will recognize that virtual teams are the wave of the future. At the same time, a good leader will recognize that not all situations and people are suited for virtual structures. Recognizing when not to go the virtual route can be as important a leadership task as identifying opportunities for using virtual teams. In the event that a team leader decides that recruiting the best talent from across the globe for the team is ideal, it is critical for him/her to get top management support on the idea of creating a virtual team. Companies where the top management buys into the idea have very successfully adapted the virtual workplace model. For instance, at Sun Microsystems more than a third of the employees do not have their own offices but use special Java smart-card-enabled flat-panel monitors and keyboards that can bring up their desktop screens no matter where they are physically located. Deloitte & Touche has 90,000 employees in 130 countries, and to facilitate information sharing between virtual team-members the company uses a Web-based tracking system that allows its employees to track the status of any project from anywhere in the world (Solomon, 2001). Investment of this magnitude into creating a virtual workplace will only take place if there is significant top management commitment to the idea of utilizing these technologies.

After securing the support of top management, the next most important step creating a virtual team is selection of team members. The team leader, if she has input in determining the composition of the team, must try to select employees that can function effectively without close supervision or direction. Several behavioral instruments are available to those who wish to identify personality types and to get an idea of a person's preferred style of handling situations. For instance, the DISC Personal Profile System is an instrument that describes personalities using the four dimensions of Dominance, Influence, Steadiness, and Conscientiousness. This instrument gives an indication of the degree to which an individual utilizes each of these dimensions in different situations and is an effective tool to use for virtual teams because it uses observable behavior not just from face-to-face interactions but also from e-mails and telephone conversations. While these behavioral tools are not infallible, in most cases they provide fairly good insight into personality types and can be used as selection tools or as a guide to dealing with the different personality types already present in a team. They can also help the team leader better understand his or her own preferred styles of decision making, thus opening up opportunities for improvement.

Once the team is in place, it is the team leader's responsibility to build trust and provide direction. The goals must be communicated clearly and frequently to the team, preferably using more than one communication medium. It also helps to create a sense of identity for the team—a common theme, logo, or credo that reinforces a shared purpose will help individuals develop pride in their team and create a sense of purpose. Getting the team together for at least one face-to-face meeting in the initial stages is an investment worth making because it fosters trust and a sense of identity. In addition, the team leader must, whenever possible, visit his or her team members in remote locations to reinforce her commitment to the team and to minimize feelings of isolation. By encouraging personal interaction whenever possible, the team leader can create the one thing that virtual teams find hardest to develop—trust. Giving people credit for their ideas and achievements can also enhance mutual trust and respect. The team leader must make an effort to develop skills to facilitate virtual meetings, which, in all likelihood, will be far more numerous than the face-to-face ones. Preparing ahead of time, soliciting input from team members, and sticking to the schedule and agenda are all essential aspects of good virtual meetings.

The virtual team leader must be aware that the leader's role changes when the composition of the team changes from homogeneous to diverse. In a homogeneous team, a leader's role is primarily that of a mentor and coach, with emphasis on helping team members fit into an existing culture. However, leading a diverse team requires the leader to take on the role of facilitator and catalyst, to shape an evolving culture, and to be aware of other cultural norms (Gardenschwartz &Rowe,

1994). It is a well-documented fact that strong relationships within teams can enhance creativity, motivation, and morale and create better decision-making processes (Walther & Burgoon, 1992). However, allowing a culture to evolve in a virtual environment is easier said than done. Since informal social settings are an essential part of the team's growth and bonding process, the task of creating the virtual equivalent of water-cooler chat falls on the team leader. Using ICTs to create social spaces where team members can interact beyond work-related issues is key, as informal encounters create common context and support group work (Kraut et al., 1993).

Merging individual cultures to form a single unique team culture is one of the most important tasks of the team leader, second only perhaps to building trust. The informal interactions can be used as opportunities to educate team members about gender, culture, and other differences and to instill in them the Platinum Rule "Do unto others as they would have done unto them" instead of the Golden Rule "Do unto others as you would have them do unto you". Sharing of emotions and mental models are an essential part of building trust among team members who may never have a chance to see each other (Nonaka & Takeuchi, 1995). Strong mutual trust and respect can lessen the need for long complex messaging systems—shared contexts will allow for effective messaging even with simple low-richness media and, hence, smoother communications.

Keeping all these factors in mind, the virtual team leader must not only carry out all the functions of a traditional team leader, but must also remember at all times the following issues that are specific to virtual teams:

- The team may be virtual but the people are very real, and because they are in a virtual environment their emotions may be much harder to read.
- In virtual teams problems may be less apparent than in traditional teams.
- The leader must not ignore nonperformers simply because they are out of sight.
- The leader must avoid paying more attention to physically closer members if she wants the team to have a perception of parity.
- The leader must walk the talk—and practice the Platinum Rule!
- The leader of a virtual team must be familiar with the technologies that facilitate the effective functioning of her team.

✦ PROJECT TEAMS

Another type of team that has gained popularity in the recent years is the Project Team. A project team is usually created to complete a specific task, typically a multidisciplinary task, within a predetermined time frame. Project teams are temporary in nature—team members are drawn from various functional areas and the group is disbanded when the assigned task is completed. Like any other team in today's multicultural society, project teams are often composed of individuals that demonstrate a wide variety of diversity elements, such as race, class, age, and gender.

Project teams have many advantages. Having people from different functional areas work together on a project helps to ensure a holistic approach to problem solving. However, since every project is different, leading project teams requires an in-depth understanding of that particular project's specific needs, life cycle, and limitations (Kloppenborg, Shriberg & Venkatraman, 2003).

The life cycle of a project can be divided into four distinct stages. The first stage, **initiating,** is when the need is identified and the scope of the project determined. The next stage is **planning,** where the details of the project and final composition of the project team are worked out. The third stage, **execution,** is the one that takes the most time and resources. This is when the deliverables are created and turned over to the customer. In the final stage, **closing,** the project team is disbanded, its members reassigned, and the results are evaluated.

Barriers to Effective Project Teamwork

One of the biggest challenges of leading a project stems from the unique nature of each project. There may be no clear precedents to help guide the decision-making process or to give an indication of things that might go wrong.

As in any other team situation, interpersonal problems are a major barrier to effective teamwork. Members of a project team are often faced with the problem of confused loyalties. Sometimes dual reporting relationships to the functional manager and the team leader cause role conflicts and prioritization problems. Since project teams are temporary, team members may have issues with group identity, and their effectiveness may be undermined as a result of not having a sense of belonging with the group. Teams with very diverse members may become ineffective if there are too many divergent viewpoints or if members bond more closely with others that are similar to them and not with those that are perceived as different.

Leading Project Teams

Kloppenborg et al. (2003) define project leadership as "the systematic application of leadership understanding and skill at each stage of the project life-cycle." Specific leadership tasks that are critical at each stage are detailed in Table 10-1.

In order to be well equipped to deal with problems that might arise in execution of a project, the leader must understand clearly the constraints within which she has to operate. These constraints include resources (financial and human), time, and technology. An important activity at the start of the project is identifying these constraints and the risks involved. In the planning stage, it is crucial to develop detailed plans and obtain the approval of major stakeholders, since one of the most common causes of project failure is the lack of management and end-user buy-in (Kelly & Stalnaker, 2002). Ensuring that the goals of the project align with the organization's goals can go a long way in gaining top management support. The execution stage requires leaders to carefully monitor and control any deviations from plan and to ensure that customer acceptance is obtained for the deliverables. Finally, the leader must remember that the closing

TABLE 10-1   **Stage Specific Tasks of Project Leadership**

Leadership Task Type	*Initiating*	*Planning*	*Executing*	*Closing*
Priorities	Align project with parent organization	Understand customer's priorities	Authorize work	Audit project
Details	Perform risk analysis	Oversee detailed plan	Monitor & control	Terminate project
Integration	Justify & select project	Integrate project plans	Coordinate work	Capture & share lessons
Human Resources	Select key participants	Select other participants	Supervise work	Reassign workers
Human Relations	Determine team operating means	Develop communications plan	Lead teams	Reward & recognize
Promotion	Develop top management support	Motivate all participants	Maintain morale	Celebrate completion
Commitment	Commit to project	Secure key customer approval	Secure customer acceptance	Oversee administrative closure

SOURCE: Kloppenborg, Shriberg, Venkatraman, Project Leadership, Management Concepts, 2003.

stage is as important as any of the other stages—it is important to make sure that successes are celebrated, team-members appropriately re-assigned, and lessons learned are documented.

In addition to the leadership tasks identified in Table 10-1, a project leader needs to address interpersonal issues that team members may face. As with other types of teams, effective and regular communication is essential at all stages. Ensuring fun and energetic interactions can play an important role in building a sense of cohesion among team members. In the case of project teams, this can be a challenging task considering that there are often time and resource constraints. However, given that the lack of cohesion can lead to project failure, an emphasis on cohesion can have many benefits. Increased team cohesion often leads to increased team stability, and making sure that the team is stable over the life of the project and that members remain with the project from the beginning to its completion can also help in creating a sense of accomplishment among team members (Ammeter, 2002).

In order to manage professional and personal diversity in the project team, the leader must encourage the team to find common ground in their technical expertise and must keep the team focused on the deliverables. The leader must understand personalities and group affiliations, value differences, and express genuine interest in the backgrounds of individual team members (Miller et al., 2000).

₂ proceeding sections have highlighted three forms of teams—tradition-al, and project—and the nuances of effective leadership in each of these ₁ₒᵣₘₐₜₛ. The following profiles add depth to our understanding of successful team leadership by examining the techniques of two acknowledged masters in team-building, one (Dean Smith) in the area of athletics and the other (Barry and Eliot Tatelman) in business.

DEAN SMITH
Teacher of Teamwork

Upon arriving at the University of North Carolina, Chapel Hill, in 1961, former head basketball coach Dean Smith proceeded to fashion one of the leading college athletics programs in the country. Not only are the Tarheels arguably the most successful college basketball team of all time, but the program has also avoided scandal and managed to have an excellent record for graduating its basketball players both during and immediately following Smith's tenure.

Smith's teams were known for their cunning defenses, their discipline, and above all, their unselfishness. Coach Smith stressed teamwork as the highest priority. No matter how talented the players are individually—and he has coached Michael Jordan, Rasheed Wallace, Jerry Stackhouse, Vince Carter, and dozens of others who have gone on to successful NBA careers—Smith wanted no part of a star system at UNC. Instead, he placed a higher value on assists than points. As a result, few of his players have averaged 20 points per game, and that's more than okay with him.

He reportedly never promised playing time, even to stellar prospects. When the newcomers arrived on campus, he assigned them an underling role to upperclassmen. For instance, they may have been asked carry the film projector and chase loose balls in practice.

In addition to the stress on unselfish play and teamwork, Smith instituted many other innovations, including huddling at the free throw line before foul shots and allowing tired players to take themselves out of the game.

Despite an incredible overall win/loss record (851–247) and coaching the 1976 U.S. Olympic team to a gold medal, Smith for years was dogged by the media for never winning an NCAA title, even though his teams made several trips to the Final Four and the championship game.

When asked about it, he said "If we win, I won't be a better coach."

When the 1981–82 team finally obtained the coveted NCAA title with a last-second win over Georgetown, Smith's players were happy to have won for him. Guard Jimmy Black, who had endured his mother's death and his own near-fatal car accident, said, "In my times of tragedy, he [Smith] has always been there to lean on. This is our way of repaying him for being a shoulder."

Frequently deflecting praise to his players, Smith that night asserted that his protégé, Georgetown's John Thompson, had outcoached him. "And I don't think I'm a better coach now because we've won a national championship...If we lost, I'd have another shot; I'd feel for those kids who wouldn't have another chance. Just because they won, I won't like them any more than last year's team," he said.

Despite the effect on future seasons, Smith has repeatedly counseled those projected to be among the top five picks in the NBA to enter the draft. This has meant losing the services of such notables as Jordan, James Worthy, and many others, most of whom have returned to earn their degrees.

Long after they've left the team, the players frequently return to visit Smith and keep in close contact with him and with each other. Michael Jordan, for instance, gave Smith his 1991 NBA championship ring. They report that more than simply being a coach, he has been a friend and a teacher, concerned with their lives beyond basketball.

A shoe contract he signed with Nike near the end of his coaching career was far different from the contracts many coaches sign: it covered the entire athletic department of the university, providing shoes and apparel for twenty-four university teams; funded the basketball team's international exhibition tour; and paid the university as well. Rather than pocketing the money himself, as most coaches do, Smith donated the entire signing bonus ($500,000) to charity. He also earmarked $45,000 of his annual $300,000 endorsement salary from Nike to a fund that helps former players finish their degrees and divided the rest among his assistants and office staff.

(For more information visit http://www.hoophall.com/halloffamers/SmithDean.htm.)

BARRY AND ELIOT TATELMAN
Fun, Families, Furniture

Most companies would give anything to have Warren Buffet call them "one of the most phenomenal and unique companies that I have ever seen. The reputation...from their employees, their customers, and the community is unparalleled. This company is a gem!" Chairman and CEO of Berkshire Hathaway Inc., Buffet offered this high praise for Jordan's Furniture, a decidedly unconventional furniture operation centered in the Boston area. Buffet's comments came with the announcement that Jordan's Furniture would merge with a Berkshire Hathaway subsidiary.

Brothers Eliot and Barry Tatelman celebrated the merger in a typically innovative way: They gave every member of their 1,200-person organization a bonus of 50 cents for every hour worked for Jordan's. Since most of the employees have been with the company for ten or twenty years and more, it meant a tidy little sum. The longest-term employee pocketed $40,000.

Such generosity is nothing new to the brothers Tatelman. In 1970, they inherited the store begun by their grandfather Samuel Tatelman (and subsequently run by their father, Eddie Tatelman) in 1928 in Waltham, Massachusetts, and have exercised a variety of employee-pleasing options ever since. Recently, a spontaneous staff holiday meant flying the company's 1,200 employees to Bermuda for a day-long beach party and barbeque.

The investment has been worth it, not only in being able to hire excellent salespeople during an unusually tight labor market, but also in keeping customers happy to return to Jordan's.

"You're only as good as your weakest link," says Barry. "Our stores are exciting, our values are good, the entertainment factor is there, the service is incredible." But what stands out above all else is Jordan's staff. "Our people smile and are genuinely happy to be where they are," he says.

And who could blame them? Jordan's four sites are nothing like stuffy furniture stores—they're theme parks that emphasize family fun and good corporate citizenship. The company is affiliated with a host of local charities, including local Big Brothers and Big Sisters and the Massachusetts Adoption Resource Exchange. For the latter, Jordan's hosted an "adoption party" that drew more than 2,000 people and resulted in at least six children finding adoptive families. Staff members get involved in the charity events, deriving a sense of satisfaction that mere paychecks can't supply.

The stores themselves are marvels: a Bourbon Street simulation complete with Dixieland band and Mardi Gras regalia, a $2.5 million laser-enhanced thrill ride called the Motion Odyssey Movie, a huge screen Omnimax theater that shows the latest releases, in-house full-service family restaurants, and hourly animatronic entertainment versions of The Beatles, Elvis, and The Supremes.

The Tatelmans use Las Vegas-style marketing designed to bring people into their stores in the same way casinos use entertainment to lure people to gamble. "We were going to bring people to a furniture store for something other than furniture and make them walk through the whole store," explains Eliot.

Especially for families, the stores have become weekend destinations, and they also sell furniture—enough so that 1999 sales figures neared $250 million. Jordan's has incredible market identity despite spending only 1 to 2 percent of their gross revenues on advertising.

One industry analyst attributes their success to credibility. "The number one reason for their success is that people believe in the company," says Britt Beemer with America's Research Group in Charleston, South Carolina. "The more you get people to believe in the company, the less you have to keep lowering and lowering and lowering your prices to get people to buy from you."

✦ Chapter Summary

There is no doubt that teamwork enhances an organization's productivity. However, with changes in technology and workforce composition, teams today vary widely in structure and roles. While there are some commonalities in the way all teams function and desirable team leadership skills, there are also key leadership differences depending on the time and space limitations of the team. Virtual and project teams, both of which are becoming increasingly popular, provide unique challenges that require different leadership skills than the skills needed to lead traditional teams. In order to ensure effective functioning, it is important for a team leader both to anticipate challenges that may arise based on the nature (e.g., virtual versus project) of the particular team he or she is leading and to adapt his or her leadership approach to address team-specific challenges that may arise.

✦ CREATE YOUR OWN THEORY ✦

Do leaders always need to be team players? In what contexts is teamwork paramount? Is working well in teams consistent with your view of the attributes of the ideal leader for the twenty-first century?

Now let's revisit our opening Leadership Moment. If you were coaching a girls' soccer team, which would be more important to you—winning or developing teamwork skills in your players? Does one lead to the other? Would you be likely to share the viewpoints of some of the parents that certain players should get less playing time because they are not as skilled as the others, or do you have the perspective that, at age ten all of the girls should play for approximately equal lengths of time (including your own daughter)? Would your answer be different if the girls were five years old? How about if they were all sixteen? What if you were coaching a team of boys instead of girls? What distinctions might you make? What does that say about your leadership style?

✦ Key Terms

adjourning

closing

execution

forming

groupthink

information and
   communication technologies

initiating

norming

performing

planning

project teams

social loafing

traditional teams

storming

virtual teams

✦ Questions for Discussion and Review

1. Describe the various stages of group development.
2. How does an organization benefit from having people work in teams?
3. What are some of the issues that are faced by traditional teams?
4. How is leading a virtual team different from leading a traditional one?
5. What are some of the key responsibilities of project leaders in the different stages of a project's life cycle?

PART IV

Current and
Future Approaches

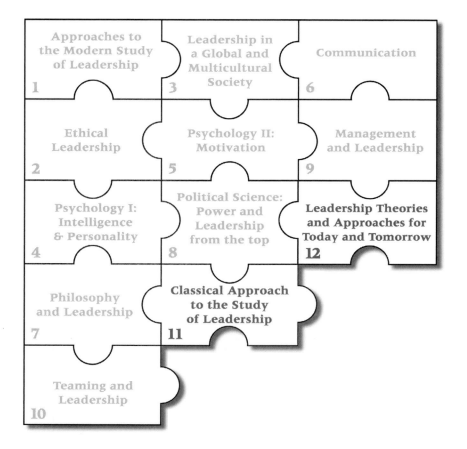

Classical Approach to the Study of Leadership

■ ■ ■

LEADERSHIP MOMENT

You are the newly hired principal of Roosevelt High School. One of the leading complaints about your predecessor is that she played favorites. As a result, you have inherited a staff that mostly views you with suspicion. In reviewing the backgrounds of the school professionals, you notice that there is a wide range of experience and skills. There are twenty teachers aged twenty-four or younger, yet there are also thirty-four who have been at the school for more than twenty years. In addition, an increasing number of specialists (speech therapists, psychologists) report to you that they felt slighted by the previous principal, who they feel worked to keep them isolated from the "real school workers" (i.e., teachers). The students generally ignore you—they only really saw the previous principal when they were in trouble. As for the community, your school's standardized test scores are declining and they expect a turnaround—fast.

1. *What would you do?*
2. *How would you attempt to understand and manage the diverse backgrounds and perspectives of school personnel?*
3. *What might some of your first steps be in this process?*
4. *To whom would you look for guidance in this process? Who are potential allies?*

t we've seen what the related disciplines have contributed to leadership
ais chapter looks at the various theories that are or have been popular in
_____ip literature. We'll touch on trait theory, behavioral management
approaches, and situational approaches. It is fitting that our discussion begins
with the seminal work of John Gardner, the former U.S. Secretary of Health,
Education, and Welfare, and current professor at Stanford University. His book,
On Leadership (1989), lists ten functions of leadership:

1. Envisioning goals
2. Affirming and regenerating important group values
3. Motivating others toward collective goals
4. Managing the processes through which collective goals can be reached
5. Achieving unity of effort within a context of pluralism and diversity
6. Creating an atmosphere of mutual trust
7. Explaining and teaching
8. Serving as a symbol of the group's identity
9. Representing the group's interests to outside parties
10. Renewing and adapting the organization to a changing world

These functions describe an ideal state that can be used as a benchmark to
measure the effectiveness of any leader.

This list should be examined in terms of another well-known leadership theorist, Warren Bennis, former president of the University of Cincinnati. Bennis (1985)
proposed his own list of competencies for leaders, based on a five-year project that
studied ninety effective, successful leaders in corporations and the public sector.

He concluded that there are four major competencies:

1. Management of attention—the ability to attract others, not only through
   a compelling vision, but also through communicating commitment
2. Management of meaning—to make dreams apparent to others
3. Management of trust—to let others believe in one's constancy and focus
4. Management of self—understanding one's skills and using them well

◆ TRAIT THEORY

Trait theory, usually seen as the first among leadership theories, was very popular during the second part of the twentieth century. Simply stated, this theory
suggests that the traits of successful leaders should be studied and emulated. The
enormity of the challenge is daunting. How can people who seek to practice leadership gain the needed traits?

One answer can be seen in Gardner's fourteen leadership attributes, which
he says "seem to be linked with higher probabilities that a leader in one situation
could also lead in another":

1. Physical vitality and stamina
2. Intelligence and action-oriented judgment

3. Eagerness to accept responsibility
4. Task competence
5. Understanding of followers and their needs
6. Skill in dealing with people
7. Need for achievement
8. Capacity to motivate people
9. Courage and resolution
10. Trustworthiness
11. Decisiveness
12. Self-confidence
13. Assertiveness
14. Adaptability/flexibility

Gardner utilized a five-year field study of organizations and interviews with hundreds of leaders. To what end do leaders employ these traits? Gardner asserts that leaders should focus on building and rebuilding community—on working for the common good. And their primary renewal task, he says, is "the release of human energy and talent."

James M. Kouzes and Barry Z. Posner also made a major contribution to trait theory in their book *The Leadership Challenge*. In the early 1980s, more than 1,500 managers responded to their survey, in which they asked, "What values do you look for in your superiors?" Of the 225 values, characteristics, and attitudes compiled from the answers, the top four were being honest, forward looking, inspiring, and competent. They called these four characteristics *being credible*. See their essay later in this chapter for more information about Kouzes and Posner's theory.

Many others have composed lists of leadership characteristics, typically including such traits as energy level, height, general cognitive ability, and, to a lesser extent, particular technical skills and knowledge about a group's task. See Table 11–1 for a summary of effective physical, social, and personal leadership characteristics.

✦ BEHAVIORAL THEORIES OF LEADERSHIP

The behavioral approach to studying leadership assumes that leader behaviors rather than personality characteristics are the elements producing the most effect on followers. Significant research on this perspective was conducted at the Ohio State University and the University of Michigan.

The Ohio State Studies

The **Ohio State studies** examined the effects of two dimensions of leader behavior: *consideration* and *initiating structure*. Consideration refers to the leader's awareness of and sensitivity to subordinates' interests, feelings, and ideas. Leaders high in consideration are typically friendly, prefer open communications, focus on teamwork, and are concerned with the other person's welfare.

TABLE 11-1 **Personal Characteristics of Leaders**

Physical:	Active
	Energetic
Personality:	Alert
	Creative
	Ethical
Social:	Skilled interpersonally
	Can enlist others in goal
	Sociable
	Cooperative
Intelligence:	Good judgment
	Fluent in speaking
	Knowledgeable
Work-related traits:	Task-oriented
	Tactful
	Driven to excel
	Responsible
	Ethical

Initiating structure is a leader behavior marked by attention to task and goals. Leaders who are high in initiating structure typically present instructions and provide detailed, explicit timelines for task completion.

Since the two behaviors are independent of each other, researchers tested the effectiveness of four combinations of leader behaviors: high initiating structure–low consideration (HIS–LC), low initiating structure–high consideration (LIS–HC), high initiating structure–high consideration (HIS–HC), and low initiating structure–low consideration (LIS–LC). The high initiating structure–high consideration style was associated with the best performance and greatest satisfaction. These leaders both met the needs of their subordinates and were effective in accomplishing their task and/or goals.

University of Michigan Studies

Similarly, in the late 1950s, researchers including Rensis Likert looked at the behavior of effective and ineffective supervisors. The **University of Michigan studies** concluded that supervisory behavior could be analyzed in terms of *employee-centered* and *job-centered behavior.* Employee-centered supervisors were found most effective. To these researchers, supervisors exhibited either one or the other of these patterns; there was no middle ground, no combination of behaviors.

The Leadership Grid

Robert Blake and Jane Mouton developed the concept of the **Leadership Grid** (see Figure 11–1), which graphically depicts the characteristics of leaders based on some of the dimensions examined in the Ohio State and University of Michigan studies. Questionnaire responses were used to rate managers on a scale from one to nine for two dimensions: concern for people and concern for production. An individual's scores on these two dimensions were then plotted, with a score of (9,9) equaling the ideal leader ("team" style).

Based on a person's location on the grid, Blake and Mouton (1964) identified four other distinct management styles. Most managers fall near the (5,5) point on the grid, indicating a "middle of the road style." These managers rate in the middle range on the concern for people scale and in the middle range on the concern for production scale. Those scoring high on concern for people and low on concern for production scales demonstrate a "country club" style. Those scoring low on people and high on production are called "authoritarian" managers.

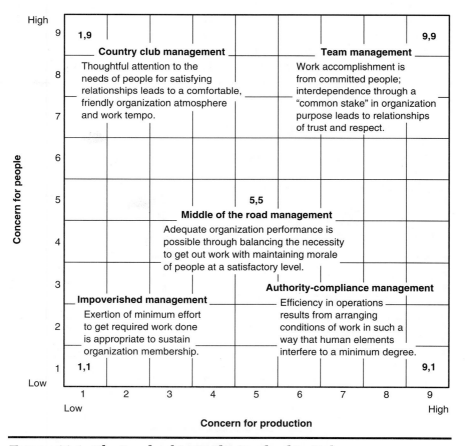

FIGURE 11-1 The Leadership Grid® Leadership Styles

SOURCE: *Leadership Dilemmas—Grid Solutions.* p. 29, by Robert R. Blake, Ph.D. and Anne Adams McCanse. Copyright © 1991, by Robert R. Blake and the Estate of Jane S. Mouton, Austin, Texas. The Grid® designation is property of Scientific Methods, Inc. Gulf Publishing Company, Houston, Texas. Used with permission. All rights reserved.

Finally, managers scoring very low on both scales are said to have an "impoverished" style.

Although Blake and Mouton concluded that managers perform best when working under a (9,9) team style, there is little substantive evidence to support this claim; some question whether a (9,9) is even possible, since often a leader is forced to make a decision that favors either people or production.

◆ WELL-KNOWN THEORETICAL APPROACHES TO LEADERSHIP

Leaders can lead in many ways depending on their style. As shown in Figure 11–2, leaders vary from a boss-centered approach (where decisions are made and announced) to a subordinate-centered approach (where subordinates make their own decisions defined by the leader). Leaders also vary on the element of the leadership situation that they stress. The elements include the leader, the follower(s) (we prefer the term *collaborator*) and the situation itself. For instance, if a group of people are "meeting" and the fire alarm rings, the situation takes priority and the group must deal with the fire. Many theorists center upon followers' needs and the leader's job is defined as meeting those needs. This will be discussed at some length in Chapter 12. There is also an emerging literature on leaders meeting their own needs. While the term "situational leadership" is used differently by different authors, a common way of using this term is to describe

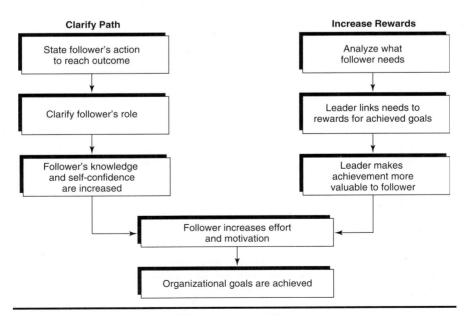

FIGURE 11-2 Continuum of Leadership Behavior

SOURCE: J. Donnelly, J. Gibson, J. Ivancevich, *Fundamentals of Management,* 9th edition, 1995. Irwin Professional. Used with permission.

the balance that is maintained among the needs of the leader, the follower, and the situation. The rest of this chapter will describe various popular leadership models and theories.

Situational Leadership Model

Hersey and Blanchard (1969) developed the best-known situational leadership model, which has been revised by both authors and others numerous times (see, for example, Blanchard, Zigarme, & Zigarme, 1985). Simply stated, situational leadership is being able to adopt different leadership styles depending on the demands of the situation at hand.

Hersey and Blanchard's model provides a framework for analyzing the needs of a situation and identifying the leadership style best suited for it. According to this model, a leader may respond in four fundamental ways to one or more followers—directing, coaching, supporting, or delegating—depending on the followers' need for support and direction.

- Situation 1 (S1)—Directing: This is a situation requiring high direction and low support (e.g., when a leader is explaining a task for the first time to a new staff member). The leader defines the roles and makes the decisions, leading to predominantly top-down, one-way communication.
- Situation 2 (S2)—Coaching: This is when the leader must act like a good coach and give the follower both high support and high direction (e.g., during a timeout in a basketball game when a coach is complimenting players on their good work and explaining in detail the strategy). The leader still makes most of the decisions, but solicits inputs from followers, and the communication is more two-way.
- Situation 3 (S3)—Supporting: In S3 situations, the leader gives high support but very little direction (e.g., when a leader is supervising people who have more technical knowledge and is trying to encourage them to keep going on a difficult task). The leader facilitates the decision-making process, but the follower is in control.
- Situation 4 (S4)—Delegating: This is a situation where the leader shares the mission and goals with the followers and they will have full responsibility to execute. The follower decides when, if at all, to involve the leader in the decision-making process.

Each of these approaches is appropriate in certain situations and inappropriate in others. The effective leader is adept at choosing the most suitable response. Recognizing that the appropriate leadership style also depends on the nature of the follower, Hersey and Blanchard further expanded their model to include the development level of the follower as measured by the latter's competence and commitment. The follower's development levels are described as follows:

- D1—Low competence, low commitment: This is when the follower lacks the skill as well as the motivation needed to complete the task.
- D2—Some competence, low commitment: The follower has some skills but cannot complete the task without assistance.

- D3—High competence, variable commitment: The follower is very skilled but is lacking somewhat in the motivation to complete the task.
- D4—High competence, high commitment: The follower is highly skilled and experienced, and needs no direction from the leader to complete the task.

It is important to note that these development levels are also situation-specific. A follower may be very skilled (D4) with respect to certain tasks but may drop to a D1 level when faced with an unfamiliar task. According to Hersey and Blanchard, it is the leader's responsibility to adapt the leadership style (S1-S4) to the corresponding development level (D1-D4) of the follower. For instance, in the example of the new staff member, if the leader were to adopt an S4 style instead of the S1 style and give the staff member no guidance on tackling the new job, the follower would probably feel lost and demotivated and the job would not be completed to everyone's satisfaction. Being able to adopt the right style is crucial to the leader's effectiveness and also allows the follower's development level to rise to D4, the most desirable level.

Path–Goal Theory

Path–Goal theory simply states that a leader must motivate followers: leaders are successful if they can successfully motivate their followers, as shown in Figure 11–3.

In order to utilize the Path–Goal theory effectively, House demonstrates the need to select the leadership style that best fits the situation (see Figure 11–4). Directive, supportive, achievement-oriented, and participative approaches are all appropriate for different situations.

The leader must consider five expectancy factors in assessing followers:

1. *Followers' valences* (a valence is one's perspective about what is important). Leaders can help followers identify and pursue an outcome that is under the leader's control.

2. *Followers' instrumentalities*. Leaders can make sure that high performance means satisfying outcomes.

3. *Followers' expectancies*. Leaders can reduce followers' frustration by overcoming barriers.

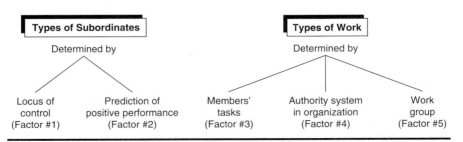

FIGURE 11-3 Leader's Role in the Path–Goal Model

Directive

- Emphasizes management functions such as planning, organizing, and controlling
- Gives specific guidelines, rules, and regulations to organization members
- Clearly spells out expectations for group members
- Typically improves performance when tasks are unclear or organization is unstable

Supportive

- Emphasizes concern for well-being of group members
- Establishes an emotionally supportive work environment and develops mutually satisfying relationships among group members
- Group members who are unsure of themselves prefer this style
- Typically improves performance where tasks are dissatisfying, stressful, or frustrating

Achievement-Oriented

- Emphasizes setting challenging goals and high expectations for performance
- Continually pushes for work improvement
- Group members expected to assume significant responsibility
- Typically improves performance with achievement-oriented team members and with those working on ambiguous and nonrepetitive tasks

Participative

- Emphasizes consultation with group members and takes their suggestions seriously when making decisions
- Typically improves performance of well-motivated employees who perform nonrepetitive tasks

FIGURE 11-4 House's Path–Goal Theory: Leadership Style

4. *Equity of rewards.* Leaders raise the levels and types of rewards available for good performance.
5. *Accuracy of role perceptions.* Leaders specify clearly the routes for effective performance.

Exercise 11–1 is helpful in bringing these concepts to life.

Combining Situational Leadership and a Continuum of Leader Behavior

In considering the appropriate leadership style, some leaders use the continuum of leadership behavior (see Figure 11–2), choosing either a directive, supportive, participative, or achievement-oriented approach (see Figure 11–4) based on the leadership of the expectancy factors that fit the situation.

- **Directive:** Authoritarian. Collaborators know precisely what is expected and when, but have no say in decision-making.
- **Supportive:** A directive leader who nonetheless shows concern and interest in collaborators.
- **Participative:** A leader who enlists and accepts others' ideas, but still makes the decision.
- **Achievement-oriented:** A leader who establishes challenging but possible goals for collaborators and fully expects their achievement.

With the five expectancy variables, the four leadership styles, and the knowledge that situational and follower factors also affect the process, the Path–Goal theory can become very complicated. As you might expect, wise individuals select a leadership style based on elements of the task, the situation, or the subordinates. They may fluctuate, too, between leadership styles, depending on which one promises the best results in a given situation.

For example, **participative leadership** produces satisfaction in situations in which the task is not routine and the collaborators are themselves not authoritarian. **Directive leadership** results in high satisfaction and performance only when collaborators have great needs for clarity. **Supportive leadership** produces satisfaction among collaborators only when the task is highly structured, and **achievement-oriented leadership** yields improved performance only when collaborators express commitment to goals.

◆ Chart Summary

Centers on:
Expectancy theory, which suggests that people calculate the advantages of different levels of effort (e.g., if I practice the piano for eight hours, how likely is it that I will do well at the recital?); performance (e.g., If I do well at the recital, how likely is it that I will get a record contract?); and values (e.g., how much do I want a performing career?).

Useful for:
- Predicting to which tasks people will devote their energy
- Understanding the complexity of the factors involved in practicing leadership

◆ IMPLICATIONS FOR PRACTICING LEADERSHIP

Effective leaders make sure appropriate rewards are available for followers (the goal) and then help them find the best way to achieve it (the path). Practicing leadership involves helping others see that the more effort and energy they put into a task, the greater the chance of accomplishing it. *Plus*, leaders must make sure that achieving the task will have valuable consequences.

Leadership Skills Needed
- Ability to identify and communicate with others
- Ability to use motivation to encourage activity
- Ability to accurately assess the situation and the collaborators
- Flexibility in determining when to use each of the four styles

What Approach Is Most Effective

Research (Mitchell, Smyser, and Weed, 1975) shows that others' satisfaction with a leader depends not only on the leader's style, but also on certain variables of the follower. For example, some studies showed that not everyone was satisfied with participatory leadership approaches. In fact, those who were happiest with participating in decisions were people with an internal locus of control—who thought that outcomes were directly related to their behavior. Conversely, those with an external locus of control—who felt that the outcomes depended on factors outside their control—were more satisfied with a directive leader.

Another collaborator variable that affects leader style is the collaborators' perception of their own abilities to perform the tasks.

Situational Factors

- The task—is it in itself motivating? Routine?
- The authority system—are there standards for performing the task?
- The primary work group—is there an accepted way of performing the task?

The Path–Goal model is very comprehensive. It sees leadership within organizations as helping members clarify their goals and identify the best ways to achieve those goals.

Cognitive Resources Theory

In this theory, Fred Fiedler and his colleagues (Fiedler, 1986; Fiedler & Garcia, 1987) focus on the impact of the leader's intelligence and experience since these two cognitive traits affect group performance. Naturally, the theory is more complicated than that simple summary. The cognitive traits interact with leader behavior (directive, nondirective) and with elements of the situation (interpersonal stress and the nature of the group's task).

A fairly recent theory, the Cognitive Resources theory has not been as yet the subject of much research to validate its assumptions. Yukl (1995) points out methodological problems and weaknesses in the theory. The Cognitive Resources theory is useful, however, because it focuses on the ability of the leader and collaborator, a component that few other models explore.

According to Cognitive Resources theory, directiveness (giving specific instructions) is most effective when leaders are competent, relaxed, and supported. Because the group is prepared, a directive style is the clearest way to communicate with them. However, when leaders experience stress, experience becomes more important than ability. Low support means the group is less receptive and the leader will have lower effectiveness. A nondirective leader (who does not give specific instructions) with high group support makes group member ability more critical. Weak support, however, gives more power to variables outside the leader or the group members.

Multiple Linkage Theory

Yukl (1995) looked at the interaction of "managerial" behavior and situational factors on the performance of the manager's work group. He recognizes the importance of six intervening variables that are aspects of member motivation and ability.

These intervening variables interact singly or in combination with situational variables comparable to Kerr and Jermier's (1978) *substitutes* and *neutralizers.*

Yukl offers two major propositions for the **Multiple Linkage theory:**

1. In the short term, unit effectiveness is greater when the leader acts to correct any deficiencies in the intervening variables.
2. In the longer term, unit effectiveness is greater when the leader acts to make the situation more favorable. After extinguishing fires, in other words, leaders should focus on the situation rather than directly on the intervening variables.

Among the long-term actions he cites are:

* Cultivating better relationships with suppliers, finding alternative sources, and reducing dependence on unreliable sources
* Undertaking long-term improvement programs to upgrade personnel, equipment, and facilities
* Modifying the work unit's formal structure to solve chronic problems and reduce demands on the leader to perform troubleshooting (Yukl, 1994)

This approach is illustrated by Louella Thompson (profiled at the end of the chapter).[1]

Life Cycle Model

In an interesting turnabout, Paul Hersey and Kenneth Blanchard (1969) envision that the effectiveness of leaders' styles depends largely on their collaborators' job experience and emotional maturity. This is the **Life Cycle model.** Maturity is defined as the ability to perform a job independently, the tendency to assume additional responsibility, and the desire to achieve success.

Hersey and Blanchard outline four types of leader behaviors:

1. Telling (best for group members with low levels of maturity)
2. Selling (effective with members at moderately low maturity levels)
3. Participating (effective with moderately high levels of maturity)
4. Delegating (best with those at the very highest maturity levels)

The model posits two basic decision styles: task orientation and relationship orientation.

1. This approach is illustrated in the profile on Doctors Without Borders.

As group members become more "ready" (mature), leaders should change their behaviors to reflect this increased maturity. Increased maturity is defined as an increase in collaborator readiness and ability. As collaborators mature, leaders should begin to focus on supportive behavior and less on task behavior until followers reach the highest phase of maturity, a stage Hersey and Blanchard termed *high readiness.*

At this stage, followers have become skilled, confident, and self-sufficient. When followers reach this stage, the task of the leader is to delegate and thus serve as a low-task, low-relationship leader. In Hersey and Blanchard's Life Cycle model, the following leadership skills are needed:

- Ability to identify followers' maturity for specific tasks
- Ability to diagnose demands of situations
- Ability to choose the appropriate decision style to match task and follower requirements

The model has been well received by leadership practitioners, perhaps in part because it is intuitive and focuses on the followers' feelings of competence, as well as on their behaviors.

Leader–Member Exchange (LMX) Model

The **Leader–Member Exchange model,** or the **LMX model,** developed by George Graen (1975), operates on the premise that all subordinates are not treated equally. Because of a combination of time constraints and human nature, the model assumes that leaders tend to spend disproportionate amounts of time with a select group of subordinates who are, thus, the *in-group.* Those in the in-group tend to perform at a higher level than subordinates who fall in the *out-group.*

Graen says that early on in the relationship, a leader determines whether another person will be part of the in-group. Precise criteria for making this determination are unclear, but some suggest that the decision is affected by three characteristics of the subordinates/collaborators:

1. Characteristics similar to the leader's
2. A higher degree of competence than members of the out-group
3. Higher levels of extraversion than out-group members

Research on the LMX theory is still preliminary and questions exist about the ways in which leaders make the determinations of in- versus out-groups. What is clear, however, is that leaders invariably devote more time to certain employees and that the selection process is not a random one.

Kouzes and Posner in *The Leadership Challenge* (1994) illustrate how leadership and management must blend. The following essay was specifically written for this text.

The Ten Most Important Things We've Learned about Learning to Lead

by James M. Kouzes and Barry Z. Posner

1. Challenge Provides the Opportunity for Greatness—in Leading and in Learning to Lead

Draw a line down the middle of a piece of paper. Now think of the leaders you admire. Write the names of leaders you admire in the left-hand column. In the right-hand column, record the events or situations with which you identify these individuals. We predict that you will have associated the leaders from business with corporate turnarounds, entrepreneurial ventures, new product/service development and other business transformations. For those leaders in the military, government, the community, the arts or the church, clubs and student organizations, we predict a similar association with transforming events and times.

When we think of leaders, we recall periods of turbulence, conflict, innovation, and change.

But we need not investigate well-known leaders to discover that all leadership is associated with pioneering efforts. In our research, we asked thousands of people, both individual contributors and those in management positions, to write personal best leadership cases. It struck us that these cases were about significant change. When the participants in our studies—be they college students or senior citizens, from communities or corporations, from the boiler room to the boardroom—recalled doing their personal best as leaders, they automatically associated their best with changing, innovating, and overcoming difficulties. These personal best leadership cases illustrate that challenging opportunities provide "ordinary" people the chance to demonstrate extraordinary leadership actions. "The biggest lesson I learned from my personal best [involving his college baseball team]," Karl Thompson explained, "is that you will never know if something will work if you don't try it."

A similar realization came when we asked people how they learned to lead. They responded overwhelmingly: "trial and error." Experience, it appears, is indeed the best teacher—but not just any experience. To describe how their "personal best leadership" and learning experience felt, people used the words "exciting," "exhilarating," "rewarding," and "fun." Dull, routine, boring experiences—in the classroom or in the boardroom—did not provide anyone anywhere with the opportunity to excel or to learn. Only challenge presents the opportunity for greatness. Leaders are pioneers—people who take risks in innovation and experiment to find new and better ways of doing things. Learners are also venturers.

2. Leadership Is in the Eye of the Beholder

Constituents choose leaders. Leaders cannot be appointed or anointed "superiors." Constituents determine whether someone is fit to lead. Power and position may offer the right to exercise authority, but we should never, ever, mistake position and authority for leadership. Only when our constituents believe that we are capable of meeting their expectations will we be able to mobilize their actions.

When we view leadership from this perspective, the relationship is turned upside down. From this vantage, leaders serve their constituents; they do not boss them around. The best leaders are the servants of others' wants and desires, hopes and dreams. And to be able to respond to the needs of others, leaders must first get to know their constituents. By knowing them, listening to them, and taking their advice, leaders can stand before others and say with assurance, "Here is what I heard you say that you want for yourselves. Here is how your own needs and interests will be served by enlisting in a common cause."

This notion of leaders as servants flies in the face of the leaders-as-heroes myth perpetuated in comic books, novels, and movies. Yet it is the single most important factor in that dynamic relationship between leader and constituent. Unless we are sensitive to subtle cues, we cannot respond to the aspirations of others. And if we cannot respond to their aspirations, they will not follow.

3. Credibility Is the Foundation of Leadership

We also researched the expectations people have of those whom they would be willing to follow. We asked more than 25,000 people from a range of organizations around the globe to tell us what they admired and looked for in their leaders. According to this data, people want leaders who are honest, forward-looking, inspiring, and competent.

While these results aren't surprising, they are extraordinarily significant to all leaders, because three of the four characteristics comprise what communications experts refer to as "source credibility." When determining whether or not we believe someone who is communicating with us—whether that person is a teacher, newscaster, salesperson, manager, parent, or colleague—we look for trustworthiness (honesty), expertise (competence), and dynamism (inspiration). Credibility is a leader's single most important asset, and it should be protected and nurtured at all costs. Personal credibility is the foundation on which leaders stand. We call this the *First Law of Leadership*—if you don't believe in the messenger, you won't believe the message. This is precisely what Michael Cole learned as a 16-year-old T-ball coach: "Once the kids [ages 4–8] saw that I wanted what was best for them as well as sharing in their excitement, they became a lot more trusting of me."

4. The Ability to Inspire a Shared Vision Differentiates Leaders from Other Credible Sources

While credibility is the foundation, leaders must envision an uplifting and ennobling future. The one admired leadership quality not a criterion of source credibility is "forward-looking." We expect leaders to take us to places we have never been before—to have clearly in mind an attractive destination that will make the journey worthwhile. "Leadership isn't telling people what to do," says Anthony Bianchi, who organized a ski trip to the Italian Alps for American college students studying in Florence: "It's painting a picture of an exciting possibility of how we can achieve a common goal."

To distinguish ourselves as leaders, we must be concerned with the future of our groups, organizations, and communities. If there is no vision, there is no business. The domain of leaders is the future. The leader's unique legacy is the creation of valued programs and institutions that survive over time.

Equally important, however, is the leader's capacity to enlist others to transform the vision into reality. We found that the ability to inspire others to share the dream—to communicate the vision so that others come to embrace it as their own—was what uplifted constituents and drew them forward. Leaders in any endeavor must demonstrate personal enthusiasm for the dream. Only passion will ignite the flames of our constituents' desires.

5. *Without Trust, You Cannot Lead*

While we asked people to recount *their* "personal best leadership" experiences, they typically came to realize that it wasn't really "*my* best; it was *our* best. Because it wasn't *me; it was us.*" Leaders can't do it alone! In fact, no one ever achieved an extraordinary milestone all by himself or herself—it is a team effort (and notice there is no "i" in the word team).

At the heart of these collaborative efforts is trust. Leaders genuinely desire to make heroes and heroines of others. Without trust, people become self-protective and controlling. Similarly, when there is low trust, people are likely to distort, ignore and disguise facts, ideas, conclusions and feelings. People become suspicious and unreceptive. A trusting relationship between leader and constituents is essential to getting extraordinary things done.

Leaders create a caring climate—a climate of trust. For people to disclose their needs and feelings, to make themselves vulnerable, to expose their weaknesses, to risk failing, they must truly believe they are safe. For example, in learning to parachute jump, people will probably not be eager to jump if they do not trust the instructor or the equipment. Trust must be established before people will risk learning something new.

Another primary task of leadership is to create a climate in which others feel powerful, efficacious, and strong. In such a climate, people know they are free to take risks, trusting that when they make mistakes the leader will not ask "Who's to blame?" but, "What did we learn?"

Involvement and participation are essential to create this climate. Giving free choice and listening to others are other important elements of a trusting environment. Leaders focus on fostering collaboration, strengthening others and building trust—on giving their power away—as the most effective strategies for enhancing the power of everyone.

6. *Shared Values Make a Critical Difference in the Quality of Life at Home and at Work*

Credibility—that single most important leadership asset we mentioned earlier—has at its root the word "credo," meaning a set of beliefs. Every leader must begin by asking, "What do I stand for? What do I believe in? What values do I hold to be true and right?" Through our research, we found that people who reported greater compatibility between personal values and the values of their organizations also reported significantly greater feelings of success in their lives, had greater under-standings of the values of their managers and coworkers, were more willing to work longer and harder hours, and felt less stress at home and on the job. Shared values are essential for personal and business health.

Shared values provide a sense of alignment, so that, just like a rowing team, everyone is pulling in the same direction. Feeling aligned is empowering, creating a sense of freedom and personal integrity. When people feel that their personal val-ues are in synch with those of their organization, our research indicates they are personally more successful and healthier. They feel liberated and in control of their lives. Shared values enable everyone to experience ownership in the organization.

7. *Leaders Are Role Models for Their Constituents*

When we asked people to define credibility behaviorally, the most common response was, "Do what you say you will do." People believe in actions more than in words, in practices more than in pronouncements. It's simply not sufficient to communicate values and beliefs. We must live them, and leaders are expected to set the example for others.

Mindy Behse, for example, reported that when she was captain of her high school swim team, her teammates watched what she did: "I couldn't ask anybody to do anything I wasn't willing to do. I had to take practices very seriously." Blaine Thomas learned quickly that being captain of his baseball team meant that peo-ple not only watched what he did on the field, but off the field as well. And, he pointed out, "I couldn't be one kind of a leader, with certain standards on the field, and then be some other kind of person or leader off the field with differ-ent, especially lower, standards." As the team leader of a group of student painters during the summer, Mike Burciago observed that his willingness to do his share of the "grubby work" made it easier to get others to voluntarily do their share as well.

Credibility is earned minute-by-minute, hour-by-hour through actions con-sistent with stated values. Values are often considered the soft side of manage-ment, but based on our research, we would say that nothing is more difficult than to be unwaveringly true to one's guiding beliefs.

8. *Lasting Change Progresses One Hop at a Time*

When we asked Don Bennett, the first amputee to reach the 14,410-foot summit of Mt. Rainier, how he was able to climb to that height, he replied, looking down at his one leg and foot, "One hop at a time." When preparing for the climb, he would imag-ine himself on top of the mountain 1,000 times a day. But when he started to climb, he'd look down at his foot and say, "'Anybody can hop from here to there.' So I did."

Big results from small beginnings. "Our goal seemed enormous; so we broke it down into parts and gave one part to each member," is how Richard Cabral accounts for the success of his high school organization in hosting a dinner for more than 300 people, including parents and the city's mayor. Progress is always incremental. The key to lasting improvement is small wins. Choosing to do the easy things first—those that can be accomplished quickly and inexpensively by a team with a local champion—is the only sure way to achieve extraordinary things in organizations. Referring to his own struggles against the seemingly insolvable problem of South Africa's apartheid, Bishop Tutu noted: "You eat an elephant...one bite at a time!"

9. *Leadership Development Is Self-Development*

Leaders take us to places we have never been before. But there are no freeways to the future, no paved highways to unknown, unexplored destinations. There is only wilderness. If we are to step into the unknown, we must begin by exploring the inner territory.

Leadership is an art—a performing art. And in the art of leadership, the instrument is the self. A musician may have a violin, an engineer a workstation and an accountant a computer. But a leader has only himself or herself as the medium of expression. Leadership development, then, is essentially a process of self-development.

The self-confidence required to lead comes from learning about ourselves—our skills, prejudices, talents, and shortcomings. Self-confidence develops as we build on strengths and overcome weaknesses. As Larry Olin, captain of his college tennis team, learned: "You must be confident in yourself before you can expect others to be confident in you."

People frequently ask, "Are leaders born or made?" We firmly believe that leadership can be learned. Certainly, some people are more predisposed to lead than others. But this is true of anything. Leadership is definitely not a divine-like grace given to a few charismatic men and women. It is a set of learnable practices. We believe it is possible for ordinary people to learn to get extraordinary things done. There is a leader in everyone, and the greatest inhibitor to leadership development is the belief that leadership cannot be learned.

Developing ourselves as leaders requires removing the barriers, whether self-imposed or imposed by the organization, and understanding that development is a continuous improvement process, not an event, a class, a book, or series of programs.

10. *Leadership Is Not an Affair of the Head,*
It Is an Affair of the Heart

Leadership is emotional. Period. To lead others requires passionate commitment to a set of fundamental beliefs and principles, visions, and dreams. The climb to the summit is arduous and often frightening. Leaders encourage others to continue the quest by inspiring them with courage and hope.

In our study of leadership, we often asked our interviewees how they would go about developing leaders, whether in school, business, government, or volunteer organizations. Major General John Stanford, then Commander of the U.S. Army's Military Traffic Management Command, gave a memorable reply: "When people ask me that question, I tell them I have the secret to success in life. The secret to success is to stay in love." Not the advice we expected from a Major General or from any of the people we interviewed, but the more we thought about it, the more we realized that leadership is an affair of the heart. Constituents will not follow unless they are persuaded that their leader passionately believes in his or her view of the future and believes in each of them.

More than ever before, there is a need for people to answer the call for leadership—to seize the opportunities for greatness. Only by looking inside our hearts will we know when we are ready to take that first step along the journey to the future.

James Kouzes and **Barry Posner** are co-authors of two award-winning and best-selling books on leadership: *The Leadership Challenge: How to Keep Getting Extraordinary Things Done in Organizations* (San Francisco: Jossey-Bass, 1995) and *Credibility: How Leaders Gain and Lose It, Why People Demand It* (San Francisco; Jossey-Bass, 1993). Kouzes is CEO of The Tom Peters Group/Learning Systems (Palo Alto, Calif.) and Posner is Professor of Organizational Behavior and Managing Partner, Executive Development Center, Santa Clara University (Santa Clara, Calif.).

DOCTORS WITHOUT BORDERS
Healing Humanity

What has more than 5,000 legs and appears in the wake of natural and man-made disasters across the world?

The answer: Doctors Without Borders, an organization of more than 2,500 medical professionals who serve people in all manner of crises across the globe.

Begun in France in 1971, the organization offers health care to people would who have no access otherwise. The members witness atrocities but take no sides in the political disputes that may have brought about the disasters.

Because they send representatives into trouble spots even before being asked, their presence has caused some diplomatic and political tension. But that hasn't kept them from showing up and helping out.

Typically, the group sends a team of people to an area to lay the groundwork for the actual medical care. This advance team asks refugees what kinds of medical care they need the most, then works with local authorities to set up more permanent solutions.

For its humanitarian work in such locales as Uganda, Kosovo, China, the Philippines, and Sri Lanka—eighty locales at last count—Doctors Without Borders won the 1999 Nobel Peace Prize. "As entire families are chased from their homes in East Timor and as thousands more are targeted in conflicts around the world,...the Nobel Prize is an important confirmation of the fundamental right of ordinary people to humanitarian assistance and protection," said the group's spokesman, James Orbinski.

(For more information visit http://www.doctorswithoutborders.org/.)

LOUELLA THOMPSON
Founder of "Feed the Hungry"

Since 1987, Louella Thompson has been working on an all-consuming assignment. That year, the Middletown, Ohio, hairdresser says God told her, "Open the door and feed whoever comes. Don't ask any questions."

For the past twelve years that's exactly what the seventy-four-year-old has done, fixing hot meals for free carryout or delivery for several hundred people a month. (That doesn't count the donuts, juice, and coffee she hands out to a steady stream of children and adults each morning.) She chose the fourth Saturday of the month for the hot meals because by that time, many people's budgets were stretched to the breaking point.

Thompson supervises volunteers from all over the area, and graciously accepts donations of food, money, clothing, and old roasting units (her crowded kitchen now has five electric units in addition to her original stove). There are "five or six" freezers scattered throughout her combination house/office/soup kitchen.

For six years she was a regular presence at county commissioner meetings, promoting the Feed the Hungry project. Her mission of feeding and not asking questions has captured the city's attention, bringing donations and volunteer help from groups and individuals. Community groups, including adults on probation and mentally retarded young people, schedule weekly sessions to help out with bagging food or peeling apples or helping in some other specific way. Thompson welcomes all contributions—of time, service, and money. "I'm not hard to please," she says. "Whatever people want to do to help feed the hungry, that's all right with me."

Her biggest project sits on the lot next to her house: a partially completed two-story community kitchen, which she envisions serving not only the nutritional needs of the community but also its spiritual needs by providing meeting areas for drug and alcohol recovery groups.

The building would have been completed long ago, she acknowledges, if she had accepted government money. "But to do that, I would have to ask the people I feed questions about their work, etc. I won't do that."

As a result, the building has been five long years in the making. Currently, the shell is up and the walls are framed, but there is little progress beyond that. She's waiting, patiently, for the electrician who volunteers his time to complete the blueprints so that the city can approve them.

Thompson shies from being called a leader. "God is the leader," she asserts. "I just do what He tells me to." Rev. Martin Luther King Jr. exemplifies leadership for her. "He was humble. People tried to use him, but he kept on doing what he had to do," she says.

For her, that meant visiting the presidents of the local banks—not to ask for money, but to inform them of her plans. "I wouldn't see anyone else but the presidents. I had no fear," she says, smiling at the memory of marching into those executive offices and waiting for an appointment.

Her rewards for leading this effort against hunger? "I just enjoy seeing people happy. It makes me happy to see people eating good food." Her generosity is contagious. Often, people drop off food, saying they were returning the favor of eating there. "They know how it feels to be hungry and get a good meal," she says. "I feel real good to see them giving to someone else."

On a larger scale, her efforts have inspired several other food programs in the community. "I'm glad to see them popping up in other places, because the times are hard. And they're going to get harder before they get better," she says, noting that she meditates each day to find the guidance and energy to persist.

Asked how she maintains her vigorous schedule, she admits to getting tired sometimes, especially after staying up the entire night to help prepare the community meal. "I just work it," she says with a shrug.

She maintains a confidence in people's willingness to help. "I just love that I don't have to call people to help. They just do it. That way, I don't feel like I'm making them do it. I feel if I leave it open, they'll do it for themselves, not to please me."

Her advice to younger people: "Search yourself. Let your mind tell you what to do."

(For more information visit http://www.odjfs.state.oh.us/women/Halloffame/bio.asp?ID=294.)

✦ Chapter Summary

This chapter begins with a review of trait theories of leadership, featuring the work of such prominent leadership experts as John Gardner, Warren Bennis, James Kouzes, and Barry Posner. Behavioral theories are also addressed, beginning with the Ohio State and University of Michigan studies. A section on situational approaches includes reviews of Path–Goal theory, Continuum of Leader Behavior, Cognitive Resources theory, Multiple Linkage theory, Life Cycle model, and Leader–Member Exchange model.

✦ CREATE YOUR OWN THEORY ✦

In this chapter you have been exposed to a broad range of major leadership theories, from trait to behavioral to situational. Did you find yourself nodding to yourself more when reading about a particular approach? If so, which approaches fit best with your own view on leadership? Can you imagine situations in which a behavioral approach would be most effective and other situations in which a situational perspective would be more effective?

Now let's revisit our opening Leadership Moment. What factors must leaders of large systems, such as school principals, consider when attempting to bring about change? What tack would you take were you in this principal's shoes, and what are the strengths and pitfalls of such an approach?

✦ Key Terms

achievement-oriented leadership

Cognitive Resources theory

directive leadership

LMX model

Leadership Grid

Life Cycle model

Multiple Linkage theory

Ohio State studies

participative leadership   supportive leadership

Path–Goal theory   University of Michigan studies

Situational Leadership Model

◆ Questions for Discussion and Review

1. According to Gardner, what should be the primary aims and tasks of leaders?
2. What are some of the historical assumptions behind the characteristics of great leaders?
3. What were the primary similarities and differences between the University of Michigan studies and the Ohio State studies?
4. Select five leaders. Where would their leadership style fall on the Leadership Grid, and why?
5. In what situations do you feel a directive leadership style would be most appropriate? A supportive style? Participative style? Achievement-oriented style?
6. In which situations would a relationship-oriented leader be most effective? A task-oriented leader?
7. Of the numerous leadership theories proposed, which speaks to you most, and why?
8. How are the leadership theories in this chapter reflective of American culture? How might other cultures view these approaches?
9. Do you think that there are any universal attributes of leaders, or are leadership traits always culturally and/or situationally bound?

◆ Online Self-Assessment Tool

Are you more task oriented or people oriented? To see where you fall on Blake and Mouton's Leadership Grid, take their online quiz at: http://www.nwlink.com/~donclark/leader/bm_model.html.

◆ Exercises

Exercise 11–1   Using Path–Goal Theory to Select a Leadership Strategy

Directions: Think of a group of which you are or have been a member. This can be a student organization (SGA, activities board, sorority/fraternity, etc.), a team (sports, debate, chess, etc.), an institution (church, Boy/Girl Scouts, college, etc.), or a workplace. Use what you have learned about Path–Goal theory to select an appropriate leadership style for that particular organization.

Name of group/organization: _____

Evaluating two sets of contingency factors—types of subordinates and types of work. Rate each factor by circling the appropriate indicator below.

Factor #1—*Locus of Control:*
In this organization, members feel like it is:

	High	Medium	Low

Factor #2—*Prediction of Positive:*
In this organization, members think that their:

Performance: Will Be   May Be   Probably Will Be
       Successful   Successful   Unsuccessful

Factor #3—*Members' Tasks:*
In this organization, they are:

     Repetitive   Combination   Nonrepetitive

Factor #4—*Authority Within the:*
In this organization, the authority system is:

     Authoritarian   Mixed   Democratic

Factor #5—*Work Group:*
In this organization, there are:

High Morale	Mixed	Low Morale
and		and
Satisfying		Unsatisfying
Relationships		Relationships

Based on your analysis of the organization's contingency factors, which of House's four leadership styles would be best suited? Circle the most appropriate leadership style.

Directive   Supportive   Participative   Achievement-Oriented

Key

Using the key on page ____, how well did your analysis of the five contingency factors match the selection of the most appropriate leadership style?

Directive Style: Factor #1—Low
                      Factor #2—Maybe → Probably Not
                      Factor #3—Ambiguous
                      Factor #4—Authoritarian
                      Factor #5—Low Morale

Supportive Style: Factor #1—Low
                      Factor #2—Maybe → Probably Not
                      Factor #3—Combination
                      Factor #4—Mixed → Democratic
                      Factor #5—Low Morale

Participative Style: Factor #1—Medium → High
Factor #2—Will Be Successful
Factor #3—Nonrepetitive
Factor #4—Mixed → Democratic
Factor #5—High Morale

Achievement-Oriented Style:
Factor #1—High
Factor #2—Will Be Successful
Factor #3—Nonrepetitive
Factor #4—Mixed → Democratic
Factor #5—Mixed → High Morale

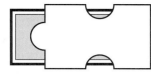

CHAPTER 12

Leadership Theories
and Approaches for
Today and Tomorrow

■ ■ ■

LEADERSHIP MOMENT

You have recently been elected to your first term on the local school board. Over the past several years, discontent has been growing about the students' declining test scores. This has been a concern of yours as well, since two of your children attend schools where there has been a particularly sharp decline. Although most schools within the district have been experiencing difficulty, one school, Smith Elementary, in the most affluent section of town, has been thriving. Not only are test scores on the rise at Smith, but, not coincidentally, each year this school is granted a larger portion of the overall budget, and parents compete to have their children placed at Smith. Morale has plummeted at the other district schools, whose staff members feel that they are being asked to do more with less money and fewer staff.

The State Board of Education has threatened to dramatically reduce funding unless your district's overall test scores rise. In response, a proposal has been made that all students must take math and reading exams at the end of each year before advancing to the next grade. Widely supported, the proposal is being hailed by other school board members as the solution to the declining test score issue. You are not so sure that this is the case. At this week's board meeting you must take a position on this issue.

1. What would you do?

2. What factors will play a role in your decision?

In the midst of the heyday of the industrial approach to leadership, the seeds of a new paradigm of leadership were being planted. Several scholars broke with mainstream thinking about leadership and began to describe it in radically different ways. As we saw in previous chapters, the industrial view of leadership:

- Saw leadership as the property of an individual
- Considered leadership primarily in the context of formal groups or organizations
- Equated concepts of management and leadership

However, the reality of leadership as experienced by many did not always fit these circumstances. Leadership occurred outside of formal organizations and was sometimes practiced by those other than designated leaders. As Kuhn (1970) taught us, no paradigm can explain all of the facts of a particular phenomenon. Several authors began to explore the aspects of leadership not captured in the old story of leadership. Their ideas served as a bridge from the industrial to the postindustrial perspectives of leadership (Figure 12-1). We turn now to three of these transition theories to examine their assumptions about leadership.

◆ THE GENESIS OF A NEW PARADIGM: SERVANT LEADERSHIP

In his work *The Leader as Servant* (1970), Robert Greenleaf made a radical departure from the industrial paradigm of the leader as an all-knowing, all-powerful hero. Instead, he proposed that "the great leader is seen as servant first" (p. 2). Greenleaf's conclusion was based on the changes he saw emerging in U.S. society at the time, namely, the questioning of power and authority and the emergence of cooperation and support as more productive ways for people to relate to one another. Greenleaf explains:

> A new moral principle is emerging that holds that the only authority deserving one's allegiance is that which is freely and knowingly granted

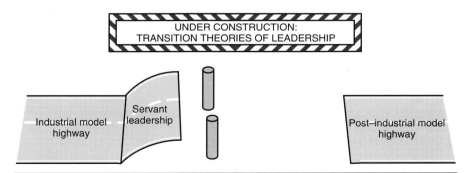

FIGURE 12-1   Under Construction: Transition Theories of Leadership

by the led to the leader in response to, and in proportion to, the clearly evident servant stature of the leader. Those who choose to follow this principle will not casually accept the authority of existing institutions. Rather, they will freely respond only to individuals who are chosen as leaders because they are proven and trusted as servants. To the extent that this principle prevails in the future, the only truly viable institutions will be those that are predominantly servant-led. (p. 4)

Greenleaf (1970) fleshed out this notion of **servant leadership** by stressing that the servant leader is servant first. The servant leader takes care to ensure that other people's greatest needs are being met and that those people, while being served by the leader, "become healthier, wiser, freer, more autonomous, more likely themselves to become servants" (p. 7). According to Greenleaf, servant leaders:

- Listen first so they may understand a situation
- Develop their intuition and the ability to "foresee the unforeseeable" (p. 14)
- Lead by persuasion, forging change by "convincement rather than coercion" (p. 21)
- Conceptualize the reforms they seek and lift others to see the possibilities as well
- Empower by creating opportunities and alternatives for those being served

Servant leaders possess the self-awareness to recognize that their own healing is the motivation for leadership. They also grasp that the connection between the servant leader and the led is "the understanding that the search for wholeness is something they share." And finally, as a change agent, the servant leader recognizes that the first step to changing the world is changing oneself.

The image of servant leader contrasts with the industrial paradigm of the leader as a power-wielding authority figure. Here we see the leader as one whose first responsibility is to consider the needs of others and to create conditions where the led can become leaders themselves. To illustrate the idea of the leader as servant, Greenleaf tells the story of John Woolman, an American Quaker who almost single-handedly rid the Society of Friends (Quakers) of slaves. What Greenleaf particularly remarks on is the method that Woolman used to bring about this change—gentle, yet clear and persistent persuasion. Greenleaf elaborates:

Although John Woolman was not a strong man physically, he accomplished his mission by journeys up and down the East Coast by foot or horseback visiting slaveholders—over a period of many years. The approach was not to censure the slaveholders in a way that drew their animosity. Rather, the burden of his approach was to raise questions: What does the owning of slaves do to you as a moral person? What kind of an institution are you binding over to your children? Man by man, inch by inch, by persistently returning and revisiting and pressing his gentle argument over a period of thirty years, the scourge of slavery was eliminated from this Society, the first religious group in America formally to denounce and forbid slavery among its members. (p. 21)

#2   John Woolman was a man with a personal conviction that led him to seek change in his organization. He achieved his objective through what Greenleaf calls *convincement* rather than *coercion.* In the process, he made his Quaker brothers and sisters leaders in their own right. This is the essence of servant leadership.

◆ TRANSFORMATIONAL LEADERSHIP

James MacGregor Burns extended the debate about what makes up leadership by conceptualizing it as occurring in two forms, transactional and transformational. He arrived at this conclusion through analysis of the leadership functions of such political figures as Mahatma Gandhi (profiled in Chapter 7 on philosophy), Franklin Roosevelt (profiled in Chapter 8 on political science), and Mao Tse-tung (profiled in Chapter 13 on military leadership). In prefacing his work, Burns (1999) noted that the concept of leadership in this century had "dissolved into small and discrete meanings" (p. 2). In seeking to generalize about the leadership process across time and cultures, he wanted to establish a school of leadership where none existed. In addition, Burns desired to unite the previously unconnected roles of leader and follower. These, then, became the foundational assumptions that underscored his perspectives of leadership (Figure 12-2).

#3   According to Burns, **transactional leadership** is a barter, an exchange of wants between leader and follower. The transactional leader satisfies followers' needs by entering into a relationship of mutual dependence in which the contributions of both sides are recognized and rewarded. The transactional leader helps followers achieve their goals; thus, we follow the transactional leader because it is obvious to us that it is in our own best interests to do so (Kellerman, 1983). The image of leadership as transaction has assumptions in common with the industrial paradigm of leadership.

Transformational leadership, by contrast, goes beyond the notion of exchange. Burns (1979) proposed that transformational leadership includes two

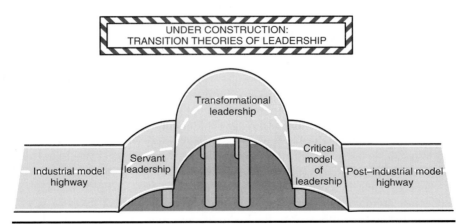

FIGURE 12-2   Under Construction: Transition Theories of Leadership

essential elements—it is relational, and it deals with producing real change. He explains: "Transformational leadership occurs when one or more persons engage with others in such a way that leaders and followers raise one another to higher levels of motivation and morality" (p. 20). This approach is a commingling of their needs and aspirations and goals in a common enterprise. The purpose of this engagement with followers, Burns tells us, is to bring about change. In fact, in his estimation, the ultimate test of practical leadership is the realization of intended, actual change in people's lives, attitudes, behaviors, and their institutions. Transformational leadership has a moral dimension as well, because those engaged in it "can be lifted into their better selves" (p. 462). This articulation of the moral dimension sharply distinguishes transformational leadership from the views of leadership promoted by management scientists.

Mahatma Gandhi, in particular, epitomized Burns's ideal of the transformational leader. Gandhi's leadership was *causative* in that the nonviolent and egalitarian values he espoused changed people and institutions in India. His leadership was *morally purposeful,* because his objective was to win individual liberty for his countrymen and women by freeing them from the oppression of British rule. His leadership was *elevating* in that he raised his followers to higher moral ground by engaging them in nonviolent activities to achieve social justice. In so doing, Gandhi asked for sacrifices from his followers rather than merely promising them goods and favors.

Burns's seminal work enlightened us to see that leadership is about transformation. It is a relationship between leaders and followers in which both are elevated to more principled levels of judgment. It is about leaders and followers engaged in a change process. It is about power *to* rather than power *over.* Burns and Greenleaf's ideas began to transform our notions of leadership.

✦ A CRITICAL MODEL OF LEADERSHIP

William Foster (1986) and other critical theorists (e.g., Smyth, 1989) honed in on the concept of leadership as transformation by examining the content of the change that the leadership process might produce. They specified that leadership should address social reconstruction: "Leadership is and must be socially critical, it does not reside in an individual but in the relationship between individuals, and it is oriented toward social vision and change, not simply, or only, organizational goals" (p. 46).

Transformational leaders and followers may be mutually pursuing a vision of greatness, but the critical question becomes "whose vision is it?" In the critical perspective, for transformational leadership to actually transform, it must prompt those engaged in the process to question the assumptions on which their vision is based.

Thus, **critical transformational leadership** requires reflection and analysis: it asks on whose behalf we use our power and makes a place for all voices and arguments to be heard regardless of race, class, and gender (Quantz, Rogers & Dantley, 1991). The critical model of leadership focuses on changing the human condition, and as such, its type of leadership can spring from anywhere. It is not confined to the organizational hierarchy. In this view, leadership is a political and courageous act to empower followers to become leaders themselves.

And finally, Foster (1989) asserts that critical transformational leadership is not "a special or unique occurrence, one that is found only in certain grand moments of human history. Rather, it happens in everyday events, when commonplace leaders exert some effect on their situations" (p. 52).

A good example of leadership from the critical perspective is the work of Brazilian educator Paulo Freire. Rejecting the standard educational pedagogy that helped maintain the social systems oppressing Brazilian peasants, he developed teaching methods he called *liberation education*. First Freire taught the peasants to critique the system that kept them in economic slavery, and then he taught them about the possibility of reforming that system so their voices would be heard and their needs would be recognized equally with the wealthier citizens in the society (Freire, 1970). His leadership empowered his followers to initiate change on their own behalf.

◆ LEADERSHIP SKILLS FOR THE FUTURE

Several common themes emerge from an analysis of this chapter's three perspectives on leadership (servant, transformational, and critical models).

1. *Leadership is a relationship, as opposed to the property of an individual.* It is conducted with leaders and followers, and followers are essential parts of the equation. The role of the leader is to serve followers and to empower them to become leaders themselves.

2. *Leadership entails change.* Both leaders and followers experience change, originating within themselves and then emanating outward to the community. Leadership requires critical reflection and analysis in order to determine whether the vision of change being pursued is inclusive or whether it excludes or diminishes some members of the community.

3. *Leadership can be done by anyone, not only those who are designated as leaders.* Alternative perspectives on leadership gained credence because they more fully captured some aspects of our experience with leadership than did the conventional view. Because the alternative perspectives raised questions that could not be addressed by the industrial paradigm of leadership, they prompted the search for a new paradigm of leadership for the twenty-first century.

◆ THE POSTINDUSTRIAL PARADIGM OF LEADERSHIP

In his 1991 book, *Leadership for the Twenty-First Century*, Joseph Rost offered a new definition of leadership that he quite boldly proclaimed as the postindustrial paradigm of leadership. One does not pronounce a new paradigm without substantial evidence of its need. And so it was with Rost. He built a convincing

argument for why the industrial paradigm of leadership is no longer
explain both the realities of leadership we experience and the kind c
we need in a twenty-first-century world.

What are the realities that prompt us to establish a new paradig
ship? U.S. culture is in the midst of a major shift in the ways that we make sense of
our world. The globalization of the economy, the rapid and continual change resulting from new technologies, the information explosion, and the increasing diversity
of our population create a reality that is messy and ambiguous rather than orderly
and predictable (Rogers & Ballard, 1995). As a result, we are moving away from a
mechanistic world view in which objectivity, control, and linear causality are
supreme, to a **relational approach,** a world view that recognizes the more contextual, holistic, complex, and relational aspects of the natural world in which we
function (Zohar, 1997; Wheatley, 1992; Kuh, Whitt & Shedd, 1987).

Among the consequences of the shift from a mechanistic worldview are the
changes in organizational structures and cultures that have been the hallmark of
the past fifteen years (Rogers & Ballard, 1995; Peters, 1992). Table 12-1 contrasts
the culture of the bureaucratic/mechanistic forms of organization with emerging
ad hoc models of organization. The latter are rapidly gaining credibility because
they more effectively respond to the kind of environmental turbulence that
marks our current reality.

Recent research and practice suggest that conventional models of organization are not as suited to understanding events and actions in uncertain, dynamic
times; thus, organizations are transforming themselves in order to better respond
to change. A key activity of the modern organization is to continuously learn and

TABLE 12-1 Organizational Culture Transformations

Old Culture (disappearing bureaucracy)	New Culture (emerging adhocracy)
hierarchy, specialization	transient units
division of labor	reorganization
slow to change	fast moving
roles sharply defined	roles flexible and temporary
chain of command	fluid, participative roles and structures
self-interested outlook	social responsibility is central to success
stable, predictable environment	accelerating change and need for innovation
vertical power	horizontal power, relationships
communication slow, only as needed	communication fast and lateral
simple problem solving	complex problem solving
staff/line distinctions	team approach
emphasis on efficiency	emphasis on people

SOURCE: Adapted from P. Harris, "Innovating with High Achievers," *Training & Development
Journal*, 34, 10 (1980), pp. 45–50.

to master new knowledge in order to innovate, solve problems, and maintain productivity. The quality movement of the 1980s and 1990s is a manifestation of the move away from machine-like forms of organization and management to more team-centered, collaborative approaches.

In a similar vein, Rost (1991) debunks the industrial paradigm of leadership because of its grounding in a mechanistic world view. He argues that the industrial paradigm of leadership is industrial because it takes a bureaucratic view of organizations; it has an individualistic focus because it asserts that only great leaders practice leadership; it is dominated by a goal achievement sense of purpose; it promotes a self-interested outlook on life; it accepts a male model of behavior and power (known as leadership style); it articulates utilitarian and materialistic ethical perspectives; it is grounded in rational, linear, and quantitative assumptions about how the world works, and it asserts a managerial perspective as to what makes organizations tick. Although these characteristics may have been appropriate for a world that was more stable, they are not as relevant in a time of rapid change. In the context of our increasingly complex and ambiguous world, Rost extends the work of Burns, Greenleaf, and Foster and offers a postindustrial paradigm of leadership for our consideration.

Rost's definition—"Leadership is an influence relationship among leaders and their collaborators who intend real changes that reflect their mutual purposes" (1991, p. 7)—includes four essential elements of leadership:

1. *The relationship is based on influence rather than positional authority.* Noncoercive persuasion is used to influence people in the leadership relationship. The influence is multidirectional, coming from all members, rather than only top down. People are free to agree or disagree and to choose to stay in or leave the relationship.

2. *Leaders and their collaborators practice leadership.* The word *collaborators* instead of followers is favored because it more closely fits the values of this perspective. The interactions of leaders and their collaborators form the essence of leadership, not the individual behaviors of the leader. In a leadership relationship, collaborators are active rather than passive. Leaders are those who at a particular moment commit more of their resources (i.e., their expertise, their passion, their political savvy) to influence the process.

3. *Collaborators and their leaders intend real change.* Rost notes that "*Intend* means that the leaders and their collaborators do not have to produce changes to practice leadership, only intend them and then act on that intention" (p. 7). Thus, the very act of initiating a change movement marks the time when leadership occurs, in contrast to the industrial paradigm that leadership happens when any goal has been achieved. **Real change** connotes that the changes are substantive attempts to transform people's attitudes, behaviors, and values.

4. *The changes that the leaders and their collaborators pursue reflect their mutual purposes.* The changes represent what *both* leaders and

collaborators desire in a shared enterprise, rather than merely accomplishing the wishes of the leader.

Several important implications are embedded in this definition of leadership. Collaborators choose the leaders with whom they wish to affiliate, and they may or may not be people who hold authority over them. Thus, leadership is not confined to those in power in the organizational hierarchy. Leaders and collaborators often change places in the ebb and flow of the leadership process. A number of leadership relationships may be present in any organization, and the leaders in one relationship may be collaborators in another.

Leadership is episodic, a stream of activities that occur when people intend a specific and real change for their organization or group. One is not a leader all of the time, but rather, when one chooses to exert the most influence on the change process. Rost (1991) elaborates: "Leadership is people bonding together to institute a change in a group, organization, or society. Leadership is a group of activists who want to implement a reformist agenda. Leadership is a band of leaders and collaborators who envision a better future and go after it" (p. 6).

When first introduced to Rost's conceptualization of postindustrial leadership, we may find it difficult to get a fix on just what it entails. Conditioned by our industrial paradigm lenses to view leadership in a particular way, much like the blind men and the elephant in the Indian tale, we have difficulty seeing beyond our own narrow perspective. In particular, we have been so enmeshed in viewing leadership and management as one and the same that untangling these concepts becomes difficult. Similarly, we have problems conceiving of leadership as not grounded in positional authority—hence, not naturally accruing to those managers at the top levels of the hierarchy. Yet in order to separate leadership from management, these distinctions are important.

Rost's work challenges us to clearly distinguish between these two concepts. In the industrial paradigm, leadership has been understood as good management, even though it was implied that a manager was somehow less effective than a leader. The industrial paradigm confers much more desirability to being considered a leader than a manager, a perspective captured in the oft-quoted words of Bennis and Nanus (1985): "Managers do things right; leaders do the right thing." While managers are pedestrian, leaders are visionary.

In the postindustrial paradigm, the two concepts are defined as distinct activities. One is not better than the other; they are simply different—and equally important—processes in a postindustrial world. Rost (1991) envisions the two roles playing out in formal organizations in this way:

> Leaders and collaborators are the people involved in a leadership relationship....Managers and subordinates are the people involved in managerial relationships....The two sets of words are not synonymous. Leaders are not the same as managers. Collaborators are not the same as subordinates. Managers may be leaders but if they are leaders, they are involved in a relationship different from management. Subordinates may be collaborators, but if they are collaborators they are involved in a relationship different

than management. Leaders need not be managers to be leaders. Collaborators need not be subordinates to be collaborators. (p. 150)

Rost asserts that the way in which influence is exercised is an important distinction between leadership and management. In his view, leadership is a relationship in which only noncoercive influence behaviors are acceptable, rather than one wherein all legitimate behaviors (including authority and other forms of coercion) are acceptable.

✦ SOME ADDITIONAL POSTINDUSTRIAL MODELS OF LEADERSHIP

Just as Rost specifically offered a new definition of leadership and labeled it the postindustrial paradigm, other scholars have also proposed new views of leadership in the face of the dramatic changes occurring in Western culture as we enter the new millennium. For example, Bensimon and Neumann (1993) draw from their own research, their analysis of others' research, and their own experiences in organizations to describe the ideal leader in the future. They conclude that the age of the heroic, solo leader is over. **Collaborative leadership,** they insist, is necessary to respond to the information-rich and complex environment of the twenty-first century. One mind can comprehend only so much; we need the combination of many minds to understand and solve complex problems. As Bensimon and Neumann see it:

> The ideal leader will be someone who knows how to find and bring together diverse minds—minds that reflect variety in their points of view, in their thinking processes and in their unique capacities as well as unique limitations.... Moreover, as the world grows more complex...it is likely that we will stop thinking of leadership as the property or quality of just one person. We will begin to think of it in its collective form: leadership as occurring among and through a group of people who think and act together. (p. 12)

In a study of college presidents and their administrative teams, Bensimon and Neumann found that the team builders who encouraged their teams to think in diverse rather than similar ways and to engage in a variety of tasks rather than following a strict division of labor were more likely to be associated with effective leadership. The authors conclude that the ability to build and maintain diverse, "thinking" teams is a critical skill for twenty-first century leadership.

Similarly, Margaret Wheatley (1992) advances the new paradigm of leadership in her work, which compares leadership and the new sciences of quantum and chaos theories. She notes, as have others, that the conventional (industrial) perspectives of organizations and leadership are heavily grounded in the principles of Newtonian physics, specifically, the belief in objectivity, linear causality, and control. These influences produce an emphasis on structure and parts, as well as on "our desire to control a reality that is slippery and evasive" (p. 25). In particular, the belief that we can control nature and thus organizations and people makes the

Newtonian frame so seductive, and also so difficult to relinquish. However, Wheatley argues that the new sciences offer a much more realistic perspective on organizational reality and a better foundation for leadership in a new world.

In quantum physics she finds the grounding for participatory leadership: "...the quantum realm speaks emphatically to the role of participation, even to its impact on creating reality" (p. 143). She asks, if the universe is participatory, how can we fail to embrace this in our organizations and our leadership practices?

The participatory nature of reality has also focused attention on relationships. In her words, "Nothing exists at the subatomic level, or can be observed, without engagement with another energy source" (p. 14). Thus, in the frame of the new science we move from the separateness and objectivity of the industrial view of leadership to recognizing that leadership is always context-bound and that the context of leadership is established by the relationships we value. The lenses of the new science show us that leadership is a relational act.

Danah Zohar (1997) has continued and extended Wheatley's examination of the new science and its implications for leadership. In particular, Zohar argues that the separation of our lives into "public" and "private" realms is a legacy of Newtonian science. For example, in our public or work life, we are asked to engage our mental/intellectual abilities. We reserve our emotional and spiritual capacities for our private life with family and friends. Framing our world holistically (as we do in the new science), where everything is connected to everything else, we begin to recognize that it is an illusion to think that we bring only our intellectual self to our work in organizations. The recognition of the unbroken wholeness of our universe, and thus the drive to create connected, holistic organizations, compels leaders to take account of people's emotional and spiritual dimensions as well as the mental. As a result, there is a burgeoning interest in understanding and developing emotional intelligence (Goleman, 1998), as well as in nurturing the spiritual dimension of leaders and collaborators (Zohar, 2000; Mitroff & Denton, 1999). An emphasis for twenty-first century leaders is to create environments that call on and nurture all dimensions of the self—mental, emotional, and spiritual.

Writing from the Center for Creative Leadership, Drath and Palus (1994) offer yet another take on postindustrial leadership. They suggest that leadership is "meaning-making in a community of practice," and they contrast this definition with the conventional view in which leaders use dominance or influence to get followers to do what the individual leader wants. The Drath and Palus view of leadership is grounded in **constructivism,** which asserts that reality is a socially constructed phenomenon known only through our perception of it; that is, we use our own perceptual filters to make sense of what we experience. This meaning-making can be achieved individually or with others (socially). We are driven to make sense of things because meaning-making is an important human activity. It is, in fact, the way we come to understand ourselves and our world.

From this constructivist base, Drath and Palus propose that leadership accrues to those who can frame the experiences of those engaged in a shared activity in such a way that helps the group make sense of its actions. Leadership is the process of providing frameworks by which members of a community make sense of what they are doing, why they are doing it, and what they have learned from it.

ing-making happens through such processes as identifying vision mission, framing problems, setting goals, arguing and engaging in ue, theory building and testing, storytelling, and the making of contracts and agreements....From an individual perspective, it is not so much that a person is first a leader and then creates meaning; it's more that, in making meaning a person comes to be called a leader....It is the process of participating in making meaning in a collective sense that makes leaders out of people. (pp. 10–11)

Here again, we see that leadership is a relational process in which everyone in a community is engaged. The question for the leader, then, becomes not how to get individuals to do what needs to be done, but rather, how to create communities in which everyone, even those on the margins, can make important contributions. Bensimon and Neumann (1993) hold strikingly similar views with Drath and Palus about the purpose of leadership as meaning-making. They, too, define leadership as the shared construction of meaning.

Leadership requires skill in the creation of meaning that is authentic to oneself and to one's community. It also requires the uncovering of meaning that is already embedded in others' minds, helping them to see what they already know, believe and value, and encouraging them to make new meaning. In this way, leadership generates leadership. (p. xv)

Rost, Bensimon and Neumann, Wheatley, and Drath and Palus are among the pioneers in defining new images of leadership. No doubt, as we move into the twenty-first century, the postindustrial paradigm of leadership will continue to be refined, modified, and elaborated on. Although still in its infant stages, with much work to be done before postindustrial leadership is widely accepted and fully embedded in our theory and practice, this leadership paradigm offers one clear theme: the age of the individual leader-hero is gone. As we look to the new millennium, leadership must be understood as a relationship, a collaborative process, a community of believers pursuing a transformational cause.

We started this chapter with a discussion on servant leadership. In today's world, a well-known example of servant leadership is Mother Teresa. During her lifetime, she achieved leadership status through serving and advocating for the poor in India and across the world. The other two profiles—those of Cleaster Mims and Aaron Feuerstein—exemplify some of the other ideas presented in this chapter. Cleaster Mims's work clearly addresses socially critical issues, while Aaron Feuerstein's leadership is an example of leadership as a collaborative process.

MOTHER TERESA
Saint of the Gutters

Mother Teresa was immersed in projects for helping the poor of India and of the entire world until her death in 1997 at age 87. Through her service to the ill and destitute, she proclaimed her message that the poor must be loved because a loving God created them.

As founder of the Missionaries of Charity, Mother Teresa started rescuing the poor people who were literally dying in the streets of Calcutta. Writer Dominique LaPierre remembers first seeing her washing the wounds of a dying man:

> So emaciated that he looked like a living skeleton. His flesh seemed to have melted down, leaving only skin over his bones.
>
> Mother Teresa was gently speaking to him in Bengali. I will never forget the eyes of this wretched, dying man. His suffering, staring look progressively changed to an expression of surprise, and then, of peace, the peace of someone who suddenly feels he is loved.
>
> Sensing my presence behind her, the nun turned around. I suddenly felt terribly awkward to have interrupted a dialogue which I could feel was unique. I introduced myself.
>
> Mother Teresa called a young European volunteer who was passing by with a washbasin in his hands.
>
> "Love him," she told him, "Love him with all your strength."
>
> She...invited me to follow her toward the small waiting room that separated the men's and women's wards.
>
> There was a table and a bench, and on the wall a poster which said: "The worst misery is not hunger, not leprosy, but the feeling to be unwanted, rejected, abandoned by everyone."
>
> These words summarize the universality of Mother Teresa's work.
>
> Detractors who accuse her of not providing any real medical treatment to the destitute people who are brought to her homes, and whom she is the only one to rescue, should know that half of them are able to leave her "dying homes" on their feet after a few days, having regained dignity and enough strength, thanks to the loving care received.
>
> Mother Teresa believed that the poor are not just the millions who are starving, but also the millions of excluded, lonely, untouchable, or homeless people. These people most needed the human touch of things like love, justice, hope, and dignity.
>
> She said, "The most terrible disease that can ever strike a human being is to have no one near him to be loved. Without a heart full of love, without generous hands, it is impossible to cure a man suffering of loneliness."
>
> She told reporters in England: "I have walked at night in your streets. I have entered your homes. I have found in them more poverty than in India. I have found the poverty of the soul, the lack of love."

LaPierre said,

> Each time I return with my wife to Calcutta to visit the dispensaries and the schools I support with the royalties from my book, *The City of Joy,* we never fail to attend Mother Teresa's 5:45 A.M. Mass in her convent headquarters, set in the very heart of the teeming megalopolis.

As sole decoration on the walls of the large room that serves as a chapel in the daytime and as a dormitory for the novices at night, there is a simple crucifix with the inscription that says, "I thirst."

...What an emotion to rediscover around her all these dark-skinned Indian novices who tomorrow will join their Japanese, European, Australian and American sisters in some 500 orphanages, leprosy homes and rescue centers in more than 100 countries on the five continents.

The order of the Missionaries of Charity cannot accept all the postulants knocking at the door of its novitiates: today it has more than 5,000 sisters, 500 consecrated brothers and more than 4 million lay co-workers.

In 1979, she won the Nobel Peace Prize. Some complain that Mother Teresa could use her charisma and fame to attack the roots of poverty, but she said: "Fortunately there are in this world people who fight for justice and human rights, who struggle to change the structures. The daily contact of our sisters is with people who do not even have a scrap of bread to feed themselves.

"Our mission is to consider the problem on an individual rather than a collective basis. Our concern is for one person, not a multitude. We are looking for the human being with whom Christ identified himself when he said, 'I was hungry and you fed me.'"

LaPierre said,

If this uncommon woman has succeeded in developing so quickly in the whole world the congregation she founded in 1950, it is thanks to an exceptional reunion of gifts and remarkable qualities, among them a faith to lift mountains and a leadership that may sometimes appear tyrannical, an indomitable will to rely for everything only on divine Providence, an exceptional charisma which has conquered the public as well as the media and those who govern the world, an innate gift for organization and a rare capacity to adapt to all situations and face all problems.

For sure, so many qualities represent many handicaps to surmount for the woman who will succeed her. Let's hope the day will come as late as possible and let's quell our fears for the future.

As Mother Teresa has so often said: "The work is not mine but God's. I am only a small pencil in His hand."

From Dominique LaPierre, "Mother Teresa Is Still Offering a Hand at 84," *The Cleveland Plain Dealer*, Dec. 19, 1994.

(For more information visit http://www.nobel.se/peace/laureates/1979/teresa-bio.html.)

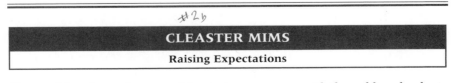

#2 b

CLEASTER MIMS

Raising Expectations

Cleaster Mims knew that something major was wrong with the public schools. As a high school English teacher, she felt that the urban system where she taught put students "on a conveyor belt from the school house to the jailhouse."

Her experience with high schoolers and with boat people and other immigrants to whom she taught English as a second language showed her that too many students were pigeonholed in terms of their socioeconomic status. Too many students who could achieve were left to languish because not enough was expected of them.

"Kids don't fail," she insists, "teachers fail. And colleges that turn out teachers who cannot teach fail."

The cost of low expectations to the individual is enormous, she said, but the cost to society is even more immense. "We assume someone coming from a certain environment can't achieve, and we end up pushing people to the back of the line who could find a cure for cancer or AIDS."

While listening to a talk by educator Marva Collins, Mims saw the parallels between her experience and the philosophy of Ms. Collins's West Side Preparatory School in Chicago: the pursuit of academic excellence. She determined to start a school in Cincinnati, Ohio, that would demand nothing short of that.

Working with volunteers in the community, she found space in a church basement and made do with cast-offs for supplies and furniture. "We didn't even have books the first year," she says, noting that she eventually bought the school's classical literature at a local Goodwill store.

Now, in the eighth year of the school's operation, what began as a basement program with 41 students has expanded to more than 300, and Mims is converting a recently purchased facility into a boarding component.

Asked about her leadership, Mims deflects credit: "I feel that I'm chosen. When God chooses you, you cannot not do it and find any happiness in life," she says. As the president, CEO, principal, and founder of the school, she says, "The buck stops with me. But I'm not above sweeping the floors."

Although her university teaching career as a professor in oral communications at Xavier University limits her to being at the school only two days per week, she says she has empowered the teachers to carry on without her. "I had a vision about the school and I've been able to pass it on."

She said, "One has not been successful until they have enough to give away."

She attributes much of her success to the hard work and persistence she learned from her upbringing in the South, where she benefited by attending black schools with high-caliber faculty. In those days, she explains, black professionals were severely limited in the types of jobs they could get, so all-black schools profited from their talents. She herself never felt the sting of lowered expectations, and she hopes to help other children avoid it as well.

"We need a metamorphosis of the mind."

AARON FEURESTEIN

The Miracle at Malden Mills

It was nearly 11 p.m. when he heard the news. Aaron Fuerstein, CEO of Malden Mills of Lawrence, Massachusetts, had been celebrating his seventieth birthday on December 11, 1995, with family and friends when he first was told of the six-alarm fire that was ravaging his plant.

Most employees were certain that this was the end of Malden Mills, best known as the primary source of the fleece material used by L.L. Bean and Patgonia to make jackets and pullovers. Said union representative Paul Coorey in a 1997 *Life* interview, "We were ready to hear that it was over."

Added employee Jim Gillett in a 1998 article in *George* magazine, "He was 70 years old and was going to get a big insurance settlement. Why would he want to run the risk of trying to rebuild?"

Coorey and Gillett had good reason to expect dire news. In addition to the absolute destruction to the physical plant, for years there had been a considerable case to be made that the 90-year-old family business would be far more profitable if it relocated out of greater Boston and into an overseas locale, where labor costs were considerably less. Now that all but one small building of the plant was gone, it was unfathomable to expect that Feurstein, who had already kept the plant in the Lawrence longer than most had anticipated, would do anything but take the $300 million in insurance money due to him and his family and close the plant down.

Then an extraordinary thing happened. While the smoke was still smoldering at the plant, Feurstein stood in front of his 3,000 employees on December 14 and made a startling announcement. He stated that not only was the plant going to rebuild in Lawrence, but that all 3,000 employees would receive their full December paychecks plus a $275 Christmas bonus. And this would be no simple holiday cheer. In January he again announced that all employees would be paid an additional month wages and benefits. In February, he made good on this pledge for a third month. By March, most employees had returned to full-time work. By midsummer, this figure was at 85 percent, leaving approximately 400 jobless. Feurstein did not forget these displaced employees, extending their health benefits, providing support for them in finding new employment, and guaranteeing all their old jobs back when a new plant opened in 1997. By September, 1997, all but seventy employees were back to work at Malden Mils. During the rebuilding process, he opened a training center where employees could work to improve their math, language, and computer skills in anticipation of the opening of a new plant.

An orthodox Jew, Feurstein leads through a combination of a strong religious beliefs, particularly as this applies to helping others in times of crisis, and hard-nosed business acumen. Said Feurstein in a *Parade* interview in 1996, "Hillel (the great Hebrew scholar) said, 'In a situation where there is no righteous person, try to be a righteous person.'"

Some call Feurstein a visionary, some call him a fool for "wasting" millions in pay and benefits to employees while significant portions of the mill were closed. Said Feurstein in a 1997 *Life* story, "Other CEOs feel I'm sort of a stupid guy who doesn't know what to do with his money. But treating the workers fairly is good for the shareholder. I consider our workers an asset, not a cuttable expense.…When you do the right thing, you'll probably end up more profitable that if you did wrong."

Said Coorey, "He's unique, this company is unique. What he did here has put food on the tables of Merrimack Valley families for years and years."

Unfortunately, Malden Mills filed for bankruptcy in 2002. However, Feurstein's extra-ordinary skills will be remembered by all who were directly or indirectly involved with the company at the time.

✦ Chapter Summary

The story of leadership from the postindustrial perspective is quite different from the stories we have told until now. For the greater part of this century we have conceived of the leader as a person apart, whose purpose was to provide us with a vision to follow and with answers for our uncertainties. The postindustrial world does not offer us such simple solutions. In a time of rapid and complex change, it is unrealistic to expect one person to be the expert who solves all our problems. We need a different kind of leadership for a new world.

This chapter chronicles the evolution of the postindustrial paradigm of leadership. Several models of leadership served as precursors to the new paradigm, specifically servant leadership, transformational leadership, and the critical model of leadership. These models broke with the industrial paradigm view in several major ways: by describing leadership as a relationship versus the property of an individual, by defining leadership as a change process, and by recognizing that leadership is not confined to those who hold positional authority, but rather, is something that can be performed by anyone.

These transitional theories influenced the thinking of leadership scholars and led Joseph Rost (1991) to propose a definition of leadership that he labeled the postindustrial paradigm. Rost explained: "Leadership is an influence relationship among leaders and collaborators who intend real change that reflects their mutual purposes" (p. 7). The postindustrial perspectives envision leadership as a process done by both leaders and collaborators; a process of bringing diverse minds together in a collaborative effort to enact some kind of real change; a process through which people make meaning of their experience; and a process separate from management.

✦ CREATE YOUR OWN THEORY ✦

Do you see yourself as a servant leader, a transformational leader, a collaborative leader—or perhaps some combination of the above? Do you believe in a relational approach or would you do better in a more mechanistic setting? These are but some of the questions we encourage you to ponder as you continue to develop your own theory on leadership. This chapter has presented a number of the most modern perspectives on leadership, but the perspective that matters most is your own.

Now let's revisit our opening Leadership Moment. How would a servant leader approach this situation? A critical transformational leader? If you were the new school board member, how would you proceed? Would your approach be reflective of the models put forth in this chapter? If so, in what way?

◆ Key Terms

collaborative leadership

constructivism

critical transformational leadership

mechanistic worldview

real change

relational approach

servant leadership

transactional leadership

transformational leadership

◆ Questions for Discussion and Review

1. What are the characteristics of servant leaders, according to Greenleaf? Why does he believe that servant-led institutions are most successful?

2. What are some of the primary lessons to be gleaned from John Woolman's crusade to eradicate slavery within the Society of Friends? Who are other examples of servant leaders?

3. Contrast transactional leadership with transformational leadership.

4. What are some of the core aspects of the critical model of leadership?

5. What are some of the common themes among servant, transformational, and critical models of leadership?

6. What are some of the societal and historical factors that have triggered movement away from the industrial paradigm and a mechanistic view of leadership?

7. What are Rost's four essential elements of leadership? Do you agree with his assessment? Why or why not?

8. What are some of the distinctions Rost makes between leaders and managers?

9. Think of your own experience doing leadership or your observations of leaders. Which characteristics of postindustrial leadership have you implemented yourself or seen implemented by others? What was the result? From these experiences and observations, what do you think it takes to successfully engage in leadership as a collaborative process?

10. Which elements of postindustrial leadership do you already practice? Which do you think would be most difficult for you to learn and why? Which aspects do you find most useful, and which aspects are the least useful?

11. Do you agree that the age of the individual leader is over? Why or why not?

12. Do you think that it is important to separate leadership and management and describe them as different processes? What do you see as the differences between the two?

✦ Exercises

Exercise 12–1 Understanding Transition Theories

In his book *Imaginization*, Gareth Morgan (1993) graphically illustrates that the commonly used *team metaphor* for leadership is shaded with very different meanings for different individuals. The use of the team metaphor is helpful as we attempt to understand the differences between the industrial paradigm of leadership and the servant/leader and transformational theories of Greenleaf and Burns. Using a sports metaphor, please give an example of a sport (hockey, basketball, football, rowing, soccer, baseball, swimming, lacrosse, golf, bowling, horse racing, etc.) that illustrates leadership as defined in the industrial paradigm, the servant-leader model (Greenleaf), and the transformational leadership model of Burns.

SPORTS METAPHORS

INDUSTRIAL PARADIGM	*SERVANT/LEADER MODEL*	*TRANSFORMATIONAL LEADERSHIP*
1. Sport:	1. Sport:	1. Sport:
2. This is a good example because:	2. This is a good example because:	2. This is a good example because:
3. In this sport, the leader plays what role?	3. In this sport, the leader plays what role?	3. In this sport, the leader plays what role?
4. Could this leader play this sport so that it would fit into the other two categories?	4. Could this leader play this sport so that it would fit into the other two categories?	4. Could this leader play this sport so that it would fit into the other two categories?
5. How?	5. How?	5. How?

Exercise 12–2 Understanding the Organizational Culture Transformations

Step One: Identify three examples of bureaucratic/mechanistic forms of organizations (old culture) and three examples of the emerging ad hoc models of organizations (new culture). These examples can be drawn from business, industry, politics, government, volunteer, or service organizations.

Bureaucratic/Mechanistic Organizations (Old Cultures)	*Ad Hoc Organizations (New Cultures)*
1.	1.
2.	2.
3.	3.

Step Two: Answer the following questions about the examples you have given.

1. What are the major differences between the two types of organizations? Be specific.
2. Will the new ad hoc organization be as successful over the next twenty-five years as the older bureaucratic/mechanistic organizations were for the past twenty-five years? Why or why not?
3. Which type of organization would you be most comfortable working in?
4. Which is easier to lead?
5. Do they require the same types of leaders?

Exercise 12–3   Understanding Differences between the Industrial Model and Rost's Postindustrial Model of Leadership

Directions: Part One: Fill in the chart highlighting the differences between Rost's postindustrial model and the industrial model of leadership by placing choices A–L in either the "Industrial Model" or "Rost's Postindustrial Model" column.

A. This has a bureaucratic view of organizations.
B. Relationships are based on influence rather than positional authority.
C. Collaborators and leaders intend real change.
D. Model is grounded in rational, linear, and quantitative assumptions.
E. *Leadership* and *management* are often used interchangeably.
F. Leadership is dominated by goal achievement and sense of purpose.
G. Leaders and their collaborators *do* leadership.
H. A leader's vision, style, objectives, and personal characteristics determine desired outcomes.
I. This has a flexible, multidirectional, ad hoc view of organization.
J. Leadership and management are two distinct and equally important processes.
K. Changes that leaders and their collaborators pursue must reflect their mutual purposes.
L. Model has an individualistic focus—only great leaders do leadership.

INDUSTRIAL MODEL	ROST'S POSTINDUSTRIAL MODEL
1.	1.
2.	2.
3.	3.
4.	4.

5.   5.

6.   6.

Directions: Part Two: Arrange the six descriptive phrases for each model in a point–counterpoint format, so that the descriptive phrase under the Industrial Model is balanced on the Postindustrial Model side of the chart with its opposite.

INDUSTRIAL MODEL	ROST'S POSTINDUSTRIAL MODEL
1.	1.
2.	2.
3.	3.
4.	4.
5.	5.
6.	6.

PART V

Applying Leadership

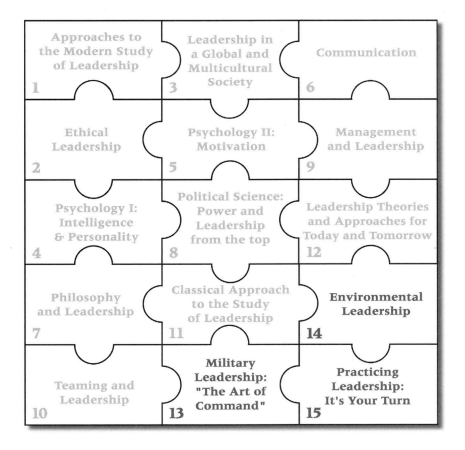

CHAPTER 13

Military Leadership: The Art of Command

■ ■ ■

LEADERSHIP MOMENT

Seeking to enhance performance, your office has decided to recruit more heavily from the armed services when hiring new personnel. One of the more recent hires, Sgt. Tina Smith, a twenty-year army vet who served in the Persian Gulf, has been assigned to your workgroup. The news of this hire has been met by decidedly mixed feelings from other group members. Some feel that hiring from the military is a very positive step and are excited to be working with somebody who has served her country and has a sense of discipline. Others worry that Smith will order everybody around (or want to be ordered around by somebody else) and won't know how to work in the "real world" of corporate America. Still others think that her military background is irrelevant. Today is Sgt. Smith's first day and you have been assigned to orient her to her new work environment and to introduce her to her new work team.

1. *What would you do?*
2. *What characteristics would you expect somebody from a military background to bring to your group?*
3. *How would you address the assumptions being made by your peers about Sgt. Smith's strengths and weaknesses?*

> Wars may be fought with weapons, but they are won by men. It is the spirit of the men who follow and of the man who leads that gains the victory

—Gen. George S. Patton

Recently a group of military officers was asked to define leadership. After reciting some of the more traditional definitions they concluded, "It would be easier to determine how many angels would fit on the head of a pin" than to come up with a definition everyone could agree on. The very act of defining leadership would, by nature, focus on a couple of elements while excluding others. As one Marine Corps Colonel, paraphrasing U.S. Supreme Court Justice Potter Stewart's famous comment on defining obscenity, put it, "It's a little like obscenity: I can't define it, but I sure know it when I see it." Laced with paradox, possession of all the leadership characteristics and abilities is no guarantee of success. What works in one instance may fail a leader in another. Leadership is not determined by age, gender, race, religion or ethnic group. Part art, part science, leadership is arguably the one constant in all successful organizations.

This chapter is the first of two chapters that will highlight some of the practical applications of leadership. In this chapter, the focus will be on leadership practice in a large system, in this case the United States military. In the next chapter, the focus will be on how individuals can apply leadership principles in acting to protect our common environment and natural resources.

✦ THE STUDY OF MILITARY LEADERSHIP: (WIFM) WHAT'S IN IT FOR ME?

> There are no bad regiments, only bad Colonels.
> —Napoleon

Because leadership involves the most basic of all human behaviors, emotions and motivation, it lends itself to examination in almost any organizational setting. It is the military environment, however, which presents the adult learner with perhaps the greatest opportunity to examine and understand leadership's true nature, analyze its various elements, and emulate the behaviors of some of our nation's most successful commanders. As Lt. Gen. Walter F. Ulmer Jr. USA (retired) put it, " Military operations tend to highlight success or failure, confirm courage or hesitation, validate selflessness or ego, assess empathy or callousness, and take measure of the integration of the behavioral and management sciences."

At some point in most people's career they will work for, with, around, or lead at least one former service member. Therefore, it is beneficial to be more than casually familiar with the leadership background, values, and beliefs of these employees. Additionally, many of the most admired corporations in America seek out and provide hiring preference to former service members. General Electric, Procter & Gamble, Allied Signal, and Bank of America, to name but a few, have all decided that former service members tend to have the requisite traits of integrity, hard work, dedication. and loyalty to succeed. When the well-known motivational speaker Zig Ziggler conducted a study of *Fortune* 500 CEOs in an effort to discover what common factors or traits had proven beneficial in their rise to the pinnacle of corporate America, more than half counted their former military service as a significant factor in their success. Lastly, rarely a day goes by that U.S. military forces are not committed to some distant corner of the globe to help support the nation's political and foreign policy initiatives. U.S. citizens are given the responsibility to elect government officials who will decide when and where to commit the youth of America in order to protect the country's vital political and economic interests. It is therefore beneficial to have some understanding of the United States' military system and its ways of thinking.

> The nation that will insist on drawing a broad line of demarcation between the fighting man and the thinking man is liable to find its fighting done by fools and its thinking done by cowards.

—Sir William F. Butler

✦ BOARDROOM TO BATTLEFIELD: COMPARISON AND CONTRAST

> The test of character is not 'hanging in there' when you expect the light at the end of the tunnel, but performance of duty and persistence of example when you know that no light is coming.

—James Stockdale

It has often been said that life in the military services is unlike any other existence in the world. The differences in culture, pay, people, organizational structure, mission, and even laws are so distinct and so vast as to represent an entirely different cultural system. In recent years, increased attention has been paid to the perceived widening cultural gap between those who serve in the U.S. military and those whom they protect and obey. Although the warrior class has always seen itself as different from society at large, the military must draw its members from the large diverse pool that makes up its citizenry. And despite its much-publicized gender shortcomings, the military is probably far more diverse than any other organization in modern America. No other organization includes such a wide representation of demographic groups.

Even though each branch of service has its challenges and opportunities, people who want to advance their leadership skills and thinking may still find similarities among the branches that offer ample opportunity for thought, reflection, and personal growth.

Figure 13-1 demonstrates some of the primary similarities between military and nonmilitary organizations and will serve as a framework for our discussion. One of the most obvious differences between the military and all other organizations lies within its reason for being—its mission. The five branches of the United States military exist for a number of reasons, most notably to win the country's wars, defend the Constitution against all counter forces foreign and domestic,

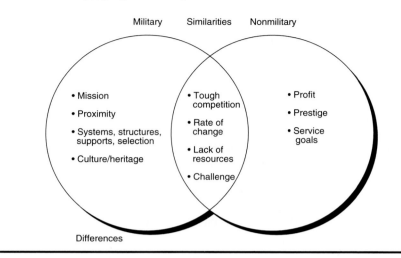

FIGURE 13-1 **Similarities and Differences between Military and Nonmilitary Organizations**

protect the country's sovereign interests and continue the country's political objectives by other means. In a nutshell, the military's mission is the management of violence. As John Lehman, former Secretary of the Navy, once put it, "The mission of our armed forces is to fight wars. To deliver violence and destruction on our enemies when our security demands it." The military doesn't decide who, what and when to fight—that decision rests within the National Command Authority (NCA)—it is elected civilians who must decide where and when vital national interests must be protected. The U.S. military is tasked with fighting and winning those battles within the parameters dictated by its civilian overseers. While the military has a particularly vital interest in preserving its nation's way of life, every organization in the world has a unique and specific mission. This **mission** dictates what authority its leaders can exercise over the resources (people, capital, and machines) furnished to them.

Another obvious distinction between military and civilian worlds is the personal proximity many people experience in pursuit of their organization's stated mission. Very few civilian occupations require the type of proximity and closeness, both physical and emotional, one would most certainly experience in the military. This may help to explain why military relationships, particularly those of individuals who have shared the hardships of combat, tend to last well beyond their time in service. What most service members experience on a daily basis, most employees and employers would consider intolerable by modern standards.

Every organization offers its leaders a unique combination of support services in the role of human resources or staff functions, such as recruiting, legal, training and development, benefits, payroll, and systems, all of which are competing for the same scarce budgetary resources necessary to function. Although these functions tend to be understaffed, underfunded, and frequently not given the support or respect they deserve, the military has always viewed the systems, support, structure, and selection business as one of its top priorities. This is evidenced by the fact that one of the most prestigious jobs a senior ranking officer can be appointed to is one that involves the selection, training, and education of other service members. Frequently referred to as the *tooth-to-tail relationships,* these vital areas have always received a great deal of attention from the military's top ranks, and those who oversee the day-to-day administrative functioning of the military in Washington. A couple of noteworthy areas are selection (recruiting, screening, and selection) and legal. The average selection period for a military officer as represented by the time he or she spends at Officer Candidate School (OCS) is about 10 weeks: 7 days a week, 24 hours a day of evaluation, testing, physical training, peer evaluations and command screenings, all of which is designed to evaluate a future officers' leadership potential. This would amount to a 1,300 hour interview, which many in the military would say is a ridiculously *short* period of time to spend evaluating a prospective leader who will eventually be entrusted with the lives of its nation's youth.

The civilian and military legal systems are also distinct. The **Uniform Code of Military Justice (UCMJ)** governs *every* facet of a service member's life, including attire, speech, grooming, conduct (on and off the job), and other personal and professional elements.

One of the most vital distinctions between the military and the rest of society lies in the military's unique core—its heritage and culture. In this age of 12-month-old e-businesses with IPOs and here-today-gone-tomorrow merger mania, the U.S. military traces its roots back more than 229 years. Perhaps no other organization in the world takes greater pride or devotes more time and resources to preserving and communicating its culture and heritage than the five services that make up the U.S. military. It is this **cultural indoctrination and transformation** that forms the foundation of all initial military training. It is the stories of great battles fought and won, of freedom preserved and evil overcome, accompanied by individual acts of heroism and courage, that help to inoculate recruits in the hope of making them better soldiers, sailors, airmen, and Marines. Eventually, when their time in the service is finished and they return to the civilian community, these stories often help to make them better citizens as well.

Although the differences between the United States military and other organizations can be vast, there are also many common frames of reference. In recent years the military, academia, scientific community, government and corporate America have all come together in order to share ideas, best practices, and even personnel. One significant common challenge includes responding to new, nontraditional forms of competition. Competition is a major battlefield, as when large corporations face pricing pressures from smaller and more nimble companies or when military forces engage in peacemaking and nation building in places like Kosovo, Panama, Haiti, Afghanistan, and Iraq.

Another area in which the military and other organizations have found a common challenge involves the rate and pace of change. For example, every organization is faced with the challenge of effectively integrating technology in order to remain competitive. Similarly, there are numerous examples of how technological advances have changed the way that warfare is waged. Just as the invention of the repeated rifle made line-and-column tactics obsolete and the machine gun, tank, and airplane relegated trench warfare to the annals of history, technological advances require leaders to develop bold new approaches to an ever-changing competitive battlefield.

A final similarity between military and other organizations is the need to effectively ration scarce resources. Many leaders can relate to the saying, "If you're short of everything but enemy, you must be in a combat zone." Precious resources—whether people, talent, equipment, or money—often must be rationed, thereby creating scarcity and shortage.

Thus, while in many ways the military culture and the culture of civilian organizations provide many contrasts, there are also many areas of overlap. The similarities between military and civilian organizations include the challenges posed by fierce competition, the rate and pace of change, and scarcity of precious resources. This common ground offers civilian and noncivilian leaders alike the opportunity to learn from each other as they share ideas, resources, and experiences and further develop their own leadership skills.

✦ FOUNDATIONS OF MILITARY LEADERSHIP

Success in battle is not a function of how many show up, but who they are.
—Gen. Robert H. Borrow

In war the chief incalculable is the human will.
—B. H. Liddell Hart

Clearly, one leadership model or style will not work well in every situation. Differences in people, resources, and environment all demand different sets of skills and abilities from the competent leader. What works in the boardroom of large corporate America would most certainly not work in an emerging e-commerce start-up or in a not-for-profit organization dedicated to feeding the hungry or raising money for the arts. While every leadership challenge is unique, there are a number of leadership fundamentals and foundations available to assist even the most novice volunteer or guide the thoughts and decisions of the most experienced corporate executive.

Over the years the U.S. military has refined its perspective on the essential leadership foundations. Although every branch of the military service has developed unique sets of core values tailored to its own beliefs, the leadership traits and principles taught to all service members are nearly identical. The fourteen leadership traits and eleven leadership principles in the lists that follow form the foundation from which the U.S. military believes that all of the demands and challenges of leadership can be met. Every newly minted lieutenant, ensign, cadet, midshipman, and NCO commits these core values to memory in an effort to ensure that the very best people lead the young men and women in the armed services.

Like blocks in an arch, each depends on the other to provide support. With core values serving as the keystone, they all serve to buttress the structure that leaders may draw upon. Just as builders must use every block in the arch to support it, so too must leaders use every element of our leadership foundation at their disposal. But just as every arch is different, requiring different shapes of building blocks, every leadership challenge is different, requiring a different use and blend of the leadership foundations.

Fourteen Leadership Traits

1. **Dependability:** The certainty of proper performance
2. **Bearing:** Creating a favorable impression in carriage, appearance, and personal conduct
3. **Courage:** The mental quality that recognizes fear, danger, or criticism but enables an individual to proceed with calmness and firmness
4. **Decisiveness:** The ability to make good decisions promptly
5. **Endurance:** The mental and physical ability to withstand stress, hardship, fatigue, and pain
6. **Enthusiasm:** The display of sincere interest and exuberance
7. **Initiative:** Taking action in the absence of orders
8. **Integrity:** Uprightness of character and soundness of moral principles; includes truthfulness and honesty
9. **Judgment:** The ability to weigh facts and possible solutions on which to base sound decisions
10. **Justice:** The ability to administer a system of rewards and discipline impartially and consistently
11. **Knowledge:** The range of one's information and understanding
12. **Tact:** The ability to deal with others without creating offense
13. **Unselfishness:** Avoidance of providing for one's own personal well-being at the expense of others
14. **Loyalty:** The quality of faithfulness

✦ CREATE YOUR OWN THEORY ✦

Military students often ponder which of these fourteen leadership traits is most important. Despite the lively discussions about the merits of each one, eventually the students almost always conclude that without integrity, nothing else really matters. Do you agree? Which of these leadership traits do you find most important?

Eleven Leadership Principles

1. *Know yourself and seek self-improvement.* Leaders are, in fact, five or more separate people. They are who they are, who they think they are, who their bosses think they are, who their subordinates think they are and, lastly, who their peers think they are. The real leader is somewhere in the middle. Leaders who work hard to know themselves and seek feedback from a variety of honest sources are better able to capitalize on their own strengths, protect (or better yet, grow out of) their weaknesses, and learn from past shortcomings and successes.

2. *Be technically proficient.* Leaders who can demonstrate technical proficiency or command of the task at hand will earn subordinates' respect.

3. *Develop a sense of responsibility among your subordinates.* Give your subordinates new opportunities and challenges that they can handle with some degree of difficulty. By expanding their boundaries and developing their own solutions, they gain confidence and valuable experience. Encourage initiative among your subordinates, and in the end you will be rewarded with employees who can run the show even in your absence.

4. *Make sound and timely decisions.* Nothing instills confidence in subordinates like a decisive leader. The ability and willingness to make tough decisions in an expeditious manner is one hallmark of good leadership. An old combat pearl of wisdom advises that "A good decision executed now, is better than the perfect solution executed too late."

5. *Lead by example.* This is the *most* important leadership principle of all. Just as the parent who says "do as I say, not as I do" is doomed to be labeled a hypocrite, so too are leaders who cannot stomach their own medicine doomed to face their subordinates' contempt and resentment. Leaders frequently underestimate the silent messages their own behaviors send to subordinates.

6. *Keep your people and look out for their welfare.* All great leaders develop a sincere interest in their subordinates' well being. This is one reason Marine Corps officers eat last, only after all the troops have been fed. The attitude that "rank has its privilege" (RHIP) often interferes with this most basic leadership principle.

7. *Keep your people informed.* When you are communicating twice as much as you think you should be, you probably have it about right. In the absence of good communication, people will make up the information they lack. Communicating is one of the hardest tasks for good leaders (see Chapter 6), and the one most susceptible to failure.

8. *Seek and take responsibility for your actions.* The old adage states that "Leaders are responsible for everything their unit does or doesn't do" and, as Gen. Norman Schwarzkopf said, "When in charge, take command." One of the best ways to develop new skills and abilities is to seek opportunities to perform outside your normal comfort zone.

9. *Ensure that assigned tasks are understood, supervised, and accomplished.* The key words here are **expectations** and **desired-end-state.** Leaders and followers need to share and understand each other's expectations, and have a clear understanding of the desired outcomes or end-states. This leadership principle is the antithesis of micromanagement, which is far too common in corporate America and destroys morale faster than almost any other leadership shortcoming.

10. *Train your people as a team.* Approximately 85 percent of all military training is accomplished in a team or unit format as opposed to less than 5 percent in the civilian world. Team training allows the organization to more rapidly develop the critical mass necessary to move the organization to the next level of performance.

11. *Employ your unit in accordance with its capabilities.* Even the best units/organizations in the world have limitations and shortcomings. Complete leaders know, analyze, and understand their organization's strengths and weaknesses. Asking an individual or group to attempt a task too far beyond their competencies without proper support or training is playing against the odds and risking unit morale and confidence.

Yours is the profession of arms, the will to win, the sure knowledge that in war there is no substitute for victory, that if you lose, the nation will be destroyed, that the very obsession of your public service must be duty, honor, country.

—Douglas MacArthur

✦ MILITARY TOOLS TO AID THE BUSY LEADER

Everything in war is simple, but the simplest thing is difficult. The difficulties accumulate and end by producing a kind of friction that is inconceivable unless one has experienced war.

—Carl von Clausewitz

There is a great deal of truth in the saying, "Show me a pilot who sits on his checklist, and I'll show you a pilot who flies by the seat of his pants." Good leaders have at their disposal a vast array of tools, techniques, and systems to enable and assist them in the day to day operation of an organization, no matter how large or small. Wise leaders use these weapons or tools to augment their own abilities and to increase the organization's effectiveness and efficacy. These aids let leaders make better, quicker, and more effective decisions in a fast moving, chaotic environment.

The **fog of war** refers to a leader's inability to deal with all of the variables and uncertainties that exist in a combat environment. Napoleon called it **friction**—the force or action that inhibits an individual or unit's ability to carry out the task at hand. In many organizations friction may manifest itself in bureaucratic delays, senior-level indecision, lack of support or resources, turf battles, office politics, and so on. This section sets forth some time-tested tools found widely throughout the U.S. military that help leaders at all levels reduce the friction or fog that clouds good decision making.

Decentralization: The Rule of Three

Many organizations have sought to improve efficiency and streamline operations by flattening their organization's structures and removing several layers of management. The effort often leaves managers or small unit leaders with a dozen or more direct reports. They feel overwhelmed, understaffed, and without the ability to properly supervise or support their direct reports.

The United States military has adopted an entirely different model, called the **Rule of Three,** that moves decision-making authority to the lowest appropriate level, yet retains a simple organizational structure designed to keep everyone's job manageable. Structurally, everyone has three (four at the most) people or things to worry about. Lieutenants who command an infantry platoon have three squads led by three squad leaders (sergeants); squad leaders have three fire-teams led by three corporals who, in turn, lead three others. Many people might view this organizational structure as overly narrow and laborious, but when the need arises, these layers disappear to streamline communications and reduce decision-making time.

Major General Perry M. Smith USAF (retired) stated, "The best leaders understand that leadership is the liberation of talent: hence they gain power not only by giving it away, but also by not grabbing it back."[1] The functional version of the Rule of Three dictates that people should limit their attention to three tasks or objectives. When used as a decision-making discipline, the rule requires leaders to distill an infinite number of possibilities to three potential courses of action (COAs). This streamlining enables leaders to evaluate relatively quickly the best, worst, and most likely scenarios prior to implementation.

Improved Feedback Loops: Seeing with Your Ears

Leaders who are serious about improving their organizations as well as their own performance seek feedback from a variety of qualified sources. All of us—even organizations—have blind spots, which if undetected limit our ability to perform at our peak. On an organizational level this mean reviewing every organizational event or activity, down to individual actions and behaviors. One reason the U.S. military enjoys air superiority over almost every theater of operations is that its pilots receive detailed reviews of their individual and the section's performance after every training mission. Such debriefings and hot washes are so vital to continuous improvement that special systems, programs, and units are dedicated to providing our warfighters with the best possible feedback on their performance.

One of the most useful tools leaders have found recently is the Multirater, or 360-degree performance reviews. These feedback tools are invaluable in helping individuals and organizations identify strengths, weaknesses, and blind spots. Whether used as a performance development tool or tied to performance measurement and compensation, Multirater feedback can be a very powerful aid in improving constructive feedback loops.

---

1. Maj. Gen. Perry M. Smith, Learning to Lead, *Marine Corps Gazette*, Jan. 1997.

Checklists and Standard Operating Procedures (SOPs)

Even though every leadership situation is unique, leaders frequently encounter situations that repeat certain patterns, such as hiring and firing employees, selecting external vendors or consultants, performing large functions or operations, and dealing with the media and regulatory authorities. Recurring patterns in these situations allow small unit leaders to develop checklists or SOPs. Just as pilots refer to checklists prior to takeoffs and landings and during emergencies, so too should small unit leaders begin to develop their own checklists to help in decision making.

Mission Orders and Commander's Intent

Several years ago the U.S. military adopted a process of communicating orders to operational forces that vastly reduced the time needed to relay instructions and improved the clarity of the message. In the past, commanders and their staffs would painstakingly construct detailed plans and instructions that, when completed, often required significant amounts of time to write, disseminate, and brief to operational units. On today's battlefield, speed and tempo of operations help forces maintain an advantage, ultimately overcoming an enemy's will to resist. Today commanders have drastically streamlined their instructions so they can provide operational forces with the essential elements for mission success:

There are two parts to any mission: the task to be accomplished and the reason or intent behind it. **Commander's intent** is a device designed to help subordinates understand the larger context of their actions. The purpose of providing intent is to allow subordinates to exercise judgement and initiative—to depart from the original plan when the unforeseen occurs—in a way that is consistent with higher commanders' aims. The task describes the action to be taken, while intent describes the purpose of the action. The task denotes what, and sometimes when and where; the intent explains why. Of the two, intent is more important. Although the situation may change, making the task obsolete, the intent is more lasting and continues to guide our actions. According to the Marine Corps Doctrinal Publication (MCDP) 1 (1997), understanding intent allows operational units to exercise initiative in harmony with the commander's desires.

> Never tell people how to do things. Tell them what to do, and they will surprise you with their ingenuity.
> —Gen. George S. Patton

OODA Loops

Not some new kind of breakfast cereal for kids, OODA is a decision-making tool developed by Col. John Boyd USAF (retired) during the Vietnam War to help leaders, particularly fighter pilots, make better decisions and, more importantly, to make decisions more quickly than the enemy. **OODA loops** notes that the essence of decision-making boils down to four interrelated functions: *observation, orientation, decision making,* and *action.* The warfighter who can accomplish these four functions the quickest gains the advantage. Much as in a Wild West gunfight, the person who observes, orients, decides, and acts quickest is able to dictate the tempo of the fight. The goal is to get inside your opponents' OODA loop and thus make better and quicker decisions.

> Speed is the essence of war. Take advantage of the enemy's unpreparedness; travel by unexpected routes and strike where he has taken no precautions.
>
> —Sun Tzu

Personnel Evaluations: Proficiency and Conduct Marks

What manager or employee hasn't dreaded the thought of the annual ritual known as the performance review? In many organizations, both parties view this most vital of all administrative leadership functions with all the enthusiasm and gusto of a root canal. That's unfortunate, because when accomplished with thought, reflection, and broad input from others, the performance review allows the leader and employee to do more than simply document past performance. It offers a chance to chart the course for individual employee development plans, discuss long-term career goals, review strengths and weaknesses, and assess an individual's overall contribution to the organization. The military performance evaluation system has traditionally consisted of two broad categories: proficiency (performance) and conduct (sharing of corporate values or behavior). By examining an individual's overall contribution to the organization within these two parameters, leaders can more effectively and efficiently document an employee's capacity for additional responsibility and growth. All things being equal, a leader would favor high conduct over performance. By demonstrating shared organizational values or behaviors, many leaders believe that performance issues will resolve themselves through experience, supervision, and counseling. Good leaders rarely miss an opportunity to counsel people about their performance and take advantage of the infinite number of teachable moments that occur each day.

✦ LEADERSHIP SKILLS ✦

Leadership Skills for the Twenty-First Century: Applying Lessons from the U.S. Military toward becoming a Better Life

---

> Make the most of yourself, for that is all there is to you.
>
> —Ralph Waldo Emerson

Obviously, there is no magic formula for developing leadership skills. It takes hard work, practice, discipline, and dedication. What serves leaders well in one situation may fail them in another. Yet in the same way that anyone who studies music can be a better musician, with a select few capable of truly extraordinary performances, so too it is with leadership. Anyone can be a better leader with practice, persistence, and experience. As the great military thinker S.L.A.

Marshall wrote in *Military Leadership* (Taylor and Rosenbach, 2005), "Great military leaders of the past possessed a certain set of qualities. These were inner qualities rather than outward marks of greatness." Although very few enjoyed acclaim in their early years, "the most successful are molded by the influences around them and have the average person's faults and vices."

As you progress in putting together your leadership puzzle and consider the U.S. military as one example of how leadership principles are applied within a large organizational structure, here are some key points to take from this chapter:

1. *Live the leadership traits and principles.* Review and reflect on them frequently. Focus on one or two leadership elements daily for a week to ten days. Keep this up for three to six months and you will have developed a more full and complete understanding of these most important leadership foundations.

2. Always keep the three C's in your mind—Character, Courage and Competence.[2]

3. Read widely and wisely as many leadership biographies as possible.

4. *Be yourself!* Use the leadership tools at your disposal and develop a style that fits your personality and mission.

5. *Remember your team.* These are the people who made you successful. Every individual life is equally precious and everyone has a contribution to make.

6. *Reward success, not failure.* Be sure you reward the right behaviors.

7. *Develop mental toughness.* Be brutally honest with yourself, and if you make a mistake, don't hesitate to make things right.

8. Develop a strong, diverse network or brain trust.[3]

9. *Take good care of yourself.* Be physically fit. The time you invest in yourself is invaluable.

10. *Avoid the cowardice of silence.* You get paid for your opinion, so make sure to voice it.[4]

There is less a line between the leader and the led than a bond.

—Leading Marines, FMFM 1-0

You have now been exposed to the basic tenets of leadership from the perspective of the United States military. Starting with George Washington, the U.S. military has produced many outstanding leaders, and through the ages, many other societies have produced countless military leaders who have made their stamp on history. What follows are profiles of two military leaders, one a product

---

2. Gen. Matthew B. Ridgway in *Military Leadership* (Taylor and Rosenbach, 2005).
3. Maj. Gen. Perry M. Smith, "Learning to Lead," *Marine Corps Gazette* (Jan. 1997).
4. *Ibid.*

of the U.S. military and the other a Chinese revolutionary, who have risen from modest beginnings to make an enduring mark on world history.

GENERAL COLIN L. POWELL
Problem Solver

When General Colin Powell's book, *My American Journey,* was published in 1995, he began a book signing tour that drew throngs of people at sites across the nation. What was the attraction?

In part, it may have been the fact that he was the first African American ever to hold such prestigious positions in the U.S. government as chairman of the Joint Chiefs of Staff and National Security Advisor. He was appointed Secretary of State in 2001 (becoming the first African American to hold this office), and announced his resignation from the position shortly after President Bush's re-election in 2004. His name was being tossed around as a candidate for president and vice president. Powell's hold on the American public, however, was also due to his integrity and to the leadership he showed during conflict.

Born of Jamaican parents, Powell grew up amid a mix of Jews, Poles, Hispanics, Irish, and Italians in the South Bronx. An indifferent student, he remembered feeling a lack of direction until he entered ROTC (Reserve Officers Training Corps) at City College. There, he says in his autobiography, he felt for the first time a sense of belonging. His admission to the selective Pershing Rifles group deepened his closeness to the military and to other young men with whom he has maintained contact throughout his career.

After accepting a commission as a second lieutenant in the infantry at Fort Benning, Georgia, Powell was sent to a unit in West Germany, where he served as platoon leader and executive officer. As he began ascending the military career ladder, he learned that to lead, one had to make decisions, often unpopular ones. A quotation he kept on his desk reminded him, "Being responsible sometimes means pissing people off."

His years within the military—which he contends is the most democratic institution in the country—were relatively free of discrimination and prejudice. Outside the service, however, he was saddened to see so much hatred and distrust among the races. At the dedication of the memorial for the Buffalo Soldiers, black soldiers who had fought courageously for the Union during the Civil War but who had received little recognition, Powell noted the injustice these brave soldiers encountered:

> I know where I came from.... All of us need to know where we came from so our young people will know where they are going. . . . I am deeply mindful of the debt I owe to those who went before me. I climbed on their backs. . . . I challenge every young person here today: don't forget their service and their sacrifice; and don't forget our service and sacrifice, and climb on our backs. Be eagles!

Powell learned in his first eight weeks these essential guidelines about the military:

"Take charge of this post and all government property in view"—the Army's first general order.

The mission is primary, followed by taking care of your soldiers.

Don't stand there. Do something!

Lead by example.

"No excuse, sir."

Officers always eat last.

Never forget, you are an American infantryman, the best.

And never be without a watch, a pencil, and a notepad.

(*My American Journey,* p. 41)

An early assignment, prosecuting three soldiers who had crashed their car, killing several Germans, had shown him that he was skilled in taking a large amount of information, shaping it, and conveying it competently and persuasively. Much of his future accomplishments serving presidents and commanding troops called on and refined this ability.

Powell's take on leadership is straightforward: "Leadership is solving problems. The day soldiers stop bringing you their problems is the day you have stopped leading them. They have either lost confidence that you can help them or concluded you do not care. Either case is a failure of leadership" (p. 52).

His combat service included two tours of Vietnam, where he earned the Purple Heart and the Soldiers Medal for rescuing his colleagues from a helicopter crash.

He completed his master's degree in business administration at George Washington University and was selected as a White House fellow during the Nixon administration. He chose to serve in the Office of Management and Budget, obtaining invaluable experience about budgetary matters that would help him enormously in his later career.

During his time serving presidents and troops, Powell has learned to get along with all types of people. He also learned the importance of acknowledging everyone's effort. In fact, "share the credit" is one of the thirteen rules he kept on his desk. He valued teamwork and cherished the existence of a sense of family in the military, of each one looking out for the other.

In many tense situations, including during the Gulf War, Powell resisted others' insistence on quick military reaction. He stressed, instead, the importance of not letting himself be stampeded into an action until he had analyzed it in depth. He vowed to take no action until a clear objective had been established.

Upon Powell's retirement from the Joint Chiefs of Staff, President Clinton had this to say of the General: "He clearly has the warrior spirit and the judgment to know when it should be applied in the nation's benefit. . . . I speak for the families who entrusted you with their sons and daughters . . . you did well by them, as you did well by America."

(For more information visit http://www.state.gov/secretary/.)

MAO ZEDONG (MAO TSE TUNG)
Revolutionary and Poet

Born in a rural village sixty miles from the capital of the Hunan Province, Mao endured the privations of poverty as well as the punishments of his harsh father, whom Mao later dubbed "the Ruling Power." Even as a young boy, he hungered for knowledge of China and the outside world. He became an avid reader, sacrificing much to attend school where he was ridiculed for his back-country ways. He excelled in debate, however, and learned early that it was possible to defy arbitrary authority.

Mao was eighteen before he ever saw a map of the world. Rather than attend school at this age, he stayed in the school library from opening until its closing, taking only enough time to eat his ration of two rice cakes for lunch. He devoured books, reveling in the folk tales and history of his native country, and also in the biographies of world leaders such as Napoleon, Peter the Great, and Americans such as Abraham Lincoln and George Washington. He later compared himself to Washington leading a rebel army against an entrenched power. He also loved to write poetry, often glorying in the delights of the natural world.

As he saturated himself with the proud history of his country, however, he also became by turns saddened and enraged at its domination by foreign powers. He was thrilled by newspaper stories of uprisings against feudal landlords across the country. Stirred by Sun Yat Sen's victory over the Manchu Dynasty, Mao signed up for the revolutionary army, but was later disillusioned when Sun was overtaken by the military and the country broke into warring factions.

Mao tossed about for a future, joining and quitting police, soap-making, and law and business schools. He finally decided on teaching. His remarkable entrance scores earned him free tuition and board for the next four years as he increased his debating skills and continued to rebel against arbitrary authority. He continued reading stories about how sheer willpower could overcome any obstacle, a belief that remained central to his life. He also entered a period of rugged conditioning, eating little and pushing his physical endurance to the limit. His prodigious physical ability would stand him well in the years to come.

After reading about the Bolshevik revolution in Russia in 1917, Mao formed communist study groups in China. He disagreed with the Marxists that the revolution would depend on the working class; instead, Mao stressed the role that the peasants would play in overthrowing the government in China.

While fighting the Nationalist Chinese led by Chiang Kaishek, Mao was captured one day and designated for beheading. He managed to evade his captors and hide, stealing back to his headquarters.

In the newly developing Red Army, Mao had set up a very different organization from traditional armies. Officers (including himself) had no special privileges: they were called leaders but wore no outward designation of rank and ate the same food as the others. Mao insisted that the soldiers show kindness and helpfulness to the peasants, helping them in whatever way they could. He told them that they must be servants of the people. This passion for serving the peasants created a love for the Red Army among the villagers, who often helped in significant ways. In addition, Mao sought to enlist women and young people in the great effort of liberating China.

Chiang encircled the Red Army, gradually tightening the stranglehold. After long deliberation, Mao convinced his soldiers that the only way to escape was through the treacherous mountains to the north. This began the Long March, a trek of nearly 7,500 miles through rugged territory, often circling back and changing directions to confuse the Nationalists. The journey was exceedingly difficult and resulted in massive deaths. Yet the Reds also took the opportunity to talk about land reform and other issues to the peasants along the way, building strong support for Mao's revolutionary ideas. Out of the 100,000 troops who began the trip, only 20,000 finished it alive. Nevertheless, the amazing feat has often been compared with Hannibal crossing the Alps, and it helped solidify Mao's growing idolization among the people of China. A personality cult was growing.

Following World War II, an out-and-out battle for control of the leadership of China erupted into civil war. Finally Chiang was defeated, moving his enclave to Formosa (Taiwan) in 1949. Mao announced the founding of the People's Republic of China.

During the next three decades, Mao showed himself as an astute strategist, a militarist who enjoyed provoking the major world powers, and a polemicist trying to overturn the cultural practices of Confucianism in China. He instigated the Cultural Revolution, asserting that artists and intellectuals needed to come from their ivory towers to work alongside the peasants. He who had been such a voracious reader now denigrated the need to read anything more than his little blue book, *Quotations from Chairman Mao.* He closed all the universities, turning high school and college students into impassioned members of the Red Guard.

Little else was available to read beyond Mao's works, and his likeness loomed everywhere. He delighted in surprising the world, as when he sent a Chinese team to the World Ping Pong championships in Japan and then allowed the U.S. team to play in China. The remarkable meeting between U.S. President Nixon and Mao was another in a long line of unexpected events. It was the first time any U.S. president had set foot on Chinese soil, and it signaled a thaw in the U.S.-China relationship. During Nixon's visit in 1972, however, Mao was in very poor health, and the country was in suspense about who would take over after his death, which came on September 9, 1977, when Mao was 82.

Summarizing Mao's life, Rebecca Steffof writes in *Mao Zedong:*

> Mao has been viewed as both a hero and a tyrant. His patriotism is undeniable; he fought valiantly to defend China against the Japanese. . . . He was a visionary who dreamed of a new China and had the force of will to reshape the world to fit his dream. Yet sometimes visionaries are dangerous. Sometimes they cannot tolerate the existence of anything or anyone outside their own narrow field of vision. Mao Zedong was an idealist who gave the Chinese people freedoms they had never known. He was also a tyrant, who ruthlessly crushed anyone who dared to dream of freedoms beyond those he offered. He may be both a savior and a villain, but one

thing is certain: In shaping the lives of one-fifth of the world's population, Mao Zedong had a greater impact on the destiny of the Chinese people than any other single person, except perhaps the emperor who first united China 2,200 years ago.

(For more information visit http://www.time.com/time/time100/leaders/profile/mao.html.)

◆ Chapter Summary

The study of military leadership in the United States is not just for those in the military; it has applications to all aspiring leaders. Current and former military men and women hold influential positions in all segments of society, and the U.S. military as a whole provides an example of the application of leadership principles on a large scale. Although each individual is different, all servicemen and women have been exposed to the same specific core values and principles. This chapter highlighted these core values and their associated tools and provides examples of their application to leadership, both within and beyond the military.

◆ CREATE YOUR OWN THEORY ◆

The U.S. military has some very distinct and clear core values related to leadership. Looking back over the fourteen leadership traits and eleven core leadership principles described earlier in this chapter, are there other ideas you would add to this list? Do you believe that these core values work best within a military climate, or do they translate to other areas of life? Which of these do you find to be most powerful and/or relevant to your own view of leadership?

Now think back to our opening Leadership Moment. If you do not have a military background and learn that you will be working closely with somebody who does, what assumptions would you make about that person? Might your assumptions be different depending on for which country or for which branch of the military the individual served? Do you see military experience as an asset of a liability? If you have a military background and/or grew up in a family or community where many have served in the military, how have your experiences shaped the way you view leadership?

◆ Key Terms

bearing

commanders' intent

courage

cultural indoctrination and transformation

decisiveness

dependability	knowledge
endurance	loyalty
enthusiasm	mission
expectations and desired end-state	OODA loops
fog of war or friction	Rule of Three
initiative	tact
integrity	Uniform Code of Military Justice
judgment	(UCMJ)
justice	unselfishness

✦ Questions for Discussion and Review

1. How does the description of military leadership put forth in the chapter overlap with conceptions of leadership expressed by other disciplines represented in this book?

2. What are the primary missions of the U.S. Armed Forces?

3. What are some similarities and differences between military and civilian life? How might these impact on an individual's personal theory of leadership?

4. Of the fourteen leadership traits listed in this chapter, what is the one that most military students agree is the most important? Do you agree with this assessment? Why or why not?

5. What is the *fog of war*? Does the concept apply only to military settings? Describe a time when you felt like you were in the fog of war.

6. What is the *Rule of Three*?

7. Which do you feel is more important when communicating to others you are depending on, task or intent? Why?

8. Why are performance reviews important?

CHAPTER 14

Environmental Leadership

■ ■ ■

LEADERSHIP MOMENT

You are a manager at a company that manufactures consumer products. Your company prides itself on ethical treatment of employees and other stakeholders, and much of your business is dependent on your company and product's reputation. Recently, the Environmental Protection Agency visited your largest plant and found that you are not in compliance with your water quality permit. Apparently, your plant is releasing more wastewater with more pollutants into a local stream than your permit allows. You are surprised that you learned about this violation from the government, as opposed to your own employees. You are also surprised to learn that most of your competitors face a similar situation, and simply pay the relatively minimal fine each year, as opposed to fixing the problem. You learn that the waterways near your plant are severely polluted by other industries, and your contribution to the problem is relatively marginal.

1.   What would you do?

2.   Do the boundaries of your leadership decision extend to nonhuman species affected by your company's actions?

3.   Would this situation prompt you to investigate other environmental impacts of your company?

4.   What personal and organizational risks are associated with paying the fine versus redesigning plant processes to minimize waste and pollution?

5.   How do your personal values factor into this leadership situation?

Imagine that your supervisor assigns you to lead a project where the end goals are undefined, multiple and often conflicting partners need to be involved, and the benefits are difficult to see and may not occur until far into the future. The short-term costs are apparent, but the benefits are intangible and long-term, and many of the beneficiaries are not even born yet! Would you volunteer for this project? Is this a leadership challenge for which you are prepared? Although this situation may seem far-fetched at first, it mirrors the situation that leaders face when dealing with environmental issues, and demonstrates some of the reasons why our environmental future tends to be overlooked in the face of everyday, seemingly more urgent demands on personal and professional time and energy. Simply put, environmental issues tend to take a back seat to the more immediate and transparent leadership challenges, despite the widely recognized importance of our natural environment to our health and happiness.

The list of global environmental problems is so staggering, serious, and overwhelming that thinking about our global environment often leads to organizational gridlock and personal denial and dissociation. Who wants to spend your time worrying not only about family, friends, co-workers and customers, but also about other species and ecosystems? However, problems such as global warming, extinction of plant and animal species, lack of clean water, air pollution, land degradation, and so on may represent the largest challenges faced by current and future generations. The long-term survival of our way of life and, in fact, all of Earth's species (including ourselves), depends on how we respond to this challenge. Important problems call for strong leadership, and this chapter is designed to apply some of the principles of leadership contained in this book and elsewhere to the thorny issue of environmental protection. As Dillon and Fischer (1992) wrote, "In its response to the various forces, leadership becomes an internal motivator for environmental behavior." This leadership can come on a personal level or in the workplace, as nearly every job is connected indirectly or directly to the consumption of natural resources and all humans impact and are impacted by their environment. To prepare you for this leadership challenge, this chapter presents motivations and tools for environmental leadership. Try to apply these thoughts to your own life as you read.

✦ WHY IS IT DIFFICULT TO BE AN ENVIRONMENTAL LEADER?

Assuming that environmental issues are prevalent and important (as the vast majority of scientists believe), why are we—as individuals, organizations, and as a species—having such a difficult time dealing with them? What makes environmental issues so difficult to provide leadership on? There are no easy answers to these questions, but there are at least four reasons why environmental issues represent a leadership challenge:

1. *Timescales.* Timing is critical in making leadership decisions. However, environmental issues often have timescales that inhibit action. **Global warming** illustrates this point. Driving your car today releases small

amounts of CO_2, which is the main greenhouse gas responsible for the current increase in global average temperature. Global warming (global average temperature has risen by at least 1°F over the past 100 years) will have greater effects in the future, and it represents a challenge on a global scale for all societies. However, the CO_2 released by your car today causes an infinitesimal increase in temperature that may not be felt for decades. This timing problem also works retroactively. The paper that you are using today to take notes on in your leadership course was once a tree, but by the time you purchase it, the impacts are far away in time and space. Why should you commit your limited personal or organizational resources to a problem that will not be fully faced during your lifetime?

2. *Individual versus collective responsibility.* Your car's impacts and all of your personal environmental impacts add up to minute problems at the global (and perhaps local) level. The same is likely to be true of your factory's releases into a local river or even the contributions of many countries to global warming, resource depletion, and pollution. However, at a collective level, we are altering the basic functioning of the carbon, nitrogen, atmospheric, and other ecological systems that sustain life. Your local river may be severely polluted by thousands of small factories. Smog is produced by thousands of individual automobiles, trucks, and other sources of pollution. But, why should you take responsibility for impacts that you are such a small part of causing? Shouldn't others with greater impacts and greater responsibility bear the burden of changing their practices? When you receive the benefits of polluting behavior (i.e., a convenient way to get to work) and everyone pays the cost (i.e., smog), what incentive do you have to change your practices?

TRAGEDY OF THE COMMONS
The Need for Collective Leadership

The classic **tragedy of the commons** scenario, outlined by Garrett Hardin in a 1968 article in *Science* magazine, takes place in medieval England. In a village, there is a public pasture (a commons) where all villagers are free to graze their cattle. For many years, the number of cattle is kept at a reasonable level because "tribal wars, poaching, and disease keep the numbers of both man and beast well below the carrying capacity of the land." However, when a period of relative peace and stability sets in, each villager begins to add more and more cattle to the commons and the village begins to expand in population (yet the commons remain the same size). The villagers directly receive benefits from the additional cattle they graze on the commons in the form of milk and meat, and perhaps even in the prestige of having a larger herd. What would you do if you were a villager deciding whether to add an additional cow to your herd?

Most likely, you would continue to add more and more cattle to your herd. Each villager acting in an individually rational way (i.e., adding more and more cattle to the commons) leads to a predictable and inevitable problem, namely overgrazing. This overgrazing eventually leads to less productive land and, ultimately, the death of most—if not all—of the cattle, and collapse of the local economy. As Hardin explains:

> "Therein is the tragedy. Each man is locked into a system that compels him to increase his herd without limit—in a world that is limited. Ruin is the destination toward which all men rush, each pursuing his own best interest in a society that believes in the freedom of the commons. Freedom in a commons brings ruin to all."

How is this relevant to environmental issues of today? Many environmental issues share similar characteristics with the village commons. For example, no country or person owns the oceans (away from the coasts), and thus every country and individual has the incentive to take as many fish as possible without regard for the health of the ecosystem and welfare of other countries. The result is the recent collapse of many global fisheries. Air crosses local and national boundaries. The acid rain that falls in New York's Adirondacks is generated largely by power plants in Ohio, West Virginia, and Pennsylvania. The pollution generated in Russia flows freely into Scandinavian countries. The greenhouse gasses emitted from our cars while commuting to work contribute to a global increase in temperature. Yet, there is little incentive to prevent air pollution because the benefits of power or industry or driving are experienced individually or locally, while the costs are spread far more widely. In each of these cases, individually rational actions create collective environmental problems. Increasing population and increasing consumption of resources leads to more and more of these "tragic" situations.

So, how does this relate to leadership? As Hardin claims, "There is no technical solution to the problem." Therefore, the solution to the tragedy must come from what ultimately becomes a collective decision. This decision could be to limit the number of cows through edict, to privatize grazing land (thus changing incentive structures in favor of long-term conservation), to charge for grazing, or to create incentives for restraint (such as making access to the commons more difficult). These solutions can be applied to most modern environmental problems through legislation, privatization, taxation, and rebates. To make these difficult yet important collective decisions, strong environmental leadership is needed.

3. *Scientific uncertainty and complexity.* There is very strong scientific consensus and evidence that global warming is occurring. However, there is no consensus on what the exact current and future impacts of global warming will be or how high temperatures will become. Scenarios range from those portrayed in the movie *The Day After Tomorrow,* which include massive, rapid, destructive climatic swings (although scientists do not, of course, believe they will happen on the

short timescale of the movie) to little more than a warmer summer and winter with additional plant growth. This uncertainty surrounds many environmental issues, in part because of the extremely complex systems at work. For example, more than 40 percent of all tropical rainforests—the ecosystems that contain the largest concentration of plant and animal species—have been destroyed, causing three to eight species of plants and animals to go extinct every hour. At present rates of estimation, 20 percent of the world's species could be gone in the next thirty years. How much would you be affected by the loss of the naked mole rat, for example? However, a particular species of plant or animal might hold the key to preventing a disease such as HIV/AIDS. Yet, without solid and specific evidence, why should individuals or organization alter current practices? In the face of scientific uncertainty, leadership becomes difficult at best.

4. *Morality.* Environmental protection is essentially an ethical choice. Humans literally determine which species live or die and how clean our air and water will be. This unique position involves serious choices and consequences. Given human capacity for moral reasoning, the questions become: Are there ethical obligations between species? For example, do you believe that the naked mole rat has an intrinsic right to exist? What ethical obligations are individuals and organizations under to protect the health of other people and communities? For example, should the United States be concerned about the impacts of our consumption of natural resources on the residents of Siberia? Do you feel physically and biologically connected to the planet? Does this affect your leadership decisions?

These complex and ambiguous circumstances constitute a leadership challenge with local, regional, national, and global consequences. This challenge applies at the personal level, as the combined impacts of individual actions at home and in the workplace drive environmental problems. This challenge applies to corporations and other organizations, which are directly or indirectly responsible for much of the world's pollution and other environmental problems. As Newman and Breeden (1992, p. 211) assert: "Of the many issues associated with **corporate social responsibility**...the environment is the most recent addition to top management's agenda. It is arguably the hardest to address, because environmental risks are less personal, less immediate and, therefore, have less apparent urgency." Given this uncertainty and complexity, it is amazing that any individuals or organizations have taken the lead on the environment, yet we are beginning to see a growing cadre of these leaders. Gladwin (1999, p. 4) observes: "I am strongly encouraged by the emergence of a well-informed and visionary set of corporate leaders who have taken up the challenge of orienting their companies to support a sustainable human future." One of these leaders, Ray Anderson of Interface, Inc. is profiled in this chapter. Environmental leaders have also risen in government, nonprofit organizations and academia (as the profile of David Orr from Oberlin College demonstrates). As you read these profiles and the rest of this chapter think about your potential or desire to become an environmental leader, despite the challenges outlined in this section.

✦ SUSTAINABILITY: A FRAMEWORK FOR ENVIRONMENTAL LEADERSHIP

To begin to move past what at first appears to be a leadership morass and into potential for visionary leadership, a framework for action is needed. This framework must recognize the long-term, complex, and interrelated nature of environmental problems (such as global warming) and solutions as well as the opportunities and rewards for success. Leading thinkers and practitioners in the field are working to put these principles into practice through the concept of **sustainability.** However, sustainability[1] is a term and concept that is much used and much abused by individuals and organizations. The many scholars and practitioners attempting to define sustainability have left few stones unturned in describing sustainability as an ideal end-state, a moral principle (Viederman 1995), an ethic (Leopold 1949), and the avoidance of ecological surprise (Holling 1986; King 1995), among other definitions. Perhaps the most basic and influential definition of sustainability comes from the World Commission on Environment and Development (also known as the Brudtland Commission) in 1987: "To meet the needs of the present without compromising the ability of future generations to meet their own needs." What does this definition mean to you? How would you describe "sustaining" your personal and professional life?

A review of definitions and conceptualizations of sustainability reveals several concepts that are integral and widespread: long-term survival, integrity and maintenance of systems, limits, interdependence, and equity. The literature also reveals an emerging consensus about the three pillars of sustainability (also known as *the triple bottom line* (Elkington 1998)—ecological, economic and social sustainability—although different analysts give priority to different pillars. The bottom line is that sustainability is about intergenerational, intragenerational, and interspecies equity in how we handle the earth's resources.

Stakeholders, defined by the Interoperability Clearinghouse as "individuals or groups with an interest in the success of an organization in delivering intended results and maintaining the viability of the organization's products and services", have traditionally been thought to be employees and stockholders. However, these emerging notions of equity represent a challenge to traditional notions of leadership, as they expand the boundaries of concern by incorporating a wider range of stakeholders. For example, decisions about building a new coal-fired power plant would undergo sustainability screens about the long-term impacts on wildlife and stocks of coal, air and water quality, health of children and adults, and the long-term economic viability of the plant and region. These analyses go far beyond the traditional notion of economic cost-benefit analysis

---

1. Note that sustainability and sustainable development are used interchangeably (unless otherwise noted) since this is common in both theory and practice.

that you were taught in your economics classes and that are the dominant way to make decisions.

While the concept of **intergenerational equity** can be traced back to Thomas Jefferson, Immanuel Kant and Edmund Burke, among others (Ball 2000), sustainability as a concept and framework has become far more influential during the past twenty-five years. "In a remarkably short time it has evolved from a concept put forward by a few scholars to a widely accepted and influential idea in the continuing debate over the future of the world" (Kidd 1992, p. 3). Mainstream magazines and newspapers have published articles about the sustainability movement, and politicians are increasingly using the concept of sustainability as a rationale for environmental action. Sustainability has great leadership potential as a concept because it crosses disciplinary, organizational, and cultural boundaries. The concept is poised to be a critical organizing principle for the twenty-first century, in part because it is not an incremental strategy for environmental and social change. Sustainability represents bold vision and potential. For example, a sustainable approach to energy use involves a holistic assessment of energy demand, consumption and conservation, not simply developing ways reduce current energy usage. This interdisciplinary approach draws heavily on the natural and social sciences as well as ethics, and is challenging for leaders to implement. Yet, as Uhl (1996, p. 1308) noted: "No other concept seems to compare to it in terms of its ability to cut across virtually all disciplines and in its fundamental importance to the human enterprise." Can you think of concepts that match sustainability in their broad scope and reach?

✦ BENEFITS TO LEADERSHIP ON THE ENVIRONMENT

"Setting out to 'achieve' sustainability is a bit like seeking the elusive state of economic 'equilibrium,' the nirvana of neoclassical economists: It rarely, if ever, exists—and when it does, only fleetingly," wrote Spencer-Cooke (1998, p. 103). Becoming a sustainable organization or individual, or even moving toward sustainability, is complex and ambiguous because there are no well-established, comprehensive guidelines. Would you consider yourself or your place of study or employment sustainable? Individuals seeking to be sustainable must find alternative ways of eating (such as all organic, local foods), living (such as without a vehicle and relying on solar or wind energy), and interacting (for example, without buying consumer products). Seeking sustainability on your campus means different ways of educating and running your college or university (see the "Campus Ecology" box).

✦ LEADERSHIP SKILLS ✦
Campus Ecology

This chapter emphasizes that environmental issues are difficult to act upon and that strong leadership is required. You have read about environmental leaders in many different sectors who have accomplished amazing things. However, you might be thinking: What can I, as a student, do to have an environmental impact?

The answer lies in campus environmentalism or **campus ecology,** as the National Wildlife Federation and others have called it. Students have tremendous and often unused power on college campuses, given your status as the primary customers. Recent research has shown that student demand is a main driver of environmental changes on campuses ranging from starting a recycling program to purchasing renewable (i.e., wind and solar) energy to beginning an environmental studies major or minor. For example, students at New College (California) are leading efforts to reduce energy usage by 20 percent through technology (e.g., more efficient lightbulbs) and education (e.g., asking students and others to turn off computer monitors and other energy-intensive products). Students at Northland College (Wisconsin) designed a campus landscape plan that restores habitats native to the area. A student at Ball State University (Indiana) created a video on sustainability that has aired on twelve public television stations. The possibilities are nearly endless for acquiring leadership skills and making environmental progress.

Seeking sustainability in the corporate sector is difficult as well. Even Stuart Hart (1995, p. 998)—the S.C. Johnson Chair for Sustainable Global Enterprise at Cornell University and a strong corporate sustainability advocate—does not believe that the market supports sustainability in the short-term: "For a firm, pursuing a sustainable development strategy thus implies both substantial investment and a long-term commitment to market development. There is little reason to believe that this investment will result in enhanced short-term profits." Some argue that organizational and leadership theory is systematically biased against sustainability in its focus solely on humans (excluding all other species), lack of biophysical foundations, reductionism, and shallowness (Gladwin & Kennelly, 1995; Shrivastava, 1994). In other words, organizational and leadership theory focus on short-term relationships and profits, without recognizing humans' role in the more complex web of life and in providing for future generations.

Without clear guidance or rewards, you may be asking: Why should I strive for personal and organizational sustainability? What are the possible benefits to organizations and individuals in seeking this "nirvana" of leadership and action? The following six points are designed to spur your thinking about justifications for environmental leadership and beginning the move toward sustainability:

1. *Long-term survival.* The simplest explanation for leading society toward sustainability is because it is necessary. The stresses that you and all other people are placing on essential ecological and social systems are too large. While the immediacy of ecological limits is a subject of some debate, there is no question that over the long-term, if corporations, individuals and other entities continue to degrade ecological and social systems, our species and institutions will not survive (Daly, 1996; Meadows et al., 1992). For example, all humans need clean

water to survive and thrive. Yet, if we continue to degrade our water supplies with toxic pollution, we will eventually run out of clean water. This logic applies at the organizational and corporate level as well. "The destiny of corporations is inextricably linked with the well-being of the rest of the earth; hence, companies must take a leading role in sustainable development," wrote Gladwin and Krause (1996, p. 9).

2. *Stakeholder engagement.* Leading for sustainability on an individual level means looking beyond our own needs to take into consideration the needs of the next generation as well as other species and communities. Leading for sustainability in the corporate world involves extending the traditional concept of stakeholders and incorporating new stakeholders such as local communities, the public, and ecosystems in our organizational decisions. "Prosperous companies in a sustainable world will be those that are better than their competitors at 'adding value' for all their stakeholders, not just for customers and investors," wrote Schmidheiny (1998, p. 86). Willmott (1999, p. 2) contends: "Companies need to respond by making their values and activities mirror the prevailing ethos of the new political economy. After all, companies are made up of individuals—whether they are shareholding owners, business managers or employees—and deal with individuals (customers, suppliers, lobbyists, etc.). Surely companies must reflect the emerging values of the people they deal with." For example, when deciding whether to shut down an auto factory, this framework would require companies to consider the broader implications of their actions on the local economy, plant and animal species, and so on. All stakeholders have legitimate and increasingly asserted claims, and many are rallying around sustainability.

3. *Reputation.* More and more people are becoming concerned with whether they are perceived as having an environmentally friendly lifestyle. Perhaps the best evidence of this is the prevalence of the hybrid gas-electric cars (such as the Toyota Prius and Honda Insight) at Hollywood gatherings such as the Emmys. At the organizational level, pursuing sustainability can lead to reputational gains that translate into enhanced image, improved culture and better external relations for individuals and organizations. Companies such as Patagonia and Ben & Jerry's rely on this reputation to increase their sales. These types of **intangible assets** are increasingly important for corporations in the new information economy, where value is based more on services than goods.

Many studies associate a reputation and culture of pursuing sustainability with improved employee recruitment, retention, and morale through increased organizational-personal environmental congruence (Fineman, 1998; Schmidheiny, 1998). Shrivastava and Hart (1995, p. 162) wrote, "Sustainability requires different organizational cultures and processes. Cultural values must emphasize harmonious coexistence with the natural world, view humans as part of the natural world, and acknowledge the rights of nature to exist." Hawken (1993, p. 127) added, "The question arises as to how long a company can prevail if its employees, consciously or unconsciously, perceive their products, processes, or corporate goals as harmful to humankind." Simply put, employees and customers tend to be happier when their values are reflected in their purchases and employers.

4. *Ethics.* As mentioned previously, environmental issues are—at their most basic level—ethical choices for individuals and organizations. This ethical choice represents a leadership challenge. For corporations, Hoffman and Ehrenfeld (1998, p. 70) wrote: "Firms are finding that as environmental values take hold at the deepest levels of societal structures, it becomes increasingly necessary to include those values in their corporate cultures or risk creating value systems that are dissonant with those of their employees." Although this logic is similar to the logic proposed about reputation, it differs because it probes deeper into social and organizational consciousness by addressing issues of morality, altruism, and responsibility. Although reputation can be enhanced through marketing tactics, ethical relationships result from repeated interactions and perceptions of intentions that go far beyond image. Do these considerations factor into your choices of products and employers? Corporations have an ethical obligation to pursue sustainability since these enterprises are often responsible for ecological and social degradation, and have been chartered to create value, not just money. "Long-term organizational legitimacy depends on how organizations handle their ethical responsibilities toward the natural environment," wrote Shrivastava (1994, p. 722). Individuals, also, are increasingly "taking their ethics to work," and surveys consistently reveal strong support for environmental protections. On a personal level, moving toward sustainability can provide a sense of empowerment and goodwill through taking action on important issues.

5. *Market opportunities.* Many scholars who point to the market opportunities inherent in pursuing management for sustainability place management for sustainability within the standard corporate strategy framework by looking for new market niches, competencies, and so on. For example, Hart (1995) wrote of the need for firms to develop strategic capabilities in pollution prevention, product stewardship, and sustainable development. Porter and van der Linde (1995) contend that environmental/sustainability management is advantageous because it spurs innovation and efficiency. For example, a firm trying to cut its emission of a harmful toxin might develop a more efficient way to produce its products. However, the logic of these claims has been hotly contested, most notably by Walley and Whitehead (1994, p. 2): "Environmental costs at most companies are skyrocketing, with little economic payback in sight," and few win–win solutions are left.

Therefore, it appears that sustainability may represent a market advantage for some firms. Part of the leadership advantage is to assess market opportunities related to sustainability.

6. *Regulatory avoidance.* One of the most pervasive arguments in favor of sustainability leadership at the organizational level is the avoidance of regulation. As pointed out by Post and Altman (1994) and Shrivastava and Hart (1995), among others, companies that commit to environmental improvements are likely to improve their relations with governmental entities, decrease prospects for litigation and other risks, and stay ahead of environmental regulations. The U.S. Environmental Protection Agency and state environmental regulatory agencies tend to devote their enforcement resources to those organizations with a reputation of breaking laws or trying to avoid regulations. Government regulation was the first factor to drive enterprise to manage environmental issues. However, this reason for sustainability leadership is largely outdated, since sustainability management goes far beyond regulatory compliance, and governments tend to lag far behind public consciousness in their regulations. Therefore, avoiding regulation is perhaps an argument for minimal environmental management and establishing strong governmental relationships, but is not nearly far-reaching enough to be a strong argument for sustainability leadership.

Combining these organizational and individual motivations for sustainability leadership leads to the concept of **enlightened self-interest** (Gladwin et al. 1995; Whitman 1999), which involves encouraging long-term thinking about relationships with social and ecological systems. For individuals, enlightened self-interest implies watching out for one's own interests at home and work, but also making sure that your individual actions do not unnecessarily or unacceptably impact other people or species now or in the future. You can think of this concept as an ethical and environmental screen on personal actions, such as the buying of a product. This screen consists of questions such as: Do I really need this product? What statement does this purchase make about my values? How does this purchase affect other people and the environment?

A key assumption in the emerging literature on enlightened self-interest is that organizational leaders and others are not guided by short-term profit alone because their personal values cannot be excluded from the workplace (Janis and Mann 1983). Employees not only shape the organizational culture and ethics of their place of employment, but also are shaped by it. Therefore, problems occur when an individual's personal environmental image clashes with the dominant environmental culture in his or her work environment. The classic example is an employee of a company infamous for its poor environmental record who is a member of Greenpeace in her or his personal life. DeSimone & Popoff (1997, p. 11) assert, "More and more companies are seeing shared values and a common sense of purpose among their staff as a key success factor. Making an environmental and social contribution can be an important element of these." Simply put, "being an ethical 'bad guy' can have far-reaching negative consequences," wrote Sains (2002). Greeno and Robinson (1992, p. 225-26) take this approach one step further:

> Companies are beginning to find that how they manage their environmental affairs can also contribute to how satisfied the stakeholders are with the company overall…Enlightened companies know that just reacting to growing stakeholder demands for environmental assurance is not enough. Instead, companies have to be prepared to take the lead.

Therefore, corporate environmental leadership is becoming integral to attracting stakeholders who are increasingly concerned with environmental ethics. These stakeholders—including employees, customers, and shareholders—are increasingly concerned about sustainability on a personal and professional level. A major lesson drawn from these studies is that leaders must consider the ethical and long-term consequences of action and inaction. Do you agree that environmental considerations should be factored heavily into personal and organizational affairs?

✦ TRANSFORMATIONAL ENVIRONMENTAL LEADERSHIP

Transformational leaders orient organizational systems toward a higher ethical purpose (Bass and Steidlmeier 1999). Transformational leaders also attempt to achieve value congruence and mutual respect between themselves and *followers,* as well as other stakeholders. The ties with environmental and sustainability leadership should be apparent to you: the concept of sustainability is also an attempt at creating a shared ethical and moral framework and could be a core component of **transformational leadership.** The *higher ethical purpose* of a transformational leader can be translated directly into a shared goal of organizational sustainability. A transformational leader is more than a manager, as she or he has the ability to inspire followers to work together toward stretch goals with a high level of motivation. As stated by Deluga (1988, p. 457): "The transformational manager cultivates employee acceptance of the work group mission." Using strong personal influence, transformational leaders inspire followers to meet "higher" needs through their organizations (Conger 1999). The transformational leader inspires commitment not only to the organization, but also to personal fulfillment through participation in organizational processes. This fits an environmental leadership framework because extreme motivation guided in part by personal ethics needs to be integrated into organizational frameworks to move toward the shared goal of sustainability. For example, when a local government leader expresses and demonstrates commitment to cleaning up all local toxic sites, city employees and residents might respond with great enthusiasm if they are inspired by the leader and believe that their actions will be personally and socially beneficial.

Transformational leaders focus themselves and all stakeholders on transcending self-interest and moving into long-term, shared personal and organizational ethical commitments and visions in addition to short-term gains (such as quarterly profit). As stated by Behling and McFillen (1996, p. 163), transformational leadership means "the actions of single managers appear to create extraordinarily high levels of employee commitment, effort, and willingness to take risks in support of the organization or its mission." The transformational leadership literature views leadership as a "dynamic and interactive process, whereby leaders inspire and energize followers" (Gardner and Cleavenger 1998, p. 3). These leaders must be charismatic, inspirational, and intellectually stimulating, and they must provide individualized consideration to followers. These leaders must also follow strong moral and ethic cues, thus leaving followers with feelings of trust, admiration, loyalty, and respect. Transformational leadership involves defining and communicating a vision, reinforcing involvement in this vision, and fulfillment of commitments. The outcomes of transformational leadership are often major changes in organizational mission, strategy, culture and—perhaps most important—values.

Sound familiar? The traits and characteristics involved in transformational leadership closely mimic the traits and characteristics necessary for environmental and sustainability leadership. In fact, environmental issues are an area ripe for transformational leaders in any organization or context. As the leadership profiles in this chapter demonstrate, many individuals are rising to the challenge of becoming a transformational environmental leader. On issues as complex as the environment and sustainability, leaders must have the personal charisma and gain the trust of their followers to ensure success. For example, the CEOs of several major oil companies—including BP—are now fully recognizing and developing plans to respond to global warming. Although these proclamations and actions may not fully satisfy environmentalists, they do represent the expenditure of personal capita to provide leadership on a complex and vitally important issue. Similarly, several European government leaders have made commitments to reduce their country's greenhouse gas emissions (which lead to climate change) far below the levels specified by international treaties. These instances of bold, visionary environmental leadership require a transformational perspective and following.

Since transformational leadership is one of the "important mechanisms that effects organizational change" (Pawar and Eastman 1997, p. 82) and is strongly related to organizational ethics (Carlson and Perrewe 1995), as well as long-term commitment (Bass and Avolio 1994; Carlson and Perrewe 1995), the relationship between transformational leadership and environmental leadership is not particularly surprising. The concept of transformational leadership is gaining influence in the leadership literature as a way to explain how personal characteristics and style can lead to organizational changes. This concept is starting to be applied to corporate environmentalism because it embodies the ethical orientation, motivation of stakeholders and interest in the broader community that often characterize strong corporate environmental responsibility initiatives. This concept may also be applicable to other types of leadership. Do you think there is a strong connection between transformational leadership and environmental issues? Do you know of examples of this connection?

RAY ANDERSON

From "Plunderer of the Earth" to "Eco-Hero"

Ray Anderson, the founder, former CEO, and current chairman of the board at Interface (the world's largest producer of commercial floorcovering with sales of approximately $930 million in 2003), claims that he fit the typical businessman in preparation and profile for the first fifty-nine years of his life. He built a company from scratch (relying on the "requisite 99 percent perspiration"), guiding it through rough periods and business reinventions. He even managed to give up the reigns of the company and move from "autocratic, hands-on" management to being "head cheerleader." Yet, his biggest challenge and ultimate "calling" was yet to come. He realized that his first fifty-nine years consisted of, as he put it, being a "plunderer of the earth," despite being considered a "modern day hero, an entrepreneur who founded a company that provides over 7,000 people with jobs."

His epiphany began when Interface, in response to customer questions, put together an environmental task force in 1994. Anderson was slated to give the keynote address to kickoff the task force, but he "sweated for three weeks" because he "didn't have a vision, except 'obey the law, comply, comply, comply.'" Through a serendipitous coincidence, an employee provided him with a copy of Paul Hawken's influential book *The Ecology of Commerce* at around this same time (we recommend that all business people and environmentalists read this book and the more recent book by Hawken, Lovins & Lovins titled *Natural Capitalism*). As he says: "I read it, and it changed my life. It hit me right between the eyes…Hawken's message was a spear in my chest that is still there." Soon thereafter, he calculated the material extracted annually from the Earth to produce Interface's products. The amount came to a staggering 1.2 billion pounds, of which 800 million pounds was of "irreplaceable, non-renewable, exhaustible, precious natural" resources that were "burned up" and "gone forever." His company was not doing anything illegal, although Anderson realized that he was externalizing many of the costs of operation and thus was a *legal thief*. He posed this relatively simple thought to himself and his employees and colleagues: "THIS CANNOT GO ON FOREVER INDEFINITELY, CAN IT?"

Anderson was soon hooked on the idea of creating the **next Industrial Revolution** because "the first one is just not working out very well, even though I am as great a beneficiary of it as most anyone." Anderson realized that no companies or individuals are sustainable, so he set a goal for Interface to be the first industrial company to "attain environmental sustainability, and then to become restorative." By restorative, Anderson means to "put more back than we take, and to do good to Earth, not just no harm." The model for doing this is natural systems, where there is no waste. Talk about a grand leadership vision! Anderson describes it as a "mountain to climb that's higher than Everest."

Anderson explained his thinking in the following manner: "Once one understands this (environmental) crisis, no thinking person can stand idly by and do nothing. Denial is alluring, even seductive, but once you get past denial, you

know you must do whatever you can." His leadership rationale is deceptively simple: "Unless somebody leads, no one will. At the very *least* we will give our people and our company a higher cause and a long range reason for being." This
translates into the current corporate vision:

> To be the first company that, by its deeds, shows the entire industrial
> world what sustainability is in all its dimensions: People, process, prod-
> uct, place and profits—by 2020—and in doing so we will become
> restorative through the power of influence.

Anderson has implemented this vision at Interface in significant ways, beginning with reducing waste (defined as "any cost that goes into our product that does
not produce value for our customers"). Currently, Interface diverts 13 million
pounds of material from landfills annually. Interface products are now lighter but
more durable. Through these initiatives, Interface has saved $231 million (cumu-
latively) since 1994. Its goal is zero emissions and the elimination of all toxic chemicals. Moreover, companies can lease instead of buy carpeting (called an Evergreen
Lease®), and Interface will replace and recycle worn tiles as opposed to companies
having to buy entire new flooring if one part is damaged. Interface is using renewable energy as a fuel source (approximately 12 percent from biomass or other
"green" sources), selling products with 100 percent recycled-content, using
resource efficient transportation and offsetting emissions from travel by planting
trees, engaging in community environmental service, and publicly reporting their
sustainability progress. Through these initiatives and others, Interface has reduced
CO_2 emissions by 46 percent in 2003, as compared to 1996. To implement these
initiatives and solicit feedback and suggestions, Interface is training its employees
on sustainability and the "thousands and thousands of little things" that can be done
to reduce environmental damage. There are no standard or easy measures of
progress toward what Interface calls EcoSense®, but Anderson believes that
Interface will "do well by doing good" by improving customer loyalty, increasing
resource efficiency, and setting an example.

(Information for this profile comes from Anderson's 1998 book entitled *Mid-Course Correction* as
well as Interface's Web site—www.ifsia.com.)

DAVID ORR

Building a Sustainable Future

David Orr, professor and chair of the Environmental Studies program at Oberlin
College, is an environmental visionary. He is the author of four major books (*The
Last Refuge, The Nature of Design, Ecological Literacy,* and *Earth in Mind*) and
more than 100 published articles that challenge readers to think deeply and act
on environmental issues.

Orr grew up in a hilltop home in the Allegheny Mountains of Western
Pennsylvania. Orr's father and paternal grandfather were preachers, which may

explain his preparation for and revered oratory skill, which he uses while traveling around the country giving dozens of keynote addresses to current and future leaders. This spiritual and natural background provides the foundation for Orr's strong belief in the connections between spirit, nature, and human, as well as environmental progress. He describes environmentalism as a "question of ethical design."

Translating this ethical design into physical design was the major challenge in building the Lewis Environmental Studies Center at Oberlin College. Orr asked a deceptively simply question: "Can organizations that purport to advance learning themselves learn to recalibrate their mission and operations to the larger facts of global ecological change?" In attempting to answer this question, in part through a physical structure and the surrounding space, he was told by Oberlin's administration that he must raise the funds for this building without tapping into current donors to the college.

Professor Orr used an unconventional approach to building design, using a process a series of open public sessions to create not only the "highest possible standard of ecological architecture" but also an "educational exercise in how we might stitch landscape, materials, energy, and water together" that "would cause no ugliness, human or ecological, somewhere else or at some later time." More specifically, the building goals were sevenfold:

1. Be integrated with the curriculum.
2. Evolve with advancing technology.
3. Discharge no waste (i.e., drinking water in, drinking water out).
4. Use sunlight as fully as possible.
5. Use only wood from forests certified as managed sustainably.
6. Minimize the use of toxic materials.
7. Be integrated with the landscape as a single design system.

With these goals in mind, construction began on the 14,000 square foot building in 1996 and was completed in 1998. The result is, according to the *New York Times*, "the most remarkable" of a new generation of college buildings and one of thirty "milestone buildings in the 20th century" according to the U.S. Department of Energy. The building uses less than 33 percent of the energy of comparable academic buildings because of solar cells on the roof, the orientation of the building to maximize natural heating and cooling, and extreme energy efficiency in lighting, heating, cooling, and so on. The building features a "living machine" that purifies wastewater onsite to standards that exceed the most stringent federal limits, using only plants and animals in a series of tanks and indoor gardens and rivers. The Lewis Center has geothermal wells that bring up water that is 54°F year-round and thus help with heating in the winter and cooling in the summer. The building is full of recycled, reused, and low energy-intensity materials. The landscape around the building features a forest, wetland, and pond containing plants native to Oberlin, Ohio, as well as "low-mow" grass that requires fewer chemicals and care. The building includes more than 150 environmental sensors that provide real-time data to students, faculty, and others interested in monitoring the progress of this groundbreaking building. Finally, and perhaps most importantly, the building is designed with abundant natural sunlight, open floor plans, and a large atrium to encourage professional and social interaction, thus creating a popular space on campus for classes, events, and socializing.

RACHEL CARSON
Writer, Scientist, Crusader

When Rachel Carson journeyed to a summer job at Woods Hole Oceanographic Institute in Cape Cod, it was the first time she had even seen the ocean. The sea had captivated her interest for years, however, even as a young girl on a farm north of Pittsburgh. She had studied diligently enough to win a scholarship in marine zoology at Johns Hopkins University in Baltimore. She earned her M.S. in 1932.

She was repeatedly warned to pursue some other field: women did not become scientists in the first half of the twentieth century. And if they insisted on getting their degrees, there would be no jobs for them. Nevertheless, Carson persisted, fueled in part by her overwhelming passion for the natural world and by her mother's support. She later recounted how much it meant to her when FDR appointed the first woman in the history of the United States to a cabinet position (Frances Perkins became FDR's secretary of labor). To top it off, Eleanor Roosevelt was becoming a national figure.

She found a job that combined her loves of language and science through writing scripts for the weekly radio show "Romance Under the Waters." The sea became her touchstone as she began to explain in graceful, nontechnical terms much of what scientists knew about the ocean and its life.

Carson went on to write several books about the natural world, including *The Sea Around Us, Under the Sea Wind,* and *The Edge of the Sea.* In between caring for her mother and raising children of relatives who had died, she wrote a moving book, *A Sense of Wonder,* to help young people appreciate the natural world.

A much-awarded and highly praised writer, she retired to her cottage off the coast of Maine. She could easily have lived a contented life producing more of the same type of writings. However, she took a gamble and began to research not the beauties of nature, but the spoilers of nature. Her landmark 1962 book, *Silent Spring,* charged that rampant use of pesticides was devastating the environment, killing birds and other animals, and potentially affecting humans as well. Further, she charged that government scientists had known of the damage from the chemicals but had been prevented from speaking out.

Ironically, shortly before the book was published, she was diagnosed with breast cancer. At the time scientists were just beginning to uncover links between environmental influences and diseases such as cancer.

It's hard to appreciate the commotion the publication of *Silent Spring* unleashed. Many scientific associations, including the American Medical

Association, attacked the book, and much of the media went after Carson personally. *Time* magazine called the book "an emotional and inaccurate outburst." The chemical industry spent large sums of money ridiculing her arguments in print. Some suggested she was a communist.

Upset at the unfairness of these attacks, the normally shy woman agreed to a nationally televised interview with Eric Sevareid on CBS on April 3, 1963. Her soft-spoken, articulate remarks convinced millions of viewers and swung public opinion to her side. Legislation passed the next year that tightened requirements for chemical companies.

More significantly, however, Rachel Carson had helped people understand the ramifications of tampering with the environment. As her comments on television showed, she was able to convey the bigger picture: "We still talk in terms of conquest. We still haven't become mature enough to think of ourselves as only a tiny part of a vast and incredible universe. Man's attitude toward nature is today critically important simply because we have now acquired a fateful power to alter and destroy nature. But man is a part of nature, and his war against nature is inevitably a war against himself."

She won many honors and awards for her efforts. Upon receiving the Audubon Medal (the first woman to be so honored), she asserted that "Conservation is a cause that has no end. There is no point at which we will say 'our work is finished.'"

Carson succumbed to cancer just over one year after her remarkable television appearance. She had become well known and greatly admired for her courage and dedication. She acknowledged her real reward, however, in this passage written shortly before her death: "It is good to know that I shall live on even in the minds of many who do not know me and largely through association with things that are beautiful and lovely."

✦ Chapter Summary

This chapter has followed the pattern of this book by posing many leadership questions for which there are no easy answers. Environmental issues represent a leadership need, given their critical nature. Yet, there are relatively few environmental leaders, in part because of the ambiguities and pitfalls involved in addressing environmental issues. Using a framework of sustainability to address the environment in a personal and organizational context requires expanding the boundaries of leadership and management theory and action to cross the boundaries of species and generations, and to deal directly with ethics and morality. Transformational leadership is the theoretical perspective most prepared to respond to this challenge, and many environmental leaders can be considered transformational in their approaches and outcomes.

✦ CREATE YOUR OWN THEORY ✦

This chapter was designed to challenge your own evolving notions of leadership theory. How has your leadership model evolved based on the consideration of environmental issues? Did environmental concerns/issues factor into your leadership theory before you read this chapter? Why or why not? What other types of social and/or ethical issues apply to your leadership theory? Can you envision orienting your organization or personal life around the principles of sustainability?

Now let's revisit our opening Leadership Moment. What would a transformational environmental leader do? Is this the same action you would take? What ethical leadership issues are raised by this situation? Who are the stakeholders affected by what at first appears to be solely a regulatory or business decision? What additional information would you like to have prior to making your decision? What if it is not available? What types of market opportunities does this decision raise?

✦ Key Terms

campus ecology

corporate social responsibility

enlightened self-interest

global warming

intangible assets

intergenerational equity

next Industrial Revolution

stakeholders

sustainability

tragedy of the commons

transformational leadership

✦ Questions for Discussion and Review

1. What characteristics of environmental issues make them difficult to manage in an organization? What makes them difficult to deal with on a personal level?

2. Where do you rank environmental issues among issues of concern to you? Where do you think environmental issues rank in terms of leadership challenges? What areas are more or less important?

3. What types of situations other than environmental issues does the tragedy of the commons scenario apply to? Have you experienced these situations?

4. Using an environmental issue that you have heard about in the media or in your classes, list some scientific facts and areas of uncertainty. If you wanted to set a positive leadership example on this issue, what would you do?

5. What reaction to the term *sustainability* do you have? Does it make intrinsic sense to you? Do you believe it can motivate others toward environmental action? What does sustainability mean to you?

6. Do you think that there are stronger moral obligations toward other species, people in other countries or future generations of humans? Why?

7. Which of the six points in the chapter that justify environmental leadership do you think is the most important? Why? Which is least important? Why?

8. Who would you consider a transformational leader? Why?

9. Compare the theory of transformational leadership with the theory of sustainability leadership. Where are they similar? Where are they different?

10. If you were a shareholder in Interface Carpeting, would you be happy with the program and policies that Ray Anderson has put into place? Why or why not?

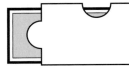

CHAPTER 15

Practicing Leadership: It's Your Turn

"The goal is for everyone's personal puzzle *not* to look the same."

This quote from the book's opening chapter helps end it, as well. You have effectively ended this portion of your leadership puzzle by completing this course of study. What does it all mean? What have you really learned? What are the *take-aways*—those ideas that make sense as you attempt to answer the ultimate final exam for this puzzle: What is leadership?

We suggest that you attempt to answer that complicated question by completing Exercise 15-1 at the end of this chapter. When finished, you should have a personal leadership road sign that briefly details the most important features of your own leadership theory. Remember, as you attempt to describe the various leadership components, this text begins and ends with practicing leadership. Therefore, answer or complete the segments as you intend to practice leadership in the real world.

Table 15–1 provides a summary of concepts, or authors, models, and theories studied.

TABLE 15-1   The Leadership Puzzle

Chapters	*Concepts to Remember*
Introduction:	"Leadership is one of the most observed and least understood phenomena on earth."
	Our basic assumptions:
	1. Where we are in our understanding of leadership is a function of where we have been.
	2. There is no one formula for leadership.
	3. Leadership is not differentiated by setting.

(Continues)

TABLE 15-1 The Leadership Puzzle *(Continued)*

Chapters	*Concepts to Remember*
	4. Our understanding of leadership requires the vantage point of multiple perspectives.
	5. Studying leadership across a range of human differences is the only way to approach the subject in the twenty-first century.
	6. Leadership can best be understood through metaphors and described indirectly through paradigms.
	7. The only leadership is ethical leadership.
	8. Good leaders are good followers.
	9. Every leader leads differently.
	10. Leadership is a verb. It is what you "do," not only how you think.
Leadership in the Modern World:	There is no one agreed upon definition of leadership.
	Leadership can be viewed, studied, and practiced based on these twelve approaches to leadership: Trait theories and other psychological approaches to leadership; group and team leadership; situational leadership theories; organizational development, change, and leadership; leadership versus management; power, politics, and leadership; charismatic leadership; vision, the human condition, and leadership; leadership formulas; ethical leadership; leadership in limited time and space; and multicultural and global leadership.
Ethical Leadership:	People cannot be successful leaders if they are not ethical.
	Executive leaders must create ethical cultures.
	An organization's credos about ethics must be lived and realized.
	The rights theory, the common good theory, fairness theory, utilitarian approach, and value ethics approach are all practiced by different organizations and people.
	The true Hero's Journey often threatens the status quo.
Leadership in a Global and Multicultural Society:	Culture is elements of learned behavior and meaning systems common to a human society.
	We learn our culture by mimicking the behaviors of those who teach us when we are children.
	The Diversity Wheel describes twenty-four dimensions of cultural differences. Each may impact how we lead at various stages of our lives.

(Continues)

TABLE 15-1   The Leadership Puzzle *(Continued)*

Chapters	*Concepts to Remember*
	Diversity can be positive, it can be negative, but it is never neutral.
	The Iceberg view of culture demonstrates that we only see a small part of the reality of any organization.
	Multicultural leaders must assume the risk of potentially losing power as a result of adopting behaviors different from those that brought them success.
	Multicultural literacy is the set of skills, insights, and attitudes that allows us to learn from diverse individuals and places on a continuous basis.
	Multicultural leaders must comprehend their own cultural influences and biases.
	Multicultural leaders create environments where they encourage teaching and learning and assist others in their own diversity journeys.
Psychology I: Intelligence and Personality:	There are numerous models for assessing intelligence, ranging from single instruments geared toward measuring global intelligence to models that view intelligence as multifaceted.
	The psychometric model, the multiple intelligence model, EI (emotional intelligence), and the triarchic theory all help leaders understand how they and others use intelligence in leadership capacities.
	The brain is an incredibly complex structure—it is not ethical and rarely accurate to view another as either wholly intelligent or not intelligent. Rather, the most useful approach is to assume that all persons have intellectual strengths and weaknesses and to attempt to put others in positions where their intellectual strengths are accentuated.
	People are neither purely the product of their genetics or of their environment. All of our personalities are shaped by a combination of our unique genetics and experiences.
Psychology II: Motivation:	A number of models have been developed seeking to understand motivation.
	Reinforcement theories, a key tool for leaders, are presented and reviewed.
	Hygiene and motivational factors need to be understood by leaders.
	Social learning theory is extremely useful for leaders.

(Continues)

TABLE 15-1 The Leadership Puzzle *(Continued)*

Chapters	*Concepts to Remember*
	Effective leaders do not rely exclusively on one motivational model, but rather, adapt their approach to best fit the personalities and needs of those they are seeking to motivate.
Communication:	Communication is a transactional process. Both the sender and the receiver of a communication filter what they hear and see into their own personal sets and the success of a given communication is based in large part on the degree to which sender and receiver are aware of and understand these sets.
	Communication is multifaceted. It can come in verbal form or it can be nonverbal. It can come through formal channels or it can come via the grapevine. One must be aware of the source and context of a particular communication if one is to interpret this communication as it was intended.
	Among the factors that can lead to communication breakdowns are differing frames of reference, selective perception, semantic problems, filtering, constraints on time, and communication overload.
	Charismatic leadership involves a relationship between a leader and the persons being led in which the leader is believed to possess inspirational charismatic qualities. Charismatic leaders are capable of introducing quantum change, sometimes for the better and sometimes for the worse (Adolf Hitler was a charismatic leader).
Philosophy and Leadership:	Leadership can be detected in philosophical works as old as the discipline itself.
	The Greeks of the classical era had no shortage of leaders.
	Remnants of the Greek portrait of a leader—decisive, physical prowess; a warrior's guile; and protection of followers—are still very widely held even today.
	Plato's notion that leaders possessed inborn traits is echoed by much of the modern literature.
	Machiavelli argued that a leader's primary task was to subordinate simply being "good" for other, more attractive ends (power, order, stability, skill at calculation, manipulation, and seeming to possess virtuous qualities). Successful princes (leaders) did not hesitate to take what they desired by force.

(Continues)

TABLE 15-1 **The Leadership Puzzle** *(Continued)*

Chapters	*Concepts to Remember*
Political Science: Power and Leadership from the Top:	Power is something used by many people for many purposes. Among these are to obtain influence. Seven common tactics for obtaining influence are reason, friendliness, sanctions, bargaining, higher authority, assertiveness, and coalition-building.
	The five sources of power are expert power (based on knowledge or competence), referent power (based on relationship and personal "drawing power"), legitimate power (bestowed by formal organization), reward power (the ability to offer and withhold types of incentives), and coercive power (the ability to force someone to comply through threat of physical, psychological, or emotional consequences).
	Another way to view power is to distinguish between personal and positional power. Positional power is derived from one's place in an organization while personal power is derived from an individual's personal attributes.
	The presidency of the United States is the most powerful position in the world. The modern-day president's powers are at once defined by the parameters put forth by the Constitutional Convention and evolution and expansion of this position since that time. FDR can be considered the first modern president. Among his legacies is the shift of power toward the president and away from Congress.
Management and Leadership:	Although the effects of management were felt more than 200 years ago during the Industrial Revolution as factories developed, it is only in this century that its impact has been systematically studied. Taylor, Fayol, and Weber were the forefathers of the burgeoning classical approach to management.
	Although the words are frequently used interchangeably, management and leadership are not the same thing. A person can be skilled as a leader or manager or both—or neither.
	Management is often described by Mintzberg's ten primary roles or Yukl's fundamental processes.
	Although classical management theory stated that there is only one best way to resolve an issue, today there is widespread agreement with the contingency theory model (House and Fieldler).

(Continues)

TABLE 15-1   The Leadership Puzzle *(Continued)*

Chapters	*Concepts to Remember*
	The quality movement gained widespread popularity in Japan after World War II as the country's businesses tried to rebuild.
	Deming (perhaps the best-known of the quality gurus) developed control charts and a fourteen-point quality plan.
	Juran published the Quality Control Handbook, which many people still consider the quality bible, and created a ten-point quality improvement model. In addition, he emphasized his trilogy: quality planning, quality control, and quality improvements.
Teaming and Leadership:	An organization or team is seen as an entity just as an individual is—it has a life cycle and a personality.
	A team may be static or dynamic.
	All teams go through five stages—forming, storming, norming, performing, and adjourning.
	Groupthink and social loafing can be a hazard to the effectiveness of all teams.
	Whether you are a leader or member, there are challenges and barriers for traditional teams, virtual teams, and project teams.
	Many of the same leadership principles can be applied to each of these three types of teams.
Classical Approaches to the Study of Leadership:	Gardner and Bennis detail the functions, competencies, and attributes of leaders.
	Behavioral theories assume that leader behaviors, rather than personality characteristics, exert the most influence on followers.
	Although the Ohio State and University of Michigan studies vary, both centered on two aspects of a manager: concern for people and concern for performance. Most individuals seem predisposed to favor one concern over the other.
Leadership Theories and Approaches for Today and Tomorrow:	James Rost has constructed what he terms the post-industrial model of leadership—the kind of leadership, he asserts, that will be absolutely necessary in the twenty-first century.
	There are four essential elements of practicing leadership as envisioned by Rost:

(Continues)

TABLE 15-1 **The Leadership Puzzle** (*Continued*)

Chapters	*Concepts to Remember*
	The leader-collaborator relationship is based on influence rather than positional authority.
	Leaders and their collaborators practice leadership together.
	Collaborators and their leaders intend real change.
	The changes that leaders and their collaborators pursue reflect their mutual purposes.
Military Leadership: The Art of Command:	Persons with military backgrounds abound in all segments of corporate, university, and private life, and the lessons of military leadership are instructive well beyond the military setting.
	The fourteen core leadership traits within the U.S. military model include dependability, bearing, courage, decisiveness, endurance, enthusiasm, initiative, integrity, judgment, justice, knowledge, tact, unselfishness, and loyalty. Many military students believe that, of all these traits, integrity is the most important.
	The eleven core leadership principles of the U.S. military are know yourself and seek self-improvement; be technically proficient; develop a sense of responsibility among your subordinates; make sound and timely decisions; lead by example; keep your people informed and look out for their welfare; keep your people informed; seek and take responsibility for your actions; make sure that assigned tasks are understood, supervised, and accomplished; train your people as a team; and employ your unit in accordance with its capabilities. Leading by example is the most important leadership principle of all.
	The Rule of Three guides the military in decision-making and in its organization plan.
Environmental Leadership:	Environmental leaders must deal with the long run when short-term costs are apparent but long-term benefits are far less obvious.
	They must motivate individuals and organizations to act morally.
	They need to be transformational leaders who are willing to disturb the status quo for the sake of future generations.
	They need to focus themselves and all other stakeholders on transcending self-interest and moving into long-term shared personal and organizational ethical commitment, effort, and vision.

Figures 15-1 and 15-2, in conjunction with Exercise 15-1, ask that you describe where and how you intend to practice leadership in your own life.

Piece #1:
What is the central "thing" in your leadership model?

(Almost all of the models and authors in the text build upon a main organizing idea or issue they feel most important in leadership: credibility, vision, traits, relationships, etc.)

Piece #8:
Leadership practiced this way means pursuing what?

Piece #10:
Why is this leadership model different than what currently exists? If it is not different, explain why you have elected for the status quo.

Piece #6:
Describe the relationships in the organization/group that exist as a result of using this leadership model.

Piece #5:
What are the core values that your leadership model emphasizes?

Piece #2:
In your leadership model, describe a leader's traits.

Piece #9:
Describe the world outside your organization/group you will have to face as a leader.

Piece #11:
How do you plan to start DOing leadership?

Piece #4:
In your leadership model, what are the leader's most important tasks?

Piece #3:
In your leadership model, describe the skills of an effective leader.

Piece #7:
Describe the culture of the organization/group that would exist if your model was used.

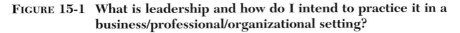

FIGURE 15-1 What is leadership and how do I intend to practice it in a business/professional/organizational setting?

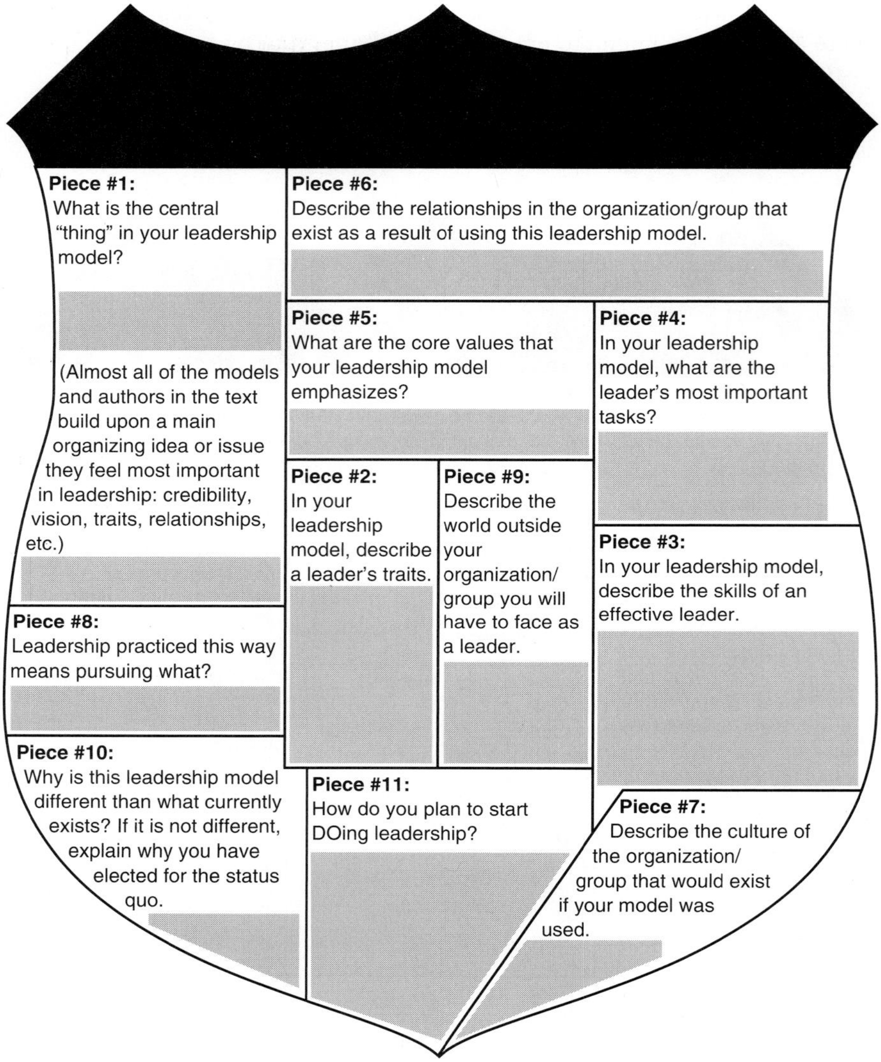

Piece #1:
What is the central "thing" in your leadership model?

(Almost all of the models and authors in the text build upon a main organizing idea or issue they feel most important in leadership: credibility, vision, traits, relationships, etc.)

Piece #6:
Describe the relationships in the organization/group that exist as a result of using this leadership model.

Piece #5:
What are the core values that your leadership model emphasizes?

Piece #4:
In your leadership model, what are the leader's most important tasks?

Piece #2:
In your leadership model, describe a leader's traits.

Piece #9:
Describe the world outside your organization/ group you will have to face as a leader.

Piece #3:
In your leadership model, describe the skills of an effective leader.

Piece #8:
Leadership practiced this way means pursuing what?

Piece #10:
Why is this leadership model different than what currently exists? If it is not different, explain why you have elected for the status quo.

Piece #11:
How do you plan to start DOing leadership?

Piece #7:
Describe the culture of the organization/ group that would exist if your model was used.

FIGURE 15-2 **What is leadership and how do I intend to practice it in my personal/social life?**

✦ Exercise

Exercise 15-1   What Is Leadership?
Key for Figures 15-1 and 15-2

What is leadership? How do I "do" leadership in my everyday life at work, home, and play? How do I intend to practice it in a business/professional/organizational setting and in my personal/social life?

Piece #1: What is the central thing in your leadership model? (Almost all the models and authors studied in the text build on a main organizing idea or issue they think most important in leadership credibility, vision, traits, relationships, and so on.)

Piece #2: In your leadership model, describe a leader's traits.

Piece #3: Using your leadership model, describe the skills of an effective leader.

Piece #4: In your leadership model, what are a leader's most important tasks?

Piece #5: What are the *core values* that your leadership model emphasizes?

Piece #6: Describe the relationships in the organizational group that exist as a result of using this leadership model.

Piece #7: Describe the culture of the organization/group that would exist if your model were used.

Piece #8: Leadership practiced this way means pursuing what?

Piece #9: Describe the world outside your organization/group that you will have to face as a leader.

Piece #10: Why is this leadership model different from what currently exists? If it is not different, explain why you have elected for the status quo.

Piece #11: How do you plan to start practicing leadership?

REFERENCES

Aguayo, R., *Dr. Deming: The American Who Taught the Japanese about Quality*. New York: Simon & Schuster, 1990.

Albanese, R. and D. D. Van Fleet, *Organizational Behavior: A Managerial Viewpoint*. Hinsdale, IL: The Dryden Press, 1983.

American Heritage College Dictionary (3rd ed). Boston: Houghton Mifflin, 1993.

Aquinas, T., *On Kingship*. Toronto: Pontifical Institute of Medieval Studies, 1982.

Archer, J., *Mao Tse-Tung*. New York: Hawthorn Books, 1972.

Arnold, M., *Culture and Anarchy*. New York: MacMillan, 1925.

Ashe, A., *Days of Grace*. New York: Alfred Knopf, 1993.

Baker, D. B., *Power Quotes*. Farmington Mills, MI: Visible Ink, 1992.

Ballon, R.J. and K. Honda, "Stakeholding: The Japanese Bottom Line," *Japan Times*, 2000.

Bandura, A. "Self-Efficacy: Toward a Unifying Theory of Behavioral Change," *Psychological Review* 84(1977), 191–215.

Bass, B. M., *Stogdill's Handbook of Leadership* (rev. ed.). New York: Free Press, 1981.

Batten, J. D., *Tough-Minded Leadership*. New York: American Management Association, 1989.

Baxter-Magolda, M., *Knowing and Reasoning in College*. San Francisco: Jossey-Bass, 1992.

Beck, J. D. and N. M. Yeager, *The Leader's Window*. New York: Wiley, 1994.

Belansky, M. F., B. M. Clinchy, N. R. Goldberger, and J. M. Tarule, *Women's Ways of Knowing*. New York: Basic Books, 1989.

Belasco, J., *Teaching the Elephant to Dance: The Manager's Guide to Empowering Change*. New York: Plume, 1990.

Belasco, J. A. and R. C. Stayer, *Flight of the Buffalo: Soaring to Excellence, Learning to Let Employees Lead*. New York: Warner Books, 1993.

Bellman, G. M., *Getting Things Done When You Are Not in Charge: How to Succeed from a Support Position*. San Francisco: Berrett-Koehler Publishers, 1992.

Bennis, W., *Managing the Dream: Reflections on Leadership and Change*. Cambridge, MA: Perseus Publishing, 2000.

Bennis, W. and R. Townsend, *Reinventing Leadership: Strategies to Power the Organization*. New York: William Morrow, 1995.

Bennis, W., J. Parikh, and R. Lessem, *Beyond Leadership*. Cambridge, MA: Blackwell Business, 1994.

Bennis, W. G., *On Becoming a Leader*. Reading, MA: Addison-Wesley, 1989.

Bennis, W. G. and B. Nanus, *Leaders: The Strategies for Taking Charge*. New York: Harper & Row, 1985.

Bensimon, E. M. and A. Neumann, *Redesigning Collegiate Leadership*. Baltimore: Johns Hopkins University Press, 1993.

Benton, D. A., *Secrets of a CEO Coach*. New York: McGraw-Hill, 1994.

Berger, P. L. and T. Luckman, *The Social Construction of Reality*. New York: Doubleday, 1967.

Bergmann, H., K. Hurson, and D. Russ-Eft, *Everyone a Leader*. New York: Wiley, 1991.

Bienen, H. (ed.), *Voices of Power: World Leaders Speak*. Hopewell, NJ: Ecco Press, 1995.

Blake, R. R. and A. A. McCanse, *Leadership Dilemmas—Grid Solutions*. Houston: Gulf Publishing Co., 1991.

274

Blake, R. R. and J. S. Mouton, *The Managerial Grid*. Houston: Gulf Publishers, 1964.

Blanchard, K. and S. Bowles, *Gung Ho!* New York: William Morrow, 1998.

Blanchard, K., B. Hybils, and P. Hodges, *Leadership by the Book*. New York: William Morrow, 1999.

Blanchard, K. and S. Johnson, *The One Minute Manager*. La Jolla, CA: Blanchard-Johnson, 1981.

Blanchard, K. and N. Pearle, *The Power of Ethical Management*. New York: Fawcett Crest, 1988.

Block, P., *Stewardship*. San Francisco: Berrett-Koehler, 1993.

Bodley, J. H. *Cultural Anthropology: Tribes, States and the Global System*. Mountain View, CA: Mayfield, 1994.

Bolman, L. G. and T. E. Deal, *Reframing Organizations: Artistry, Choice and Leadership* (2nd ed.). San Francisco: Jossey-Bass, 1997.

Bryman, A., *Charisma and Leadership in Organizations*. Thousand Oaks, CA: Sage Publications, 1992.

Burke, W. W., "Leadership as Empowering Others," in Srivastra and Associates, *Executive Power*. San Francisco: Jossey-Bass, 1986.

Burns, J. M., *Leadership*. New York: Harper & Row, 1979.

Business Horizons, "Different Forms of Political Manipulation," March–April 1987.

Cantor, D. W. and T. Bernay, *Women in Power: The Secrets of Leadership*. Boston: Houghton Mifflin, 1992.

Chaleff, I., *The Courageous Followers*. San Francisco: Berrett-Koehler, 1995.

Chandler, A. D. Jr., *The Visible Hand: The Managerial Revolution in American Business*. Cambridge, MA: Harvard University Press, 1977.

Chapman, E. N., *Leadership*. Indianapolis, IN: Macmillan, 1989.

Chrislip, D. D. and C. E. Larson, *Collaborative Leadership*. San Francisco: Jossey-Bass, 1997.

Clough, M., *Cultural Audiotapes* (concept and scripts). Cincinnati: Property of Global Lead Management Consulting, 2000.

Conger, J. A., *The Charismatic Leader*. New York: Jossey-Bass, 1988.

Conger, J. A. and R. N. Kanungo, *Charismatic Leadership in Organizations* (2nd ed.). New York: Jossey-Bass, 1998.

Covey, S. R., *Principle-Centered Leadership*. New York: Summit Books, 1990.

Crosby, P., *The Absolute of Leadership*. San Francisco: Pfeiffer & Co, 1996.

Csikszentmihalyi, M., *Creativity*. New York: Harper Perennial, 1996.

Daft, R. L., *Leadership: Theory & Practice*. Forth Worth, TX: Dryden Press, 1999.

Daft, R. L., *Management* (3rd ed.). Fort Worth, TX: Dryden Press, 1994.

Daft, R. L. and R. H. Lengel, *Fusion Leadership*. San Francisco: Berrett-Koehler, 1998.

Decker, C., *P&G-99*. New York: Harper Collins Business, 1998.

Deming, W. E., *Out of the Crisis*. Cambridge, MA: Massachusetts Institute of Technology Center for Advanced Engineering Study, 1986.

DePree, M., *Leadership Is an Art*. New York: Dell, 1989.

DePree, M., *Leadership Jazz*. New York: Dell, 1992.

DePree, M., *Leading without Power*. San Francisco: Jossey-Bass, 1997.

Dinkmyer, D. and D. Eckstein, *Leadership by Encouragement*. St. Lucie Press, Boca Raton, FL: 1996.

Donnelley, J. H., J. L. Gibson, and J. M. Ivancevich, *Fundamentals of Management* (9th ed.). Chicago: Irwin, 1996.

Drath, W. H. and C. J. Paulus, *Making Common Sense: Leadership as Meaning-Making in a Community of Practice*. Greensboro, NC: Center for Creative Leadership, 1994.

Drucker, P. F., *The Practice of Management*. New York: Harper & Row, 1954.

DuBrin, A., *Leadership: Research Findings, Practice and Skills*. Boston: Houghton Mifflin, 1995.

Dye, T. R., *Understanding Public Policy* (9th ed.). Paramus, NJ: Prentice-Hall, 1997.

Eales-White, R., *How to be a better...Leader*. Dover, NH: Kogan Page, 1998.

Eisenhower, D. D., *The White House Years: Mandate for Change*, 1953–1956. Garden City, NY: Doubleday, 1963.

Elashmawi, F. and P. R. Harris, *Multicultural Management 2000*. Houston: Gulf Publishing, 1998.

Etzioni, A., *The Spirit of Community*. New York: Crown, 1993.

Evans, M. G., "The Effects of Supervisory Behavior on the Path-Goal Relationship," *Organizational Behavior and Human Performance* 5(1970), 277–298.

Evans, J. R. and W. M. Lindsay, *The Management and Control of Quality* (2nd ed.). St. Paul, MN: West Publishing, 1993.

Fairhurst, G. F. and R. A. Sarr., *The Art of Framing*. San Francisco: Jossey-Bass, 1996.

Fayol, H., *General and Industrial Administration*. New York: Pitman, 1949.

Fiedler, F. E., "The Effects of Leadership Training and Experience: A Contingency Model Interpretation," *Administrative Science Quarterly* 17(1972), 455.

Fiedler, F. E. and J. E. Garcia, *New Approaches to Leadership: Cognitive Resources and Organizational Performance*. New York: Wiley, 1987.

Fiedler, F. E., M. M. Chemers, and L. Mahar, *Improving Leadership Effectiveness*. New York: Wiley, 1976.

Foster, W., *Paradigms and Promises*. Buffalo, NY: Prometheus Books, 1986.

Foster, W., "Toward a Critical Practice of Leadership," in J. Smyth (ed.), *Critical Perspectives on Educational Leadership*. London: Falmer, 1989.

Freeman, F., K. B. Knott, and M. K. Schwartz, *Leadership Education: A Source Book* (6th ed.), Greensboro, NC: Center for Creative Leadership, 1997.

Freire, P., *Pedagogy of the Oppressed*. New York: Continuum, 1970.

French, J. and B. Raven, "The Bases of Power," in D. Cartwright (ed.), *Group Dynamics: Research and Theory*. Evanston, IL: Row, Peterson, 1962.

Gardenswartz, L. and A. Rowe, *Diverse Teams at Work*. New York: McGraw-Hill, 1994.

Gardner, J., *On Leadership*. New York: Free Press, 1990.

Gates, B., *Business at the Speed of Thought*. New York: Warner Books, 1999.

Geertz, C., *The Interpretation of Cultures*. New York: Basic Books, 1973.

Gibb, J. R., "Defensive Communication," *Journal of Communication,* XII no. 3 (1961), 141–148.

Gibbs, R., *In Profile: Women Prime Ministers*. Morristown, NJ: Silver Burdett, 1981.

Gilligan, C., *In a Different Voice*. Cambridge, MA: Harvard University Press, 1982.

Goldberg, J., *Rachel Carson: Biologist and Author*. New York: Chelsea House, 1992.

Goleman, D. P., *Working with Emotional Intelligence*. New York: Bantam Books, 1998.

Goodwin, D., *Caesar Chavez: Hope for the People*. New York: Fawcett Columbine, 1991.

Gordon, T., *Leaders Effective Training*. New York: Bantam Books, 1977.

Graen, G. B. and J. F. Cashman, "A Role Making Model of Leadership in Formal Organizations: A Developmental Approach," in J. G. Hunt and L. L. Larson (eds.), *Leadership Frontiers*. Kent, OH: Kent State University Press, 1975.

Graen, G. B. and M. Uhl-Bien, "Relationship-based Approach to Leadership," *Leadership Quarterly* 6, 2 (1995), 219–249.

Granrose, L. S. and S. Oskamp, *Cross-Cultural Work Groups*. Thousand Oaks, CA: Sage Publications, 1997.

Gray, A. and J. McGuigan (eds.), *Studying Culture: An Introductory Reader*. London: Edward Arnold, 1993.

Greene, R. and J. Elffers, *Power*. New York: Profile Books, 1998.

Greenleaf, R. K., *The Servant as Leader*. Newton Center, MA: Robert K. Greenleaf Center, 1970.

Greenleaf, R. K., *Servant Leadership*. Mahwah, NJ: Paulist Press, 1977.

Greenleaf, R. K., *The Power of Servant Leadership*. San Francisco: Berrett-Koehler, 1998.

Gull, G. A., "Being Ethical," *Executive Excellence* 12, 8 (Aug. 1995), 20.

Hackman, M. Z. and C. E. Johnson, *Leadership: A Communication Perspective* (2nd ed.). Prospect Heights, IL: Waveland Press, 1996.

Hale, G., *The Leader's Edge*. New York: Simon & Schuster, 1996.

Harris, P., "Innovating with High Achievers," *Training & Development Journal* 34, 10 (1996), 45–50.

Harvard Business Review, *Leaders on Leadership*. Cambridge, MA: Harvard Business School Press, 1992.

Harvard Business Review, *On Leadership*. Cambridge, MA: Harvard Business School Press, 1998.

Hass, H. G. and B. Tamarkin, *The Leader Within*. New York: Harper Business, 1992.

Heifetz, R. A., *Leadership Without Easy Answers*. New York: Belknap-Harvard, 1994.

Helgesen, S., *The Female Advantage: Women's Ways of Leadership*. New York: Currency Doubleday, 1990.

Hersey, P. and K. H. Blanchard, "Life Cycle Theory of Leadership," *Training and Development Journal* 23(1969), 26–34.

Hersey, P. and K. H. Blanchard, *The Management of Organizational Behavior* (3rd ed.). Englewood Cliffs, NJ: Prentice Hall, 1977.

Herzberg, F., *Work and the Nature of Man*. Cleveland, OH: World Publishing, 1966.

Hess, P. and J. Siciliano, *Management: Responsibility for Performance*. New York: McGraw-Hill, 1996.

Hickman, G. R. (ed.), *Leading Organization*. Thousand Oaks, CA: Sage Publications, 1998.

Hirsch, E. D. Jr., *Cultural Literacy: What Every American Needs to Know*. Boston: Houghton Mifflin, 1987.

Hobbes, T., *Leviathan*. London: Oxford University Press, 1947.

Hofstede, G., *Culture's Consequences: International Differences in Work Related Values*. Beverly Hills, CA: Sage, 1980.

Holkeboer, R. and T. Hoeksema, *A Case Book for Student Leaders*. Boston: Houghton Mifflin, 1998.

Holman, L., *Eleven Lessons in Self-Leadership*. Lexington, KY: A Lesson in Leadership Book, 1995.

House, R. J. and T. R. Mitchell, "Path–Goal Theory of Leadership," *Journal of Contemporary Business* 3(1974), 81–97.

Hughes, R. L., R. C. Ginnett, and G. J. Curphy, *Leadership: Enhancing the Lessons of Experience* (2nd ed.). Chicago: Irwin, 1996.

Hunsaker, P. L. and A. J. Alessandra, *The Art of Managing People*. New York: Simon & Schuster, 1980.

Hunsaker, P. L. and C. W. Cooke, *Managing Organizational Behavior*. Reading, MA: Addison Wesley, 1986.

Ishikawa, K., *What Is Total Quality Control? The Japanese Way*. Englewood Cliffs, NJ: Prentice Hall, 1985.

Jaeger, W., *Paideia: Ideals of Greek Culture*. New York: Oxford University Press, 1965.

Jago, A. G., "Leadership: Perspectives in Theory and Research," *Management Science* (March 1992), 315–318.

Juran, J. M., *Juran's Quality Control Handbook* (4th ed.). New York: McGraw-Hill, 1988.

Juran, J. M., *Managerial Breakthrough* (2nd ed.). New York: McGraw-Hill, 1994.

Kanter, R. M, *When Giants Learn to Dance.* New York: Touchstone Books, Simon & Schuster, 1989.

Katzenbach, J. R. and D. K. Smith, *The Wisdom of Teams.* New York: Harper Business, 1993.

Kellerman, B., *Leadership, Multidisciplinary Perspectives.* Paramus, NJ: Prentice-Hall, 1983.

Kennedy, J. K., "Middle LPC Leaders and the Contingency Model of Leader Effectiveness," *Organizational Behavior and Human Performance* 39(1982), 1–14.

Kerr, S. and J. M. Jermier, "Substitutes for Leadership: Their Meaning and Measurement," *Organizational Behavior and Human Performance,* 22(1978), 375–403.

Kets Devries, M. F. R., *Leaders, Fools, and Imposters.* San Francisco: Jossey-Bass, 1993.

Kostner, J., *Virtual Leadership.* New York: Warner Books, 1994.

Kotter, J. P., *A Force for Change: How Leadership Differs from Management.* New York: Free Press, 1990.

Kotter, J. P., "What Leaders Really Do," in W. E. Rosenbach and R. L. Taylor (eds.), *Contemporary Issues in Leadership.* Boulder, CO: Westview Press, 1993.

Kouzes, J. M. and B. Z. Posner. *Credibility: How Leaders Gain and Lose It.* San Francisco: Jossey-Bass, 1993.

Kuczmarski, S. S. and T. D. Kuczmarski, *Value-based Leadership.* New Jersey: Prentice Hall, 1995.

Kuh, G. D., E. J. Whitt, and J. D. Shedd, *Student Affairs Work, 2001: A Paradigmatic Odyssey.* Alexandria, VA: American College Personnel Association, 1987.

Kuhn, T. S., *The Structure of Scientific Revolutions* (2nd ed.). Chicago: University of Chicago Press, 1970.

Kurtzman, J., *Thought Leaders.* San Francisco: Jossey-Bass, 1998.

Lander, H. H. and I. W. Porter, "The Effect of Performance on Job Satisfaction," *Industrial Relations* (Oct. 1967), 23.

Landy, M. and S. Milkis, *Presidential Greatness.* Lawrence, KS: University of Kansas Press, 2000.

LaPierre, D. "Mother Teresa Is Still Offering a Hand at 84," *Cleveland Plain Dealer* (Dec. 19, 1994).

Lappe, F. M. and P. M. DuBois, *The Quickening of America.* San Francisco: Jossey-Bass, 1994.

Lazo, C., *Rigoberta Menchu.* New York: Dillon Press, 1993.

Lebo, F., *Mastering the Diversity Challenge.* Boca Raton, FL: St. Lucie Press, 1996.

Levine, S. R. and M. A. Crom, *The Leader in You: How to Win Friends, Influence People, and Succeed in a Changing World.* New York: Simon & Schuster, 1993.

Lewis, P. V., *Occupational Communication: The Essence of Effective Management* (3rd ed.). New York: Wiley, 1987.

Locke, J., *The Second Treatise of Government.* Indianapolis: Bobbs-Merrill, 1977.

Lowe, J. C., *Jack Welch Speaks.* New York: Wiley, 1998.

Luthans, F., *Organizational Behavior* (7th ed.). New York: McGraw-Hill, 1995.

Lynch, R., *Lead!* San Francisco: Jossey-Bass, 1993.

Machiavelli, N., *The Prince.* New York: Signet, 1952.

Magolda, B., *Knowing and Reasoning in College.* San Francisco: Jossey-Bass, 1992.

Mandela, N., *Long Walk to Freedom.* Boston: Little, Brown, 1994.

Manz, C. C. and H. P. Sims, Jr., *Superleadership: Leading Others to Lead Themselves.* New York: Prentice-Hall, 1989.

Maslow, A. H., *Motivation and Personality.* New York: Harper & Row, 1954.

Maslow, A. H., *Maslow on Management.* New York: Wiley, 1998.

Mayo, E., *Human Problems in an Industrialized World.* New York: Macmillan, 1953.

McClelland, D. E., *Power: The Inner Experience.* New York: Irvington, 1975.

Mclean, J. W. and W. Weitzel, *Leadership—Magic, Myth, or Method?* New York: Amacom, 1992.

Mikulski, B., "Power and the Ability to Lead," in D. W. Cantor, and T. Bernay (eds.), *Women in Power: The Secrets of Leadership*. New York: Houghton Mifflin, 1992.

Milkis, S. and M. Nelson, *The American Presidency: Origins and Development*. Washington, DC: Congressional Quarterly Press, 1999.

Miller, D. S., S. E. Catt, and J. R. Carlson, *Fundamentals of Management: A Framework for Excellence*. St. Paul, MN: West, 1996.

Miller, J. B., *Toward a New Psychology of Women*. Boston: Beacon Press, 1976.

Mintzberg, H., *The Nature of Managerial Work*. Englewood Cliffs, NJ: Prentice Hall, 1979.

Mitchell, R. R., C. M. Smyser, and S. E. Weed, "Locus of Control: Supervision and Work Satisfaction," *Academy of Management Journal* 18(1975), 623–630.

Mitroff, I. A. and E. A. Denton, *A Spiritual Audit of Corporate America, A Hard Look at Spirituality, Religion, and Values in the Workplace*. San Francisco: Jossey-Bass, 1999.

Moreth, G., *Imaginazation: The Art of Creative Management*. Thousand Oaks, CA: Sage, 1993.

Morrison, A. M., *The New Leaders*. San Francisco: Jossey-Bass, 1992.

Murphy, E. C., *Leadership I.Q.* New York: Wiley, 1996.

Nair, K., *A Higher Standard of Leadership: Lessons from the Life of Gandhi*. San Francisco: Berrett-Koehler, 1994.

Nanus, B., *Visionary Leadership*. San Francisco: Jossey-Bass, 1992.

Napolitano, C. S. and L. J. Henderson, *The Leadership Odyssey*. San Francisco: Jossey-Bass, 1998.

Nehru, J., "Nehru: The First Sixty Years. 1947 Correspondence Referring to Gandhi," in H. Bienen (ed.), *Voices of Power: World Leaders Speak*. Hopewell, NJ: Ecco Press, 1995.

Nelson, D. L. and J. C. Quick, *Organizational Behavior*. St. Paul, MN: West, 1996.

Neustadt, R., *Presidential Power and the Modern Presidents*. New York: Free Press, 1990.

Nichols, E., *Information on Culture Patterns*. Baltimore: Property of Nichols, Inc., 1995.

Northouse, P. G., *Leadership: Theory and Practice*. Thousand Oaks, CA: Sage Publications, 1997.

Otfinoski, S., *Marian Wright Edelman, Defender of Children's Rights*. New York: Blackbirch Press, 1991.

Ouchi, W. G., *Theory Z: How American Business Can Meet the Japanese Challenge*. Reading, MA: Addison-Wesley, 1981.

Paine, L. S., *Cases in Leadership, Ethics, and Organizational Integrity*. New York: Irwin McGraw-Hill, 1997.

Palmer, P., "Community, Conflict and Ways of Knowing," *Change* (Sept.–Oct., 1987).

Perkins, D. N. T., *Leading at the Edge*. New York: Amacom, 2000.

Peters, T., *Liberation Management*. New York: Alfred A. Knopf, 1992.

Peters, T., *Crazy Times Call For Crazy Organizations*. New York: Vintage Books, 1994a.

Peters, T., *The Pursuit of Wow*. New York: Vintage Books, 1994b.

Phatak, A., *International Dimensions of Management*. Boston: Kent, 1983.

Phillips, D. T., *Lincoln on Leadership*. New York: Warner Books, 1992.

Pierce, J. L. and J. W. Newstorm, *Leaders and the Leadership Process* (2nd ed.). New York: Irwin McGraw-Hill, 2000.

Piper, W. *The Little Engine That Could*. New York: Platt & Munk, 1930.

Powell, C. L., *My American Journey*. New York: Random House, 1995.

Pritchett, P. and R. Pound, *Team Reconstruction*. Dallas, TX: Pritchett and Associates, 1994.

Quantz, R. A., J. L. Rogers, and M. Dantley, "Rethinking Transformational Leadership: Towards the Democratic Reform of Schools," Journal of Education 173, 3(1991), 96–118.

Rehfeld, J. E., *Alcheming of a Leader*. New York: Wiley, 1994.

Riedinger, E. A., *Where in the World to Learn*. Westport, CT: Greenwood Press, 1995.

Robbins, S. P., *Organizational Behavior Concepts, Controversies and Applications* (6th ed.).

Englewood Cliffs, NJ: Prentice-Hall, 1993.

Robbins, S. P. and P. L. Hunsaker, *Training in Interpersonal Skills* (2nd ed.). Englewood Cliffs, NJ: Prentice Hall, 1996.

Roberts, W., *Leadership Secrets of Attila the Hun.* New York: Warner Books, 1987.

Rogers, J. L. and S. C. Ballard, "Aspirational Management: Building Effective Organizations Through Shared Values," *NASPA* 32, 3 (1995).

Rosenbach, W. E. and R. L. Taylor (eds.), *Contemporary Issues in Leadership.* Boulder, CO: Westview Press, 1993.

Rost, J. C., *Leadership for the Twenty-first Century.* New York: Praeger, 1991.

Ruettiger, R. and M. Celizic, *Rudy's Rules.* Waco, TX: WRS Publishing, 1995.

Sayles, L. R., *Leadership.* New York: McGraw-Hill, 1989.

Scholtes, P. R., *The Leader's Handbook.* New York: McGraw-Hill, 1998.

Senge, P., *The Fifth Discipline: The Art and Practice of the Learning Organization.* New York: Doubleday, 1990.

Sergiovanni, T. J., *Moral Leadership.* San Francisco: Jossey-Bass, 1992.

Shweder, R. A., *Thinking Through Cultures: Expeditions in Cultural Psychology.* Cambridge, MA: Harvard University Press, 1991.

Simons, G. F., C. Vazquez, and P. R. Harris, *Transcultural Leadership.* Houston: Gulf Publishing Company, 1993.

Sims, H. P. Jr. and P. Lorenzi, *The New Leadership Paradigm: Social Learning and Cognition in Organizations.* Newbury Park, CA: Sage, 1992.

Skowronek, S., *The Politics Presidents Make: Leadership from John Adams to George Bush.* Cambridge, MA: Belknap Press of Havard University, 1993.

Smitha, F. E., *Antiquity, A World History.* Cynthianna, KY: M. Thomas Bell Publishing, 1999.

Smyth, J., *Critical Perspectives on Educational Leadership.* London: Falmer, 1989.

Spears, L. C. (ed.), *Reflection of Leadership.* New York: John Wiley, 1995.

Srivastva, S., D. L. Cooperrider and Associates, *Appreciation Management and Leadership.* San Francisco: Jossey-Bass, 1990.

Steffof, R., *Mao Zedong: Founder of the People's Republic of China.* Brookfield, CT: Millbrook Press, 1996.

Swift, J. A., *Introduction to Modern Statistical Quality Control and Management.* Delray Beach, FL: St. Lucie Press, 1995.

Tichy, N. M. and E. Cohen, *The Leadership Engine.* New York: Prichett & Associates, 1998.

Tjosvold, D. and M. Tjosvold, *Psychology for Leaders: Using Motivation, Conflict and Power to Manage More Effectively.* New York: Wiley, 1995.

Treacy, M. and F. Wiersema, *The Discipline of Market Leaders.* New York: Perseus Books, 1995.

Trickett, E. J., R. J. Watts, and D. Birmans (eds.), *Human Diversity.* San Francisco: Jossey-Bass, 1994.

Trine, R. W., *Character Building Thought Power.* Santa Fe: Sun Publishing, 1993 [orig. 1899].

Tubbs, S. L. and S. Moss, *Interpersonal Communication.* New York: Random House, 1981.

Tylor, E. B., *Anthropology: An Introduction to the Study of Man and Civilization.* New York: D. Appleton, 1909 [orig. 1881].

U.S. Army Cadet Command, *Leader's Guide.* Fort Monroe, VA: Dec. 30, 1995.

Useem, M., *The Leadership Moment.* New York: Times Business, 1998.

Vaill, P. B., *Managing as a Performing Art.* San Francisco: Jossey-Bass, 1989.

Vaill, P. B., *Learning as a Way of Being.* San Francisco: Jossey-Bass, 1996.

Vroom V. H., and A. G. Jago, *The New Leadership.* Englewood Cliffs, NJ: Prentice Hall, 1988.

Vroom, V. H. and A. G. Jago, *The New Theory of Leadership: Managing Participation in Organizations.* Englewood Cliffs, NJ: Prentice Hall, 1988.

Vroom, V. H. and P. W. Yetton, *Leadership and Decision Making.* Pittsburgh: University of Pittsburgh Press, 1973.

Wachowski, A., *The Matrix.* Los Angeles: Warner Studios, 1999.

Waitley, D., *Empires of the Mind.* New York: William Morrow, 1995.

Walters, J. D., *The Art of Supportive Leadership.* Nevada City: Crystal Clarity Publishers, 1993.

Walton, D., *Are You Communicating?* New York: McGraw-Hill, 1989.

Walton, M., *The Deming Management Method.* New York: Putnam, 1986.

Wellins, R. S., W. C. Byham, and J. M. Wilsom, *Empowered Teams.* San Francisco: Jossey-Bass Publishers, 1991.

Wheatley, M. J., *Leadership and the New Science: Learning about Organizations from an Orderly Universe.* San Francisco: Berett-Koehler, 1992.

Wood, J. T., *The Little Blue Book on Power.* Winslow, WA: Zen-n-Ink Publishers, no date.

Yukl, G., *Skills for Managers and Leaders: Test Cases and Exercises.* Englewood Cliffs, NJ: Prentice Hall, 1990.

Yukl, G., *Leadership in Organizations* (3rd ed.). Englewood Cliffs, NJ: Prentice Hall, 1995.

Zand, D. E., *The Leadership Triad.* New York: Oxford University Press, 1997.

Zohar, D., *Rewiring the Corporate Brain, Using the New Science to Rethink How We Structure and Lead Organizations.* Collingdale, PA: DIANE Publishing, 2000.

Zohar, D., I. H. Marshall, and F. D. Peat, *Who's Afraid of Schrodinger's Cat? All the New Science Ideas You Need to Keep Up with the New Thinking.* New York: Morrow/Avon, 1997.

INDEX